TEACHING THE FUTURE

A Guide to Future-Oriented Education

by

DRAPER L. KAUFFMAN, JR.

An ETC Publication

C|P

Library of Congress Cataloging in Publication Data

Kauffman, Draper L   1946-
      Teaching the future.

      (Education futures; no. 4)
      Bibliography: p. 269.
      Includes index.
      1. Educational innovations.   I. Title.

LB1027.K275   371.3   75-15636
ISBN 0-88280-024-8
ISBN 0-88280-025-6 pbk.

Copyright © 1976 by Draper L. Kauffman, Jr.

Published by ETC Publications
Palm Springs
California 92262

Printed in the United States of America.

Preface

This book is for teachers. Specifically, it is for teachers at all grade levels who care about preparing students for adult life in a world of rapid change. Administrators, curriculum specialists, parents, and friends of education are also welcome, of course, and I think they will find much here that is of interest and value to them. But the main objective of the book is to provide a practical handbook for classroom teachers interested in future-oriented education.

The key word is *practical.* Jargon, theorizing, and rhetorical exhortations for better teaching have been minimized. So have extremely long or detailed units which can only be used under ideal circumstances. Instead, the emphasis is on teaching methods and resources which have been shown to be both effective and flexible.

The book begins with the rationale for future-oriented education and a discussion of the objectives of a future-oriented curriculum. Part II contains the heart of the book: 22 exercises on ways of thinking about the future, each of which has been successfully used (or readily adapted) by teachers in a wide range of grade-levels and classroom settings. Part III presents two longer exercises, aimed primarily at senior high school students. Finally, the appendix includes a brief history of the study of the future, a scenario for a role-play exercise, a guide to books, magazines, films, and simulation-games of special interest, a bibliography, and a glossary of basic terms.

If you are one of the several thousand teachers who have already taught a futures course or unit, you should find many new ideas here and perhaps some alternative ways of approaching the units you have already developed on your own. If you are now planning your first effort in future studies, you can use this book to benefit from the experience of other teachers and to avoid some of the pitfalls of starting completely from scratch. And if you are undecided (or simply curious) about future-oriented education, this book will help you find out what it is like, in practice as well as in principle; I hope that when you are done you will join me in the conviction that the future is an essential (and exciting) component of good education.

Acknowledgements

A great many people contributed, directly and indirectly, to this book. I would like to take this opportunity to thank them all, particularly those most immediately involved.

Throughout the research that went into the book, I drew heavily on the resources of the Future Studies Program and the School of Education at the University of Massachusetts. Particular thanks go:

—to David Schimmel, Ernest Anderson, and Sylvia Forman for their support and their substantial editorial contributions;
—to Chris Dede and Billy Rojas, founders of the graduate Future Studies Program, Paul Burnim, initiator and fellow founding director of the Future Studies Teacher Education Program, and all of the program members who contributed their ideas and their encouragement;
—to Richard Clark and the members of the Teacher Education Council, for their administrative and financial support and their willingness to take risks on an unusual and untried approach to education;
—and to Dwight Allen and all of the many people at the School of Education who have helped make it an open and supportive environment for educational innovation.

Special thanks are also due to the more than 35 elementary and secondary teachers and the more than 100 undergraduates and student teachers who helped develop the teaching methods in this book; particularly to Margaret Brosnahan, Roger Cirone, Bruce Crowder, Peggy George, Cyndy Guy, Richard Needham, Bonnie Rennell, Raymond Smith, Frank Taylor, and Kathleen Weinman, members of the review panel who contributed generously of their time and their ideas to field testing and improving the entire book.

Eight of the exercises in Section II were borrowed from, or inspired by, a particular source or individual: Edward T. Hall (Exercise 1), Donella Meadows and her colleagues (Exercises 1, 6, 7, and 8), Robert Bundy (Exercises 3 and 4), Alvin Toffler (Exercise 13), and Patricia Burke Guild (Exercise 19). Thanks are also due to Donella Meadows, *et al.*, for permission to reproduce the figures on pages 60 and 153, to Robert Bundy for permission to reproduce the materials quoted in pages 67 through 72, and to United Educators, Inc., for permission to reproduce in Appendix A portions of my article on "Futuristics" from their *Wonderland of Knowledge Encyclopedia*. (For full references, please see the "Notes" to the specific exercises or sections indicated.)

Finally, very special thanks go to my wife, Susan Kauffman, editor, production manager, colleague and companion, without whom this book could not have been written.

Draper Kauffman

Contents

Exercises

PART I
Introduction

CHAPTER I
Why Teach the Future?

Barring disasters, the students in school today will spend most of their lives in the next century. Yet their education is, in many ways, more suited to the 19th century than the 21st.

If you are now beginning a forty-year teaching career, roughly half of your students will spend not most, but ALL of their adult lives in the next century. (Some of them will live to see the 22nd century!) How well will you prepare them for the world they will live in?

Our society is changing very rapidly, and it is impossible to predict what it will be like in 50 years; we only know for certain that it will be very different from today.[1] It therefore makes little sense to base education either on the past or on one particular version of the future. What we can and must do instead is give students an understanding of the most important issues, problems, and opportunities they may face; teach them the skills they will need to continue to look ahead on their own; and prepare them to cope successfully with the dislocations and stresses of rapid change.

In this chapter we will explore the importance of future-oriented education for four "clients" of education; the individual students, the society as a whole, the institution of education, and ourselves, as individual teachers and educators.

---

[1]References are located in the "Notes" sections at the ends of the chapters.

Students

"Why do I have to go to school?" Is there a teacher, or a parent of a school-age child, who hasn't heard that question and tried to answer it? There are temporizing answers, of course: "To get an education" . . . "Because the law says you have to." But these just duck the issue. Why does the child need to be educated? Why does the law say he must?

The answers are legion. Education will help him to fit into society. It will enable him to make more money. It will enable him to choose more wisely, be a more effective citizen, enjoy the "higher" pleasures of life, be healthier, be happier, be more productive. Whatever the rhetoric, noble purpose, or direct mercenary appeal, the common theme which we din into our young people over and over again is: education is good for you because of the ways it will benefit you *in the future*.

Both the justification and the structure of our educational system are explicitly future-oriented: the child *learns*, so that the adult can *know, do,* and *be*. It therefore seems perfectly straightforward that we should attempt to provide the child with the knowledge, skills, and values that *will* be appropriate to the world which that child will live in as an adult — the world of the future.

Yet our schools seem, by and large, to ignore this fundamental fact. They act as if the child and the adult — the learner and the user of learning — exist side-by-side, simultaneously. Listening to the rhetoric, one gets the clear impression that schools in the 1970's are attempting to prepare students for adult life in the 1970's. Examining the curriculum, one can only conclude that it was designed as a preparation for adult life in the 1950's and 1960's.

Such a system makes perfectly good sense when the rate of social change is quite slow. At most times and in most societies, the best guide to the future was the past and present, and the best education for the future was an education based on an intimate knowledge of the past and present. But this kind of reasoning simply does not apply today. Our society is already profoundly different in many ways from what it was only 30 years ago. Even so, one of the few predictions we can make with any certainty about the future is that our society will change more in the next 30 years than it has changed in the last 30 years.

Education based solely on the past (and even on the present) is no longer an adequate preparation for life in the future. We have promised a great deal from education. If we as educators intend to live up to those promises, we are going to have to consider seriously the implications of rapid social change and revise the substance of education accordingly.

One of the most personal and direct consequences of the rapid pace of change in our society is the psychological disorientation that it brings. Alvin Toffler calls this disorientation "future shock":

> Future shock is a time phenomenon, a product of the greatly accelerated rate of change in society. It arises from the superimposition of a new culture on an old one. It is culture shock in one's own society. But its impact is far worse. For most Peace Corps men, in fact most travelers, have the comforting knowledge that the culture they have left behind will be there to return to. The victim of future shock does not.

Toffler goes on to describe the basic remedy for the problem of being overwhelmed by change:

> 350 years after his death, scientists are still finding evidence to support Cervantes' succinct insight into adaptational psychology: "Fore-warned fore-armed." Self evident as it may seem, in most situations we can help individuals adapt better if we simply provide them with advance information about what lies ahead.

We are in general much less shocked by, and much better able to cope with, situations which we have at least considered in advance than situations which are totally unexpected.

This is true even if we have also considered many events which never do occur. If we think through five alternative possibilities in advance, and only one of them actually occurs, we will still be better prepared to cope with that one than if we had considered none of the possibilities at all. This is fortunate, indeed, since it means that we *can* achieve our educational objective of "fore-warning" students by dealing with thoughtful forecasts of future possibilities. The task would be impossible if we needed certain knowledge of THE future, since true prediction in all but the narrowest of areas remains a practical impossibility.

Herbert J. Muller describes the educational role of such forecasts in his book, *Uses of the Future:*

> For our students, speculation about what life will be like in the year 2000 is not at all idle or academic: they will be in their prime then. To be sure, they had better understand clearly the reasons why prediction is necessarily uncertain. But on the traditional assumption that education should prepare young people for life, it should now make them aware of major developments that are not only possible but may be highly probable or virtually certain . . . and the problems most of them will raise.

In any case, as Toffler points out, actual factual data about the future is less important than a psychological orientation toward the future:

> Even more important than any specific bits of advance information, however, is the habit of anticipation. This conditioned ability to look ahead plays a key role in adaptation. Indeed, one of the hidden clues to successful coping may well lie in the individual's sense of the future. The people among us who keep up with change, who manage to adapt well, seem to have a richer, better developed sense of what lies ahead than those who cope poorly. Anticipating the future has become a habit with them. The chess player who anticipates the moves of his opponent, the executive who thinks in long-range terms, the student who takes a quick glance at the table of contents before starting to read page one, all seem to fare better.

Of course, the "richer, better developed sense of what lies ahead" comes not just from the habit of anticipation, but from the quality of that anticipation as well.

These then, are the fundamental things which we owe to our students if we seriously intend to prepare them for adult life: the available *information* about important future possibilities; the *habit* of looking ahead; and the *skill* to anticipate effectively. Any curriculum that completely ignores these basics does students a real disservice and is quite literally irrelevant to their lives and concerns.

Society

There is an old Chinese curse which goes, "May you live in interesting times!" This left-handed blessing gets its delicate irony from the fact that times which are interesting from an historical perspective are usually times of turmoil, upheaval, or catastrophe, and exceedingly dangerous and uncomfortable for the people who live in them. The joke cuts a little too close to home, however, since it is increasingly clear that we do, in fact, live in very "interesting" times.

Kenneth Boulding suggests in *The Meaning of the Twentieth Century* that our century will be seen as the second great watershed in the history of mankind. (The invention of agriculture more than 10,000 years ago was the first such watershed, and even that was spread out over an incomparably longer period of time.) He is probably right, if for no other reason than that this is the century when man first achieved the ability to destroy the entire planet and the entire human race along with it.

But the times are "interesting" not just because the dangers we face are so great, but because the problems we must cope with are so complex. It is not just the pace of change, but the increasingly interconnected nature of our society and the entire planet, that makes it so hard to cope. Each action, social innovation, or technological invention has potential impacts on many different parts of society and on many different areas of the globe. A bureaucratic error in Peru can cause hunger in Africa, inflation in Europe, and strained diplomatic relations between the U.S. and Japan. A local war in the Mid-East can change recreation and employment patterns in the West, have adverse effects on the ecology of Alaska's North Slope, and possibly precipitate a global famine.

In addition, these difficulties tend to pile up, each one reducing our ability to cope with the rest. John Platt calls this "the crisis of crises":

> What finally makes all of our crises still more danger-
> ous is that they are now coming on top of each other. Most
> administrations are able to endure or even enjoy an
> occasional crisis, with everyone working late together and
> getting a new sense of importance and unity. What they
> are not prepared to deal with are multiple crises, a crisis

of crises all at one time. This is what happened in New York City in 1968 when the Ocean Hill-Brownsville teacher and race strike was combined with a police strike, on top of a garbage strike, on top of a longshoremen's strike, all within a few days of each other.

When something like this happens, the staffs get jumpy with smoke and coffee and alcohol, the mediators become exhausted, and the administrators find themselves running two crises behind. Every problem may escalate because those involved no longer have the time to think straight. What would have happened in the Cuban missile crisis if the East Coast power black-out had occurred by accident that same day? Or if the "hot line" between Washington and Moscow had gone dead? There might have been hours of misinterpretation and some fatally different decisions.

In other words, as a result of technology, the rate of change has increased, the number and extent of the problems caused by each change have also increased, and the resultant problems tend to interact with each other to overload our ability to manage them. Franklin Tugwell describes the effect of all this in *Search for Alternatives:*

> Evidently we are involved in a multi-dimensional management crisis in our society of entirely unforeseen dimensions. The cumulative result of our pursuit of the good life is that we are spinning out ahead of us a society that is becoming less manageable, relative to our needs, than the one we leave behind. It is tragic that just as we become self-consciously committed to knowing the future and shaping it to our ends, we find our means of collective action in such disarray. And because of this we find society suffused with a growing sense of uncertainty and aimlessness, a sense that the vitality and authority of our institutions is draining away. As Amitai Etzioni has so aptly put it, our society is "adrift," moving into the future increasingly unable to steer itself or set a course.

The dilemma is compounded still further because the problems we face are increasingly long-range problems which require anticipatory action, often far in advance of the crisis point, if a disaster is to be averted. Take the case of DDT. Studies have shown that DDT takes approximately 11 years to cycle through the environment, from the time of application to the time it is at its maximum concentration in human food supplies. This means that if we wait until DDT reaches an unacceptable level before we stop using the pesticide, the levels of DDT in food will continue to grow beyond that danger point for another 11 years, with obviously lethal results. If we prefer not to be poisoned by DDT, we must anticipate the danger point and stop using DDT 11 years in advance of that point.

Another example with an even longer time horizon is population. A population with normal age structure takes roughly 70 years to stop growing *after* the birth rate has been reduced to replacement levels (approximately 2.1 children per family). During that 70 year period after "zero population growth" (ZPG) is instituted, the population would normally grow by about 50%. If, for instance, it turns out that the earth can support 6 billion people but cannot support 8 billion, then we need to achieve replacement levels of fertility in the very near future. If it turns out that 6 billion are too many, but that the current population of roughly 4 billion could be maintained indefinitely, then it is already quite a bit too late — the birth rate would have had to have been stabilized before 1960.

There are many more possible examples, some vital to our survival, and others merely important to our comfort and the smooth working of our society. On a mundane level, suppose that your city becomes choked with traffic and the city government decides suddenly that what it needs *now* is an elaborate rapid transit system. Sorry, it's too late. The city should have decided ten to fifteen years ago that it would need a rapid transit system today. Similar delay times exist for nearly every segment of our society, whether it is housing, or transportation, or energy, or social justice, or education, and in each case we must *anticipate* the need or we won't have what we need when we do need it. This requires unusual foresight on the part of citizens and government and a considerable willingness to make sacrifices in the present for their own and their decendants' future survival and well-being.

The mischief is that our society is simply not structured to make these kinds of long-term anticipatory judgments. In chapter ten we will take a detailed look at 24 specific ways that this kind of short-sightedness is built into our system. The energy crisis is an excellent recent example of the consequences. All of the substantial outlines of the problem were known well in advance, yet we waited until the Arab oil boycott of 1973 to begin to do anything serious about it. The vaunted Project Independence is a clear case of "a day late and a dollar short," and the whole energy crisis beautifully demonstrates the adage that "an ounce of prevention is worth a pound of cure."

In terms of the United States, this means that our chronically shortsighted nation is going to have to make a number of wise and far-sighted decisions in the face of a growing crisis of manageability, created in part by the rate of change, in part by the increasing interconnectedness of our society, in part by the "crisis of crises," and in part by our lack of foresight in making decisions in the past. This basic dilemma is likely to continue for at least 50 to 100 years, and the necessity for foresight will increase rather than decrease during that period.

Under circumstances such as these, we have three basic choices as a society. We can continue to try to muddle through in a short-sighted fashion, in which case it is quite likely that we won't make it through the next century intact. We can try to avoid the danger of collapse from public shortsightedness by sacrificing the substance of democracy, transferring the leadership of the nation to a hopefully farsighted elite which is not responsible to the will of the people — i.e., a dictatorship. Or, we can try to cope with our problems as a democracy by creating a citizenry that is both able and willing to deal with complex, long-range kinds of issues.

Most Americans would strongly prefer the last of the three choices, but it seems probable that *in the long run* the survival of the United States as a free nation depends directly on what education does today. We are right now educating the citizens and voters of the next half-century, and the quality of the decisions they will make will be in good part a consequence of the quality of the preparation we give them.

Education

Education in our society is an extended exercise in delayed gratification: work hard now (from anywhere between twelve and twenty-two years); reap your reward for it later — sometimes much later. But delayed gratification always depends fundamentally on *trust*. As long as we "sell" education to young people (and their parents) in terms of its future benefits, we have a fundamental obligation to them to provide them with an education that really will be of benefit. If we offer them an education that is conspicuously unconcerned with the world they will live in, they are entitled to doubt our good sense. If we repeatedly promise them intrinsic benefits that clearly will not be forthcoming, they are entitled to conclude that we are dishonest and hypocritical.

This is, in fact, what has been happening. Education, as an institution, has been steadily losing its legitimacy for the last 15 years. Young people see what goes on in school is increasingly divorced from important issues in the real world. They conclude that the curriculum is irrelevant to the lives they will lead, and that they have no *intrinsic* reason for wanting to learn it. (There are still *extrinsic* reasons, such as jobs, money, and status, but these lead to a desire to get grades and diplomas, not a desire to learn.)

This loss of legitimacy is gradually undermining education as a viable institution. If education is an arbitrary and meaningless ritual, those students whose talents are favored under the rules of the game see any route to success as fair, and cheating, cramming, and grade-grubbing increase. Those students who see themselves as being forced to submit to the process without a chance to reap some of the external rewards increasingly resent what is being done to them, and violence, vandalism, and classroom disruptions also increase. The result inevitably is that schools become less effective and therefore lose legitimacy in the eyes of parents, taxpayers, and politicians. This produces loss of parental support, increasing taxpayer resistance to school-bond issues, and growing hostility on the part of legislatures to increasing salaries and school expenses. And these, in turn, undermine further the effectiveness (and therefore the legitimacy) of education, thus perpetuating the downward spiral.

Public attitudes toward social institutions possess a great deal of inertia. An institution which is perceived as being highly legitimate can retain that perception of legitimacy for quite some time after it has become rigid and irrelevant. Unfortunately, the inertia works the other way as well. An institution that is in disrepute needs to prove itself for quite some time before it earns back its legitimacy. Compared with, for instance, the 1950's, the schools of today are in considerable disrepute, and even with a major effort at reform it will be quite some time before we regain even a semblance of smooth functioning and general credibility.

The only possible way to achieve such a restoration is to give serious attention to that much-abused word "relevance" — relevance to the fundamental needs of the students and of society. As we saw in the two preceding sections, those needs increasingly involve an explicit concern with the real problems of the future and the conceptual skills for thinking competently about the future. The future health of education as an institution will be a direct function of our ability to streamline its current glacial mechanisms for institutional change and alter its almost exclusive orientation with the past.

Teachers

So far we have been considering weighty but somewhat impersonal reasons why we should concern ourselves with the future in the classroom. Our students, our society (both U.S. and global), and our educational institutions all will benefit greatly if we do and will be harmed if we do not. This is justification enough for our concern and one should not infer that it lacks an important personal dimension. Most teachers go into teaching with a strong desire to contribute to the well-being of their students and of their country; each teacher also benefits personally when education is done well and the teaching profession is well respected.

Nevertheless, there are simpler and more immediate benefits from teaching about the future. The simplest is that it is fun. Teachers who have experimented with future studies are unanimous in reporting the tremendous popularity of these courses and units, the very high level of student interest and involvement, and equally high levels of teacher satisfaction.

Student enthusiasm for future studies courses has been high from the beginning. Priscilla Griffith taught one of the first modern courses on the future in an American high school, a course called "21st Century" taught at Melbourne high, near Cape Canaveral, in 1966/67. She describes the experience in Toffler's book *Learning for Tomorrow*, and says of the first day, "Both sections were filled to overflowing. The '21st Century' opened to a full house."

A similar story can be heard from a hundred different sources. More recently, Bonnie Rennell, who teaches social studies in North

Adams, Massachusetts, was almost overwhelmed when she offered to teach a course on the future during the fall of 1974. The student enrollment was eight times the course capacity and included nearly two-thirds of the eligible students in the school. (She was able to recruit another teacher to help out and each of them took two sections in the fall and two more in the spring, so nearly all of the students were accommodated.)

If there are teachers who truly prefer to teach students who are bored with their subjects and turned off by classes, they are a small minority. To most teachers, teaching is much more enjoyable and much more personally rewarding if the students are involved in and excited about what they are learning. And, although it is not always less effort, in an important sense teaching motivated students is easier. You may have to do a little more preparation, especially in a new and experimental field like future studies, and students may demand more of you and range more widely in their desire to learn, but you are spared the grinding effort of creating artificial motivation and discipline among students who just don't care. Furthermore, students who are interested in what they are learning learn more and remember it far better, so the ratio of teaching effort to long-term results is much smaller.

If you are not in a position to teach an entire course on the future, as Priscilla Griffiths and Bonnie Rennel were, you may reasonably be asking yourself if this has anything to do with you. In the next chapter, we will take a closer look at the question of teaching future studies courses versus "futurizing" the normal curriculum. But, whatever subject you teach, student motivation can be increased by systematically relating the subject to your specific students' future needs and concerns. "Why do we have to learn that?" is always a legitimate and serious question. It needs to be dealt with honestly and effectively at the outset and throughout the course.

Honest attention to this question of "Why?" may lead to reorganizing the material to be presented and even to changing the emphasis from some areas to others. Reorganization may be particularly appropriate in subjects like history. We teach history "logically," starting with the events that happened first. But this requires the students to learn about people and events from the distant past and remember them for months and sometimes even years before the historical sequence finally arrives at the present. It is only then, if at all, that the student is shown *why* the things he had to learn are important for understanding where we are now, how we got here, and where we are headed.

Why not be "illogical" instead and teach history backwards? Begin with the present and future, the great issues and problems facing us. Then work backwards in twenty to fifty year chunks, tracing the roots of each issue and dilemma in successively earlier periods. By the time you reach, for example, 1787 and the compromise on slavery in the Constitutional Convention, the students will know not just that it is related to current problems of race relations, but in detail *how* it is related to those problems. They will understand the significance of the event far better and remember it far longer as a result.

The same kind of approach can be used for nearly any course, consistently relating the subject to the personal present and future concerns of the individual students. Where this is done, student motivation rises and teacher satisfaction rises along with it. And while you are making your own job more enjoyable, you can also have the satisfaction that you are making an important contribution to the welfare of your students, your country, and your profession.

As a nation and as individuals, we badly need to become more attuned to the future and more competent in coping with it. Your effort as a teacher will play an important part in whether we do make it through these "interesting times" in one piece, with our civilization and our psyches intact.

NOTES

In order to keep the main text of this book as uncluttered as possible, most of the footnotes and direct quotations have been moved to these "Notes" sections at the ends of the chapters. Since, as a result, the notes contain a good deal of useful supplementary material, an effort has also been made to make the notes more readable by using a narrative style instead of the normal cryptic reference format. The numbers in brackets [ ] refer to the appropriate entries in the bibliography.

The notes for this chapter begin with a set of quotations which apply to the chapter as a whole and thus cannot easily be linked to a specific page. You may also find this section useful for discussions in the classroom or with other teachers. (The notes to chapter two begin with a similar section.) The specific page references for this chapter begin on page 21.

Change, Society, and Education:

Warren L. Ziegler:
   Among all collective enterprises, education is unique in its claims on the future. The children of this decade will be inhabitants of the 21st Century — *our* future, but *their* present.

> Marien and Ziegler, *The Potential of Educational Futures*, p. 3. [65]

Herbert J. Muller:
   Although men have tried to foretell the future ever since the ancients consulted the stars or the entrails of animals, and they have dreamed or speculated about it especially since the rise and spread in the 18th century of the historically novel faith in progress, never before have they thought about it so intensively. The obvious reason is the imperious fact of change in a technological society; continuous, often radical change, at an unprecedented rate, which has created a plain need of efforts not only to understand it but to anticipate it, if possible direct and control it. These efforts raise the basic questions of what is *probable*, what is *possible*, and above all what is desirable.

> Muller, *Uses of the Future*, p. 5. [67]

Wilbur J. Cohen:
   The radically changing values in our society, the increased tempo of scientific and technological change, the new and varied life-styles

that are evolving, and the greater leisure and the discretionary incomes which are developing are all factors affecting educational change. Who knows what the economy and environment will be like in the year 2010 when the current six year olds entering school will be the parents and voters in the society of the next century?

> Hostrop, *Foundations of Futurology in Education*, p. 101. [60]

John I. Goodlad, *et al.:*
Other generations believed that they had the luxury of preparing their children to live in a society similar to their own. Ours is the first generation to have achieved the Socratic wisdom of knowing that we do not know the world in which our children will live.

> Hostrop, *Foundations of Futurology in Education*, p. 217. [60]

Edmund J. Farrell:
Education has been failing to respond adequately to a fast-changing society, one in which new ideas, new issues, new technology, and new social patterns demand new priorities and performances from those who are at the center of the educational process, the teachers. The consequence of this failure has been a widening schism between the environment of the school and the environment of the young when out of school.

> Farrell, *Deciding the Future*, p. 3. [54]

Farrell:
The stake is crucial, and the role of formal education is paramount: as an institution, education will in large measure help shape, be shaped by, and transmit whatever values determine the future of man.

> Farrell, *Deciding the Future*, p. 104. [54]

Grant Venn:
The most significant aspect of the new technology is described by the word *change*. It is not simply a case of new sets of social and economic relationships replacing older ones, but of the new ones themselves being replaced at a faster and faster rate, with only

those adapting to change surviving. This concept of change is not new; what *is* new is the *change in the rate* of change. This has come as a result of the tremendous increase in the rate of scientific activity; significantly, the *rate* of that increase is not constant, but *exponential.*

> Farrell, *Deciding the Future*, p. 6. [54]

Neil Postman and Charles Weingartner:
The standard reply to any comment about change (for example, from many educators) is that change isn't new and that it is easy to exaggerate its meaning. To such replies, Norbert Wiener had a useful answer: the difference between a fatal and a therapeutic dose of strychnine is "only a matter of degree." In other words, change isn't new; what is new is the *degree of change.*

> Postman and Weingartner, *Teaching as a Subversive Activity*, p. 10. [68]

Postman and Weingartner:
We've reached the stage where change occurs so rapidly that each of us in the course of our lives has continuously to work out a set of values, beliefs, and patterns of behavior that are viable, or *seem* viable, to each of us personally. And just when we have identified a workable system, it turns out to be irrelevant because so much has changed while we were doing it.

Of course, this frustrating state of affairs applies to our education as well. If you are over twenty-five years of age, the mathematics you were taught is "old"; the grammar you were taught is obsolete and in disrepute; the biology, completely out of date, and the history, open to serious question. The best that can be said of you, assuming that you remember most of what you were told and read, is that you are a walking encyclopedia of outdated information.

> Postman and Weingartner, *Teaching as a Subversive Activity*, pp. 10-11. [68]

Postman and Weingartner:
Change — constant, accelerating, ubiquitous — is the most striking characteristic of the world we live in and our educational

system has not yet recognized this fact. We maintain, further, that the abilities and attitudes required to deal adequately with change are those of the highest priority and that it is not beyond our ingenuity to design school environments which can help young people to master concepts necessary to survival in a rapidly changing world.

> Postman and Weingartner, *Teaching as a Subversive Activity*, pp. xxiii-xiv. [68]

Postman and Weingartner:
  Survival in a stable environment depends almost entirely on remembering the strategies for survival that have been developed in the past, and so the conservation and transmission of these becomes the primary mission of education. But, a paradoxical situation develops when change becomes the primary characteristic of the environment. Then the task turns inside-out — survival in a rapidly changing environment depends almost entirely upon being able to identify which of the old concepts are relevant to the demands imposed by the new threats to survival, and which are not. Then a new educational task becomes critical: getting the group to unlearn (to "forget") the irrelevant concepts as a prior condition to learning.

> Postman and Weingartner, *Teaching as a Subversive Activity*, p. 208. [68]

Alfred North Whitehead:
  Our sociological theories, our political philosophy, our practical maxims of business, our political economy, and our doctrines of education are derived from an unbroken tradition of great thinkers and of practical examples from the age of Plato . . . to the end of the last century. The whole of this tradition is warped by the vicious assumption that each generation will substantially live amid the conditions governing the lives of its fathers and will transmit those conditions to mould with equal force the lives of its children. *We are living in the first period of history for which this assumption is false.*

> Postman and Weingartner, *Teaching as a Subversive Activity*, p. 11. [68]

Edwin O. Reischauer:

One cannot say that this static, sometimes backward-looking approach to education did not work in the past. The human race has muddled through with reasonable success up until now with this sort of education. But clearly this is no longer adequate. Change is now so rapid and drastic that future generations, if given an education based on the already somewhat outdated perceptions of the preceding generation, may not be able to adjust in time to the new conditions. And the rate of change goes on accelerating at an alarming pace. If the human life span were shorter — say ten years to reach maturity and ten years of productive life — the succession of generations might be fast enough to keep up with the rate of change, at least for a little while longer. But in this, as in so much else, we are stuck with our biological limitations. We are the only people we've got.

> Reischauer, *Toward the 21st Century*,
> pp. 15-16. [70]

Reischauer:

The inevitable time lag in the educational process makes these next few decades all the more crucial for the generations that lie ahead. The child entering first grade this year will not be a member of the voting public for over a decade. He is not likely to have gotten well started on his career for two decades or more. His most important period as a leader or molder of opinion, if he ever achieves such levels of prominence, lies roughly three to six decades ahead. During the intervening years he will no doubt still be learning, but his basic attitudes are likely to have been strongly conditioned, if not completely shaped, by the perceptions and prejudices he is absorbing now.

Education thus has at least a generation of time lag automatically built into it. If it in turn is somewhat behind the times, as is so frequently the situation, the lag can be still greater. . . . With the accelerating speed of change in the world, this generation gap in education becomes more serious all the time. It is frightening to imagine American leaders and the voting public facing global problems as these will probably develop during the first half of the twenty-first century with the basic attitudes and emotions about the rest of the world that American education and environmental influences are likely to instill in most of them today. In the field of education, there is no time for relaxed inattention, because the twenty-first century and its problems are already here.

> Reischauer, *Toward the 21st Century.*
> pp. 12-13. [70]

Reischauer:
  We need a profound reshaping of education if mankind is to survive in the sort of world that is fast evolving. In all human affairs, the speed of change seems constantly to accelerate and the complexity of relationships to multiply.

> Reischauer, *Toward the 21st Century,*
> p. 3. [70]

Lester R. Brown:
  The accelerating rate of social and technological change puts added stress on the educational system. A paragraph in a recent UN report describes this well: "Those now in their active years were born in an economic, social, physical and cultural environment which differs enormously from the one they may still live to see. They were taught by teachers who had been reared in a world whose features are now fading rapidly, and they are called upon to instruct a new generation whose future living conditions are still shrouded in mystery. Basic human nature remains the same, but the necessary adaptations between man and his increasingly manmade environment are now changing with greater speed than ever before." As the pace of change quickens, the focus of education must be not so much how to live, but how to adapt.

> Brown, *World Without Borders,*
> p. 114. [115]

Brown:
  If we could devise an index to measure change, we might conclude that the next three decades will bring at least two centuries' worth of change, as measured in historical terms. Should this be the case, the consequences are profound, for whereas change in the past could occur between generations, it must now occur within a generation, putting a great deal more stress on the

individual. Accelerating change is also putting an enormous burden on society, its values and institutions. In Alvin Toffler's words, "It puts us in collision with the future."

> Brown, *World Without Borders,*
> p. 349. [115]

Page References:

4.   On education's preoccupation with the past, see chapter ten, pages 219-221 and the notes. Postman and Weingartner also appeal to our own personal experience with schools:

> Perhaps you have noticed that most examinations and, indeed, syllabi and curricula deal almost exclusively with the past. The future hardly exists in school. Can you remember ever asking or being asked in school a question like "If such and such occurs, what do you think *will* happen?" A question of this type is usually not regarded as "serious" and would rarely play a central role in any "serious" examination. When a future-oriented question is introduced in school, its purpose is usually to "motivate" or to find out how "creative" the students will be. But the point is that the world we live in is changing so rapidly that a future-orientation is essential for everybody. Its development in schools is our best insurance against a generation of "future shock" sufferers. (*Teaching as a Subversive Activity*, pp. 203-204). [68]

5.   The two passages by Toffler are from *Future Shock*, pages 13 and 371, respectively. [40]

6.   The Muller quotation is from page 52 of *Uses of the Future* [67]; the Toffler quotation is from page 371 of *Future Shock* [40].

7.   On the question of whether we, in fact, live in "interesting times," Donald Michael argues that,

> . . . on the one hand, we face enormously complex issues, problems, and opportunities, and we will have to use unprecedentedly powerful means for responding

to them, especially an improving capability to do long-range planning. On the other hand, we have seen that our ability to plan and to implement those plans will continue to be seriously limited by methodological, institutional, and human weaknesses. Consequently, we will live in a period of tremendous turmoil. (*The Unprepared Society*. p. 106.) [34]

7.   Boulding's views are represented in *The Meaning of the Twentieth Century*, particularly in Chapter One, "The Great Transition." [19]

7.   The descriptions of the international reverberations from decisions made in Peru and the Middle East are not, of course, hypothetical. Nearly everybody is familiar with the effects of the Arab oil embargo, but the effects of the collapse of the Peruvian anchovy fishery are less well known. Robert Prinsky described what happened in an article in the *Wall Street Journal* on June 3, 1974:

> The Pacific Ocean waters off Peru habitually produce a huge catch of anchovies that can be processed into fish-meal to feed cattle ... After a catch of 10.6 metric tons in 1971, Peruvian fishermen had to be content with a mere 4.5 million tons in 1972 and about two million tons last year. Meanwhile the demand for alternative cattle feeds, notably soybeans, skyrocketed ...
>
> On the other side of the Pacific, the Japanese viewed the trend with alarm, for while cattle will munch soybean meal as happily as fishmeal, there isn't an acceptable substitute for soy sauce. One man's cattle feed is another man's daily diet. In Tokyo, soy prices about tripled and there was great consternation when the U.S., by far the world's biggest supplier, temporarily limited soybean exports.

The experts disagree as to whether the collapse of the fishery was the result of overfishing (catching so many adults and adolescents that there were too few left for breeding the next generation), or whether it was the result of a natural shift in ocean currents. It is worth noting, however, that for some years before the collapse ecologists such as Paul Ehrlich had been warning of over-fishing and the danger of collapse. [144]

7-8. The Platt quotation occurs on pages 4 and 5 of *Search for Alternatives* (edited by Franklin Tugwell); the Tugwell quotation is from page xii of the preface. [15]

9.   A discussion of DDT delay times occurs in Meadows, *et al.*, *The Limits to Growth*, pages 81 to 83. [105]

9.   The figures on the growth inertia of a "typical" population apply to countries like the United States which have experienced moderately rapid growth in recent generations. (See *Population and the American Future*, the report of the Commission on Population Growth and the American Future.) Societies experiencing very rapid rates of growth, as is common among third-world nations, would typically take a little bit longer to stabilize after the introduction of ZPG, and would approximately double in size during the interim period. [152]

9.   The question of the carrying capacity of the globe is discussed in Ehrlich and Ehrlich, *Population, Resources, Environment,* particularly in Chapters 4 and 8. [124]

10. Forecasts by respected authorities of the imminence of the energy crisis were so numerous that no one of them would convey the full weight of the warnings that were ignored. Perhaps this excerpt from a *Time* essay ("What Went Wrong") describes the situation best:

> No disaster, however, has been more visible from a distance — or caught people more off-guard — than the energy crisis. The failure to head it off, despite loud and repeated warnings, may some day be considered America's economic Pearl Harbor.
>
> The basic problem was obvious to anyone who could read a simple line graph. For years, American consumption of oil has been rising faster than American production of oil. After the two lines crossed in the mid-'60's, the difference had to be made up in imports, with an ever-increasing percentage coming from Arab countries that disagreed with American policy toward Israel. The possibility of a cutoff was thereafter always present and predictable, and in hindsight, it is clear that the U.S. failed on every level to prepare for it . . .

The shadows of the larger crisis have loomed over the U.S. for years. Back in the '50's, the Paley Report, commissioned by President Eisenhower, pin-pointed a coming shortage of oil and coal. The warnings increased in tempo in the '60's. Biologist Paul Ehrlich was among the decade's many Cassandras. "Using straight mathematics," he now says, "what I was predicting then was foreseeable in the late '40's and early '50's. It was a case of simple multiplication — the number of people times what we were doing."

By 1970 John A. Carver Jr., a member of the Federal Power commission, was saying: "A crisis exists right now. For the next three decades we will be in a race for our lives to meet our energy needs." Nor was the Nixon Administration unaware — or totally unaware. In a speech to oilmen in Dallas in the fall of 1970, Paul McCracken, then chairman of the Council of Economic Advisers, clearly sketched the genesis of the problem and recommended a reserve capacity in the U.S., just in case anything went wrong with foreign suppliers. It seems that nearly everybody knew. "We could see it coming," says James Boyd, who directed a federal commission that last summer predicted: "We conclude that an energy shortage, of severely disruptive and damaging proportions, is a distinct possibility in the immediate future." (*Time*, Dec. 10, 1973, p. 49.) [117]

10.   For a summary of the reasons why energy self-sufficiency is highly unlikely by the year 1980, see Les Gapay, "Elusive Goal," *Wall Street Journal*, 24 July, 1974. [127]

11.   In 1973, a Senate sub-committee commissioned Louis Harris to do a survey on "What America Thinks About Itself." The results showed that — in the midst of Watergate, soaring inflation, and an energy crisis — education was one of the ten answers most frequently given to the question, "What are our biggest problems?" (*Newsweek*, December 10, 1973, p. 40.) [316]

11.   My argument about relevance and student attitudes (i.e., that delinquency and school disruptions increase when students see

schooling as irrelevant to their own future concerns is supported by the research that Arthur L. Stinchcombe has done on student "rebels." Wendell Bell and James Mau describe the results of Stinchcombe's work in *The Sociology of the Future:*

> Arthur L. Stinchcombe in his book *Rebellion in a High School* found that differential images of the future among high school students helped to explain whether or not the students became rebels. He says that the " . . . future, not the past, explains adolescent rebellion, contrary to the hypothesis that deviant attitudes are the result of distinctively rebel biographies . . . we hold that deviant values or crippling of the ego are traceable to differences in the futures of adolescents." His argument is that adolescents whose images of their own occupational future are such that they expect to become members of the manual working class in the next labor market cohort see no clear relation between what they are doing in school and their future status. Thus, their current self-restraint is perceived as irrelevant to the achievement of long-run goals. The student " . . . reacts negatively to a conformity that offers nothing concrete. He claims autonomy from adults because their authority does not promise him a satisfactory future." (Bell and Mau, *The Sociology of the Future,* p. 33.) [2]

Margaret Mead is even more succinct:

> Going through the forms by which men were educated for generations, but which no longer serve to educate those who accept them, can only teach students to regard all social systems in terms of exploitation. (Mead, *Culture and Commitment,* p. 68.) [66]

12. In discussing the popularity of futures courses with students, there is always the question of whether the interest is genuine, or simply a response to novelty. One answer can be found in the results of a Harris poll on the attitudes of high school students toward society and education:

> They are excited by the prospect of living in a fast-changing modern society and they want their high school education to help prepare them for it — not for some

society of the past. (Quoted in Farrell, *Deciding the Future*, p. 10.) [54]

The poll was conducted in 1969, before all but a handful of futures courses had even been considered; the results of the poll are reported in *Life* magazine, on May 16 of that year.

12. The passage by Priscilla Griffiths occurs on page 202 of the Random House edition of *Learning for Tomorrow*, edited by Alvin Toffler. [78]

12. The reference to Bonnie Rennell is from a personal communication. (Ms. Rennell is now a part-time member of the Future Studies Graduate Program at the University of Massachusetts.)

13. The importance of intrinsic motivation for learning has been pointed out many times. Perhaps Postman and Weingartner give the most concise summary:

> No one has ever said that children themselves are the only, or necessarily the best, source for articulating relevant areas of inquiry. What *has* been said is that, regardless of its source, unless an inquiry is perceived as relevant by the learner, no significant learning will take place. (*Teaching as a Subversive Activity*, p. 11.) [68]

CHAPTER II
The Future-Oriented Curriculum

So far, we have discussed future studies only in general language, looking at it primarily in terms of its objectives. But what would it mean to actually put it into practice? What might a future-oriented curriculum look like?

There are three major approaches to orienting the curriculum toward the future: using the future as an organizing principle, "futurizing" the classroom, and teaching the basic skills for futures thinking. In this chapter we will explore the first two approaches at some length, and discuss the third approach as a preface to the specific exercises in futures thinking which are the focus for the rest of the book.

The Future as an Organizing Principle

Why do we teach the subjects we teach? For the most part, the curriculum has been shaped by a random mixture of historical accident, institutional inertia, and social demand. There has been no coherence, no focus, no organizing principle that allows us to say, "include this; exclude that." The result has been a hodge-podge that is very hard to explain rationally. (This is especially true of the exclusions; there are always plausible-sounding arguments for what is included.) One implication of the preceding chapter is that we would do well to organize the curriculum around one question that is already implicit in much of the public debate: What education will best prepare this student for the next seventy years?

The virtue of making this focus explicit is that it forces us to make serious long-range forecasts about society and to acknowledge our general inability to predict. We cannot know what the future will bring; the best we can do is to try to define the range of alternative possibilities. Fortunately, we do possess two important bits of information about the future: the fact of change, and the fact of uncertainty.

In our society today, both the rate of change and the degree of uncertainty are so high that it is dangerous and misleading to base education on *any* static picture of society, whether it be the present or one particular image of the future. We are left instead with the task of designing education that enables students to function and to deal with change *regardless of which of the many possible changes actually occur.*

The prospect this presents is not quite the trackless void it appears to be. We will continue (out of necessity) to make all sorts of projections from the present and assumptions about what is likely in the future. The difference lies in the way we use our projections and assumptions. Instead of trying to pick out the most likely future world and then trying to identify the best preparation for that world, we should select elements for our curriculum which will be valuable preparation for the greatest number of *different* possible future worlds. This immediately puts a great premium on flexibility and diversity; on the ability to learn a new skill quickly, instead of the possession of pretrained skills; on underlying principles, instead of factual data; and on general, as opposed to specialized, kinds of competence.

Having gotten this far, we can begin to see the outlines of a future-oriented curriculum designed around areas of competence which will be essential, whatever future actually comes about. One possible design would center on these six areas of competence:

- Access to Information
- Thinking Clearly
- Communicating Effectively
- Understanding Man's Environment
- Understanding Man and Society
- Personal Competence

The table on the next page outlines some of the basic elements of these six areas of competence. As you can see from the table, the emphasis throughout is on general skills rather than specific content. Even in the seemingly content-rich sections, like the physical sciences, the emphasis should be on the over-all conceptual framework for organizing knowledge, rather than the mass of information. It is not vital for students to be able to name the parts of the cell, for example, as long as they are aware of the cell as a complex system of interdependent parts.

If we are presently attempting to teach only a small portion of the areas listed (and not succeeding very well at that), how are we to accomplish all of this in a mere twelve or sixteen years? The answer lies in an old bromide, but one we persist in ignoring: teaching children how to think, how to learn, and how to retrieve information from where it is stored is a much more efficient process than trying to cram the raw data itself into the students' heads.

Of course, no skill, not even an abstract skill, is learned in a vicarious or abstract way. Skills are learned by practice. This means, for instance, that if we wish to teach the skills of information retrieval, students must be faced with real problems that require specific information which they must obtain from a variety of sources. But instead of choosing that information solely on the basis that they "ought" to know it, we need to balance four interrelated considerations:

- Student interest and motivation
- Utility for teaching the desired skill
- Breadth and diversity of student experience
- Intrinsic value of the information

"Intrinsic value" is placed last deliberately, since it is very difficult to claim that any one datum is essential in an age where there are far more "crucial" bits of information than any individual could possibly learn.

There is one item in the table which may cause particular comment. This is the inclusion of history and humanities under cultural anthropology in the general section on "Understanding Man and Society." The overall objective of this section is to have students gain the best possible understanding of the origins, the potential, the limitations, and particularly the considerable diversity of human nature and human societies. In order to have

TABLE 2-1

Learning Objectives For a Future-Oriented Curriculum

Access to Information
Reading
Listening and seeing
Direct experiment
Libraries and reference books
Computerized data-retrieval
Data from newspapers, businesses
    government agencies, etc.
Asking experts
Judging reliability
Managing information overload

Thinking Clearly
Semantics
Propaganda and common fallacies
Values clarification
Deductive logic
Mathematics
Analytical problem solving
Scientific method
Probability and statistics
Computer programming
General systems
Creative problem solving
Forecasting and prediction

Communicating Effectively
Speaking informally
Public speaking
Voice and body language
Cultural barriers to communication
Formal and informal writing
Grammar, syntax, and style
Drawing, sketching, still photo-
    graphy, film making, etc.
Graphic design and layout
Outlines, flow-charts, charts,
    tables, and graphs
Organization and editing
Handwriting, typing, dictating

Understanding Man's Environment
Astronomy, physics, and chemistry
Geology and physical geography
Biology, ecology, and ethology
Genetics, evolution, and population
    dynamics
Fundamentals of modern technology
Applied mechanics, optics, and
    electronics

Understanding Man and Society
Human evolution
Human physiology
Linguistics
Cultural anthropology (including
    history and the humanities)
Psychology and social psychology
Racism, ethnicity, and xenophobia
Government and law (especially
    American constitutional law)
Economics and economic philosophy
Changing occupational patterns
Education and employment
Issues in human survival
Prospects for mankind

Personal Competence
Physical grace and coordination
Survival training and self-defense
Safety, hygiene, nutrition, and sex-
    education
Consumer education and personal finance
Creative and performing arts
Basic inter-personal skills
Small group dynamics
Management and administration
Effective citizen participation
Knowledge of best personal learning
    styles and strategies
Mnemonics and other learning aids
Bio-feedback, meditation, mood control
Self-knowledge and self-motivation

some chance of anticipating how people may respond in rapidly changing circumstances, it is essential that students get a thorough exposure to the range of human responses to widely varied circumstances, past and present. History and the humanities should be an integral part of this exposure.

The trajectory of most world history courses (from the Mid-East through Greece, Rome, Europe, and England, to the United States) is much too narrow, and the emphasis at each point is still primarily on "who did what, when" instead of on gaining a real understanding of the nature of the culture and the society and the reasons why people behaved as they did. We need at least to sample a much greater variety of current and historical societies and go into each much more fully in terms of the inner workings of the society — its culture, economics, religion, environment, and technology.

Our teaching of the "humanities" is even more narrow than our teaching of history. Out of the whole broad sweep of human art and culture, most of our schools concentrate almost exclusively on one tiny sliver: critically approved writings in English during the last 400 years. Even these are taken almost entirely out of cultural context and taught instead with the intent of inculcating a particularly artificial set of esthetic standards. To devote up to a quarter of the secondary curriculum to the likes of *Ivanhoe* or (shudder!) *The Last of the Mohicans* is folly, especially as the principal effect on adult Americans seems to be to give them a distaste for books and a particular dislike of "literary classics." Literature is only one part of art, and all art can be, if used properly, a special kind of window onto other people's lives and feelings. In addition to taking a much broader view of the humanities and placing them in a more meaningful context, the secondary "English" curriculum must take a much broader and more skills-oriented approach to the many varieties of communication.

One objection to the kind of curriculum suggested here is that it contains nothing in the way of specific vocational training. Such training has its place (though that place may be with the employer rather than the school), but the need for it is a testimony to the failure of the educational system to equip students with more general skills. Furthermore, such training is only of limited benefit, since it is quite likely that any particular specialty will be transformed or made obsolete in a relatively short period of time, thus confronting the *adult* — no longer a student and probably with a family to support — with the task of learning new skills or obtaining employment for which he is not specifically pre-trained.

Sidney Harris describes the necessary shift in educational emphasis in a short essay titled, "Man Must Learn How to Learn":

> The real reason that vocational and "specialist" training is largely pointless today lies in the rapid out-dating of so much technical knowledge and skills . . .
>
> What the new society of the future calls for are versatility and flexibility and creativity. These cannot be learned in a technical sense; they are part of a liberal education, which teaches men and women how to think, not just how to put things together and make them work . . .
>
> In a recent talk, Dr. Arnold Ducoffe, Director of Georgia Tech's School of Aerospace Engineering, remarked that this obsolescence of knowledge is the big reason that today's engineering schools no longer stress the "mechanical" — but rather the "philosophical" elements in science — not how to do something, but why something is true.
>
> If we learn the reasons behind phenomena, then we can cope with changing conditions.
>
> Our pressing need is for men and women who can adapt to needs and acquire skills that are barely on the horizon today.
>
> More and more, the function of the specialist is being taken over by the machines; it is the "generalist" who can make decisions based on an imaginative projection of the future, we so desperately require to keep the wheels turning.

In terms of specific job preparation, the most useful approach may be to give students a realistic sense of what different occupations actually involve, the ways (and the rate at which) they are changing, and the realistic relationship between education and employment. Units dealing with "the world of work" are a step in the right direction, but they give only a static picture of different occupations. This needs to be complemented by case studies of the changing requirements of specific occupations, and by information on the changing overall patterns in employment, with existing jobs disappearing and new jobs being created all the time. Students must also be made aware that the educational preparation necessary for survival in a rapidly shifting job market is considerably different from the preparation they would need for some specific, supposedly unchangeable occupation.

"Futurizing" the Classroom

So far we have been talking in terms of an entire curriculum, as if a whole school were contemplating a future-oriented program. Such a situation would have important advantages for the individual teacher. Under ideal conditions, older students would enter the classroom with adequate preparation, built up in sequential steps in earlier grades. Student progress would be assessed (in a diagnostic rather than a competitive manner) in terms of the students' general mastery of the six main areas of competence, instead of being assessed primarily by tests of remembered data. And, in particular, teachers would not be judged by such an extremely narrow set of outcomes as is presently the case.

Unfortunately, most teachers who are experimenting with future-oriented education must do so on their own, in schools which are more or less traditional. Students enter the class as products of a past-oriented system. Periodically their progress is judged by examinations and "objective" tests on a very limited range of subjects. Furthermore, the teacher is also judged almost exclusively (with the exception of classroom discipline) in terms of that same narrow, pre-assigned range of content. Your own situation may be in a school that is much more open than this, but even if your school is quite conventional there are a number of important ways that you can "futurize" your classroom.

Some of these have already been mentioned. One of the most important is that of simply discussing with students the connection between what you are about to teach them and their own concerns and personal objectives. This may involve "wasting" a week or two in an exploration of the students' futures and the possible futures of our society, but if this results in greater student interest, it should be relatively easy to make up for the "lost" time. This may also involve reorganizing part or all of the course, as in the suggestion in chapter one for a "backwards" U.S. History course. (If you do something of this sort, by the way, be sure to tell the students what you are doing and why, and give them a sense of being involved in something innovative; just the fact of being part of an experiment increases interest and enthusiasm, and there is no reason for you not to take advantage of this phenomenon.)

A second important change you can make is to increase the emphasis on active learning. A great deal has been said in the last century about the importance of "learning by doing," but the typical American classroom is still depressingly dependent upon passive forms of learning, especially at the secondary levels. If you are trying to teach students a skill, such as math or reading, give them content which matters to them and a situation where they must *use* the skill to achieve their own objectives. If you have content which you must teach them, have them dig it out from sources other than textbooks or lectures, and have them demonstrate their mastery of it in some form which also requires them to master a variety of interpersonal and communication skills. If possible, get them out of the classroom into the real world and bring the real world into the classroom, in the form of people, newspapers and magazines, and real issues that are important to the public at large.

A third basic way to orient the classroom toward future needs is to *democratize* it as much as possible, for two solidly pragmatic reasons. The first has to do with the health of our political system. The Founding Fathers based our political system on the firm conviction that freedom can only be maintained if the citizens play an active, informed, and skeptical role in the political process, without fear of reprisals or intimidation. In Part III, we will take a more intensive look at some of the complex modern problems facing our democracy today. One of the conclusions reached there is that informed citizen participation is even more important today than in the past. At the same time, participating in this democracy has become more difficult, and it is more essential than ever that young people gain experience and understanding in a basically democratic environment. It is simply not reasonable to expect students to live for 12 years in an authoritarian environment and suddenly, on their 18th birthdays, become responsible defenders of democracy at the ballot box. (It is worth adding here that this is not a matter of liberal versus conservative, but of authoritarian versus democratic; the Symbionese Liberation Army and the American Nazi Party are equal threats to our freedom.)

Jerry Farber describes the danger and helps define what we do, and do not, mean by classroom democracy in his essay, "The Student and Society":

> Our schools make democracy unlikely because they rob the people, who are supposed to be sovereign, of their sense of power and of their ability to will meaningful institutional changes.
>
> The democratic ideal . . . means government of, by and for the people. It means power in the hands of the people. Our schools, however, remain less suited to this ideal than to an authoritarian society; they are more effective in teaching obedience than in fostering freedom. Our textbooks may teach one kind of political system but the method by which our schools operate teaches another. And the method wins out over the textbooks overwhelmingly. A more substantial degree of democracy will become likely only when we understand that political freedom is not merely a constitutional matter; it's also a state of mind, which can be either nurtured or blighted in school . . .
>
> A democracy cannot possibly function if its citizens are educated to be clever robots. The way to educate children for democracy is to let them do it — that doesn't mean allowing them to practice empty forms, to make pretend decisions or to vote on trivia; it means that they participate in the real decisions that affect them. You learn democracy in school not by defining it or by simulating it but by doing it . . .
>
> Democracy in school doesn't mean that a class votes on whether two and two make four, even though that seems to be the fear of some teachers. Suppose, for example, my entire history class insists that Rome fell because of its sexual laxity. Suppose we argue, I give my reasons and they give theirs. Then, in desperation, I try to impress them by detailing my academic background but they still insist that they're right. In this (unlikely) situation what relevance would grading have? What would it add to my

true authority if I were able to pass, fail, expel, what have you? My value to a class is that I can be of some kind of assistance to them. What they make of it is up to them. I'm a teacher not a cop. Democracy in school doesn't mean that we vote on what's true; it means that education isn't anything which is *done to* somebody.

The consequences of authoritarian schooling are frightening. Every so often, someone prepares a questionnaire or petition quoting the Bill of Rights from the U.S. Constitution without identifying the source, and asking people if they approve of the principles expressed. The story always makes the news because the general public always rejects overwhelmingly these fundamental guarantees of political and personal freedom as being "radical" or "un-American." That the citizens of a democracy should reject the basic tenets of democratic society is an extraordinary indictment of the failure of the educational system to prepare them for citizenship, a failure which will become increasingly dangerous as our society comes under increasing stress in the years ahead.

The second reason for democratizing education has to do with the health of our national economy. How can a nation with the highest industrial labor costs in the world compete effectively in world markets? One way is by selling *knowledge*, directly and indirectly — directly in the form of creativity, research, and education, and indirectly in the form of advanced technology and greater efficiency of production. Douglas Davis described our situation in a recent *Newsweek* article:

> The American economy is dependent upon innovation, which can only flourish within an open, "permissive" context. We are finished as the supreme manufacturing and producing economy. In the first place, we cannot compete now with other advanced industrial powers as a hardware manufacturer ("The general rule is that if it can be made abroad," says one expert, "it can be made cheaper"); we will do even worse when matched against emerging under-developed nations, who can bring to bear large armies of low-cost labor. Furthermore, the heart of this country — and particularly the younger generation rising to power — is no longer in bread-and-butter work.

Beneath the surface turn in our balance-of-payments trade relationship with the rest of the world, the nature of the American society — which means the nature of its people — has been changing. In 1900 this was a predominantly agricultural and rural nation; by 1940, it was predominantly industrial. Since 1965, an even more remarkable conversion has been taking place — into a professional, managerial and technical society. Simply put, this means that our basic skill is developing and disseminating ideas, not products. Peter Drucker has called this new sector of the economy the "knowledge sector." It is already generating one-third of our GNP. By the end of this decade, it will produce half of the GNP. If we are lucky, we will more and more export programmers, consultants, technicians, theses, reports, teachers, lecturers and art, broadly defined. Already, we see evidence of this in the GNP statistics: among the few areas where we enjoy a trade surplus now are computers, high-technology electronics and nuclear power plants.

In other words, we are going to be depending more and more for sheer economic survival on our creativity, originality, and ability to innovate, and these talents require an open and questioning environment in order to develop and flourish. Since the most important training ground for the knowledge industries is the schools, the degree of democratization of our classrooms will have a direct bearing on our economic, as well as our political, well-being in the future.

There is one further form of "futurizing" the classroom that is much harder to describe concretely. It has to do with psychological atmosphere and with attitudes toward change and toward the future. The attitudes your students bring to class may go to extremes. Some students will have a "gee-whiz" enthusiasm for all the possible new gadgets. Some will have an almost religious faith in "progress" and in the invulnerability of the United States. Some will simply delight in the roller-coaster thrill of novelty and the rapidity of change.

On the other hand, some of your students will be deathly afraid of the future. To them it is the dark, scary unknown. They will want you to give them certainty, to tell them what *will* happen, and to reassure them that everything will be all right. And there will be some students who have simply given up hope. Toffler tells of one student, a 15-year old boy, who came up to him after a class on the future and said, in effect, "This was very interesting, but it's all kind of pointless, isn't it? We're not going to make it, you know."

What can you do? Somehow, you must make the case for a middle ground between enthusiasm for change and fear of change, and between blind optimism and blind pessimism. Let's hold the question of personal attitudes toward change for a moment, and consider the problem of extreme optimism or pessimism about society. Of the two, unwarranted optimism is the easier to handle (among students; with adults the reverse is often true). The problems we face are undeniable and the dangers if we fail to cope with them are enough to pale the rosiest glasses. Your more serious problem is how to handle the pessimism that seems endemic to the middle of many future studies courses. In *Uses of the Future*, Herbert Muller describes the problem he faced in his own courses:

> In a course on modern technology I set students to exploring independently a wide variety of problems, and those who did the most thorough job of research uniformly reported pessimistic conclusions about our prospects. What troubled me was the difficult effort to maintain a nice balance: on the one hand, young people need to be clearly aware of what they are up against, the very real dangers, the good reasons for alarm about the future; on the other hand, they need to retain a hopeful spirit if there is to be any hope for the future. The most that I could say to my students was that the growing alarm was the best reason for hope.

Muller plays down the value of his own response much more than he should. The growing alarm is indeed the best reason for hope. Most of the dilemmas ahead of us are not basically technical problems. The difficulty, instead, is in generating the political and social *will to cope*, so it is quite true in these cases that, for society as a whole, understanding a problem is halfway to solving it. The real time to be frightened is when everyone else is smug and complacent and refuses to acknowledge a problem until it turns into a full-blown catastrophe.

There is still far too much complacency in the U.S. on subjects like population, resources, food, the environment, and social stability in general, but there is a great deal less than there was only a few years ago. The trick is to wake up those who are complacent without convincing the rest that things are hopeless. Frank Hopkins, a retired State Department policy planner, writes about this problem as follows:

> We must disabuse people of the notion that everything is just wonderful, that they can eat their cake and still have it, that they can indulge themselves with every form of comfort and convenience. We cannot permit anyone — older people or younger people — to be complacent. Civilization is in danger, and if we have to ring alarm bells and blow loud whistles, then that is what we must do.
>
> But we must not give people the impression that a dreadful future is inevitable, and that we should resign ourselves to despair. I find in talking to audiences that I have to adopt two completely different tones in my addresses depending on what age group I am trying to reach. I have to try to shake older people out of their over-confidence, their complacency. But I find young people already terribly worried and disturbed. They have heard so much about problems they have become apprehensive and pessimistic. Many of them display a sort of "What's the use?" attitude. Many feel that their elders have made such a mess of modern society that the best thing to do is to cop out and run for cover. They want to turn their backs on the real world, not to confront it and try to change it.
>
> Here I think is one of the great challenges to education. We are training now the generation which will be taking charge of the world in the 21st century. Somehow we must equip them for the challenges which they will be facing. We must impart to them the knowledge and skills they will need for a future society becoming ever more difficult and complex. But we must also try to instill in them hope for the future, confidence that they can influence and change it in desirable directions, a belief in their own capabilities.

In practice, the two best means for achieving these goals are an increased sophistication in long-range forecasting, and, paradoxically, a better sense of history. On the one hand, the inevitability of either progress or disaster is the kind of linear, "single future" assumption that comes from a lack of imagination or serious consideration about the real range of alternative possibilities; the more forecasting students do, the more they will realize that there are more options than just a choice between "the present extended" and disaster. On the other hand, the apparent magnitude of the problems we must deal with is partly due to a lack of historical perspective; few young people today have any grasp at all of how far we have come as a civilization in the last 300 years, and the tremendous magnitude of the problems which we have already overcome.

Let's return now to the problem of psychological attitudes toward change. People who thrive on change, even lust for novelty, have a real advantage in a "future shocked" world. The problem here is not to discourage their adaptability, but to make them aware that many others in society are much less adaptable than they are. These others constitute a fundamental limit upon the adaptability of the society as a whole, and the novelty-addicts must realize that changes for the sake of change and changes in unessential areas of society put a considerable stress on social stability and cohesion and reduce the ability of the society as a whole to cope with essential changes.

Those who fear change have a much more serious problem because, whether they like it or not, they are going to have to cope with it. Toffler has explored this dilemma, and ways of coping with it, in great depth in *Future Shock*. The simplest and most effective method of coping has already been mentioned in chapter one: "Fore-warned fore-armed." Anticipated change is much less threatening and less disruptive than unexpected change, so these students especially should be encouraged to read widely in the literature of forecasting and to do considerable forecasting of their own.

A more basic approach to helping them cope with change is to encourage them to abandon their dependence on absolutes, and to gradually shift toward a greater tolerance for ambiguity. The best way to do this is through your normal day-to-day teaching. If you — and teachers in general — routinely treat "facts" as if they were absolute certainties, students will tend to regard them as such. Then, when some of the "facts" are seriously questioned or found to be false, the effect is traumatic. Trust in all learning is shaken and all secondary conclusions based on the false data have to be re-examined.

If, on the other hand, you routinely treat even the most certain piece of information as ever so slightly tentative, a hypothesis of which you are almost (but not quite) completely positive, students will pick up *that* attitude. Then, if one of the "facts" you teach them turns out to be wrong, they will not be shocked, because you will have already forewarned them of that possibility. They will also be more likely to be a little bit skeptical and to keep an eye out for confirming evidence, and therefore be less likely to build whole belief structures that depend on the truth of any single assumption.

It may be necessary to emphasize again that this is a gradual process. It is not accomplished simply by telling students that nothing is absolutely certain, though that may help. It is an approach that must be taught primarily by example over a period of time. If you can demonstrate to your students that you have a well-integrated world-view and can nevertheless accept the possibility of being wrong in any particular, tolerating and even encouraging students to question your views, then the students will gain confidence that they can question not just your beliefs, but their own, without everything dissolving into quicksand.

This is tremendously important in a time when everything from scientific fact to basic social values to personal circumstances is subject to change almost without notice. An individual who has built absolutes into the foundation of his personality is put in an impossible position when the absolutes are threatened: either reality must be denied (insanity) or whole portions of the personality must be dismantled and reassembled (a rough definition of psychotherapy). As science fiction author Ted Sturgeon puts it, " 'Tain't what you don't know that hurts you, it's what you do know that ain't so."

One of the worst things schools do is to teach students an intolerance for ambiguity. From the classroom question and weekly quiz right up to the elaborate College Board Exams, the most important items in a student's scholastic success or failure hammer home the message: every question has *one* right answer. In the real world, of course, this is just not so. Some questions have many, equally valid answers. Some questions have no good answer, only least bad answers. And a great many have answers that are rapidly changing as circumstances change.

You can help your students to cope with the future by encouraging them to look for alternative explanations for events, by supporting them when they say "I don't know" or "It might be this, or it might be that." Help them see real-world issues in all their complexity and shades of gray, instead of simple black and white. Get them, also, to plan ahead in terms of contingencies, the different things that might happen, instead of a single fixed schedule.

In addition to a tentative, questioning attitude toward knowledge and a tolerance for ambiguity, we need to encourage the general traits of creativity and imagination. Perhaps the biggest single failing in thinking about the future is a failure to be sufficiently imaginative about what might happen; a fertile imagination is an indispensible requirement for even the most hard-headed futurist. In chapter six, we will look at some specific methods for helping students to be more imaginative about the future, but anything else you can do to encourage imagination and creativity on their part will help them to be better futurists. And, as we have already seen, these are increasingly important attributes from an economic standpoint as well.

Teaching Basic Skills for Futurist Thinking

One of the objectives of future studies is to give students a more sophisticated approach to thinking about the future. Fortunately, this does not mean that students have to learn a lot of complex and specialized forecasting methods. The biggest difference between the man in the street and the professional forecaster is not the forecaster's fancy techniques, but rather the richness of his conceptual approach. Moreover, none of the basic concepts and skills which make up that approach are beyond the understanding of the layman and very few, if presented clearly, are beyond the grasp of an interested sixth grader.

How should these be taught? All at once, in a future studies course? If so, at what age? Some basic forecasting methods, for instance, depend on at least a minimum knowledge of algebra and so cannot be taught before high school in most places; should we therefore wait until one of the high school years to introduce students to futures thinking? The disadvantage is that much of the material can be taught at an earlier age and could benefit students in the interim. On the other hand, teaching each piece at the earliest appropriate age assumes that the entire school is involved in a futures curriculum, which is generally not true.

The sensible answer is to do whichever is practical for you in your own circumstances. You will normally have to assume that your students are coming into your class without any prior preparation, so you will have to begin with the basics, regardless of the grade level you teach. If you have the chance to teach a future studies course at the secondary level, by all means do so. Your students cannot, after all, go back in time and learn the more introductory bits at an earlier age. If you teach a subject course, like math or biology, you can incorporate into it those elements of future studies which are relevant, without much fear of duplicating the efforts of other teachers. If you teach in the elementary grades, the approach that probably makes the most sense is to include one or more short units on the future in the year's work.

These answers, of course, are only common sense in a field as new as this one. However, they pose some awkward problems for the curriculum developer, since all but the most advanced topics will be taught at a number of different grade levels and under widely different circumstances.

The next eight chapters are devoted to a basic future studies curriculum. Selecting and developing the teaching methods and exercises that make up that curriculum required some hard decisions, especially in terms of audience. The more cautious course of action would have been to gear the curriculum to the high school level. However, a good deal of work had already been done on units for elementary grades, including some of the most challenging and interesting work that has been attempted (e.g., the task of finding ways to teach fifth and sixth graders to really understand exponential growth — see chapter four). The exercises in Part II have therefore been described so that, where possible, they will be useful to both elementary and secondary school teachers.

The result of this decision, however, is to demand more of you, the user. The exercises that follow have all been tested in different versions at different grade levels. In each case, the version described is the one which could be most easily adapted to the whole range of relevant age-groups. In some cases this was the middle ground, usually around grades 6 - 8. More often, however, it required more ingenuity to teach the same skill or concept to younger students and it proved easier to adapt the exercises "up" than "down"; the version given in these cases is the one appropriate to the youngest (or next to youngest) group.

Thus, in many instances you will have to use the exercises as a point of departure and do some judicious improvising instead of accepting them ready-made. Most teachers seem to do this in any case, even with the kind of highly detailed and age-specific lesson plan that underestimates teacher resourcefulness and over-estimates student uniformity. Certainly, the teachers who helped out with the development and testing process for these exercises showed no reluctance to adapt and embellish to suit the needs of their particular students.

The chapters in Part II and Part III are arranged in a useful sequence (though by no means the only one) for a separate future studies course. Beginning Part II, chapter three introduces the basic notion of the future and some preliminary ideas about forecasting. Chapters four through eight correspond to five general approaches to forecasting: trend extrapolation, intuitive forecasting and expert opinion, alternative futures and scenario writing, modelling, and simulation. In Part III, we apply a general futures approach to an intensive look at the problems threatening the survival of humanity on a global scale (chapter nine), and to the underlying problem of lack of foresight in our own society (chapter ten).

Although the topics are arranged in a sequence, many users of this book will not want or be able to use it for an extended course of study. An attempt has been made, therefore, to keep the chapters somewhat independent of each other and, where possible, to do this with the individual exercises as well, so that various bits and pieces of the whole can be incorporated where relevant into other courses with a minimum of effort. Chapters four and eight, for instance, are relevant to many science and math courses, while chapter six may be of special use to history, social studies, and English teachers.

A final note: no matter how positive the language, none of what follows is carved in stone. It is based on a discipline, long-range forecasting, which is practically brand new and which is growing and changing quite rapidly. The teaching methods which are described are a tentative beginning, not a final word. New topics, and different and better ways of doing things, will undoubtedly occur to you as you put these into practice. This is as it should be. If we are going to presume to help others cope with change, we must show that we can cope with it ourselves, and the principal source for the innovation and renewal that this requires will have to be the teacher in the classroom.

NOTES

The Nature of the Future-Oriented Curriculum:

Glen Heathers:

What chief demands on the individual does societal change impose? These demands challenge education to make changes that will meet them, insofar as education can contribute toward satisfying such difficult requirements.

In the economic realm, there is an increasing demand for workers possessing competencies in problem solving and in human relations, and for individuals who are capable of relearning their jobs or preparing for different jobs. The industrial worker's tasks increasingly will be those of creating programs for machines and trouble-shooting problems that were not anticipated in automated programs. The need for greater skills in human relations results from the increasing proportion of jobs in service occupations — teaching, social welfare occupations, jobs in government, recreational work, etc. Special provisions are needed to prepare many millions in our inner cities to obtain jobs in industry or service occupations.

In the *political* sphere, there is the need for every citizen to become prepared for responsible participation in dealing with the many critical societal problems that exist now and are certain to become more acute in the years ahead. The alternative is for our citizens to abrogate democracy through permitting control of our society by whatever special-interest groups can seize power — Fascists, technocrats, generals, unions, or corporations. Enlightened self-interest in dealing with issues and problems is at the heart of citizenship in a democracy. But effective democracy demands citizens who recognize that their interests can be served best when, through negotiation and compromise, the interests of many different groups are served.

Citizens respond tardily to events, becoming aroused to action only after problems have become acute. Thus, learning to look ahead — to see local, national, and world-wide problems in their early stages and to take preventive political action — is becoming increasingly essential for survival. An educated citizenry should be prepared to influence the direction and pace of change, rather than adjusting defensively to changes that have already taken place.

> Heathers, "Education to Meet the Psychological Requirements for Living in the Future," *Journal of Teacher Education,* Summer 1974, pp. 110-111. [82]

John and Evelyn Dewey:

If it was true in Rousseau's day that information, knowledge, as an end in itself, was an "unfathomable and shoreless ocean," it is much more certain that the increase of science since his day has made absurd the identification of education with the mere accumulation of knowledge. The frequent criticism of existing education on the ground that it gives a smattering and superficial impression of a large and miscellaneous number of subjects, is just. But the desired remedy will not be found in a return to mechanical and meagre teaching of the three R's, but rather in a surrender of our feverish desire to lay out the whole field of knowledge into various studies, in order to "cover the ground." We must substitute for this futile and harmful aim the better ideal of dealing thoroughly with a small number of typical experiences in such a way as to master the tools of learning, and present situations that make pupils hungry to acquire additional knowledge. By the conventional method of teaching, the pupil learns maps instead of the world — the symbol instead of the fact. What the pupil really needs is not exact information about topography, but how to find out for himself.

> Dewey and Dewey, *Schools of Tomorrow* p. 12. [49]

David J. Irvine:

The [educational] system must be capable of coping with increased amounts of information. The explosion of knowledge in almost every field of human endeavor requires that we develop ways of processing information so that it does not become unmanageable. Information systems are vulnerable to information overload. We can foresee the day when educational systems become so swamped with knowledge that students are exposed to confusing, perhaps almost random, bits of the total sum of knowledge. In addition, the very means of collecting, processing, storing, and disseminating information are likely to become clogged.

Organization of knowledge is becoming as important as facts. We cannot rely on each learner to supply his own organization. He must be taught how to organize his knowledge without being provided an inflexible organization which destroys creative thinking.

> Hostrop, *Foundations of Futurology in Education*, p. 79. [60]

Irvine:

Change is taking place at an accelerating pace, and the nature of change is changing. New knowledge does not merely pile onto old knowledge; it changes the old knowledge. Man's work changes not only because a machine now does his work faster and better, but also because machines are doing jobs which were not feasible using raw manpower. It is becoming less and less likely that the learning one goes through at any one stage of life will be completely adequate for a later stage. For this reason, the individual must have the necessary learning skills available when he encounters learning situations throughout his lifetime.

> Hostrop, *Foundations of Futurology in Education*, p. 80. [60]

Robert G. Scanlon:

The emphasis in schools of 1985 will be to free the individual from subject matter as bodies of knowledge and to provide him or her with higher-order cognitive, interpersonal, and achievement-competence skills.

> Scanlon, "A Curriculum for Personalized Education" *Journal of Teacher Education*, Summer, 1974, p. 121. [82]

Herbert J. Muller:

In more familiar terms, young people have more need of being flexible, adaptable, and resourceful than any generation before them, immediately through a fuller awareness of their fast-changing world, and then by developing their powers of choice. Some of the new courses on the future, I gather, attempt to do this by games presenting possible alternatives. Although the drive of science and technology will force adaptation to much change, like it or not, students will have plenty of vital options — a point that Toffler rightly emphasizes, in view of the stereotypes about our standardized mass society.

Muller, *Uses of the Future*, p. 54.[67]

Lester R. Brown:

We are severely handicapped by our educational system, which produces many highly trained specialists but few well-trained generalists. The world needs specialists, but it also needs generalists able to move between the natural and social sciences, between the academic and nonacademic worlds, and capable of seeing the forest as well as the trees. It very much needs policy advisers and political decision makers who can operate with confidence along the multifaceted interface created by the inter-action of economic, ecological, demographic, social and political forces. It needs economists who can think like ecologists, and politicians who can behave like statesmen.

Brown, *World Without Borders*, p. 350.
[115]

Louis J. Rubin:

The school of the future must emphasize decision-making skills. The goal is hardly new; indeed, one might say, as Chesterton remarked of Christianity, that it was not tried and found wanting, it simply was not tried. The importance of decision making, naturally, increases in proportion to the number and degree of decisions made. It is precisely because the citizenry of the future will be called upon to make agonizingly difficult choices in priorities, lifestyles, and social aspirations that the instructional program of the schools must treat, in varying contexts, the processes through which people examine problems, gather evidence, project probable consequences, and reach decisions.

> Rubin, "Whither Goest the Curriculum?" *Journal of Teacher Education*, Summer, 1974, p. 117. [82]

Donald N. Michael:

We must put vastly more emphasis on educating for certain intellectual abilities. We must educate people to have long-range perspectives, to think in terms of many variables related to each other as probabilities rather than certainties and related as both cause and effect of each other. We must educate for logical skill in recognizing and working through the ethically and morally tortuous dilemmas implicit in the assignment of social priorities and in the risks involved in seeking to attain them. This logical skill must be complemented by deep familiarity with the history of ideas and of comparative ethics, since the recognition and resolution of ethical issues is as much a matter of extrarational factors — historical accident and traditional values — as of purely rational assessments. We must educate so people can cope efficiently, imaginatively, and perceptively with information overload.

> Michael, *The Unprepared Society*, p. 108. [34]

John I. Goodlad, *et al.*:

The education of the 21st century man is necessarily an enabling process rather than an instructional one. It requires opening the whole of the world to the learner and giving him easy access to that world. This implies enormous respect for the child's capacity to learn, and with the granting of respect goes, by implication, the granting of freedom.

> Hostrop, *Foundations of Futurology in Education*, pp. 217-218. [60]

Dean C. Corrigan:

Margaret Mead, at a meeting in Washington, captured the educational implications of the new technology when she stated, " . . . to the multiple functions of an educational system we must add a quite new function: education for rapid and self-conscious adaptation to a changing world." She further sharpens the problem: "No one will live all his life in the world into which he was born, and no one will die in the world in which he worked in his maturity." Very much the same point of view was expressed by Peter Drucker some time ago: "Since we live in an age of innovation, a practical education must prepare a man for work that does not yet exist and cannot be clearly defined." The exactitude of his prediction is already visible.

> Corrigan, "The Future," *Journal of Teacher Education*, Summer, 1974, pp. 100-101. [82]

Werner Z. Hirsch:

The demands which the world of tomorrow will make on education and the effectiveness of innovations to meet them are, of course, matters of great uncertainty. It therefore appears more appropriate to select a model that provides for flexibility (one which is not sensitive to rather wide differences in future conditions) rather than a model that produces the best solution — but only if a correct estimate of the future has been made. In short, in evaluating different innovations, we should select a model which reflects our preference for educational innovations, will work well under many divergent contingencies, and will yield a reasonably satisfactory performance even under a major misestimate of the future.

> Hirsch, *Inventing Education for the Future*, p. 18. [56]

John A. Dow:

Changes to be Expected:

How can schools interest students in the mastery of knowledge for its own sake when it is obvious to the students that the enterprise is an anachronism in a society where knowledge is constantly changing? Clearly it cannot be accomplished given the present structure of education. Schools must change *what* is taught as well as *where* and *how* it is taught. The following are some of the changes which can be expected in the near future:

1. Schools will have to provide a better basic repertoire of skills as well as attitudes of flexibility.

2. More stress will be placed on the acquisition of concepts, retrieval and sorting skills, and experiences which equip the individual to assimilate further knowledge.
3. Educational programs will focus on learning how to learn and the ability to identify what it is that is important to learn.
4. Instruction will become more responsive to student needs, at a time, place, and in a manner conducive to their requirements.

Need for New Curricula:

If schools are to fulfill their role in educating individuals to function as effective citizens in an information-loaded environment, new curricula must be designed to meet these needs.

1. Curricula that help individuals develop skills in recognizing and rejecting irrational arguments, in perceiving subterfuge, and in rejecting logical distortion when it occurs in public media
2. Curricula which emphasize problem-centered activities, inquiry training and training dealing with complex and dynamic interrelationships, and application of common sense
3. Programs which provide "upending" cognitive, perceptive and evaluative experiences, and opportunities conducive to "unlearning"
4. Programs which provide skills and experience in gathering, utilizing, organizing, augmenting and disseminating a knowledge base
5. Curricula devoted to giving individuals the cognitive skills for integrating information, and a framework within which to sort out the diverse values to which they are exposed.

If schools are not successful in accomplishing this task, there is a danger that individual citizens will lose confidence in their ability to deal with the volume, complexity and diversity of information available to them, thus deferring their citizenship responsibilities to demagogues.

Dow, "Alternative Futures for Education"
Journal of Teacher Education, Summer,
1974, pp. 139-140. [82]

Kenneth Boulding:

If all environments were stable the well-adapted would simply take over the earth and the evolutionary process would stop. In a period of environmental change, however, it is the adaptable not the well-adapted who survive.

> Boulding, *The Meaning of the Twentieth Century*, p. 23. [19]

Page References:

31. In *Deciding the Future*, Edmund Farrell quotes one of the members of his panel on the future of English teaching, concerning adult American reading habits:

> The reading of self-chosen books on one's own initiative, apart from school requirements, apparently reaches a peak in Grade 8 and declines thereafter with each increment in age and education until the great majority of American adults read hardly any books. This seems to be true in spite of the paperback revolution. (Farrell, *Deciding the Future,* p. 142.) [54]

In *Hooked on Books*, Daniel N. Fader suggests some of the reasons why:

> Attitude only follows performance where children are performance-oriented, and even with such children the attitude may not be the one that educators intend to foster. When reading and writing are made means to the end of school success, what happens to performance-oriented children when that success has been attained? To put the question another way, what happens when the performing child becomes the school-graduated (performance-certified) adult? As any librarian or bookseller will tell us, the average modern adult avoids bookstores and libraries as though they were leprosaria. Had the goal of modern, performance-oriented education been the creation of unwilling readers and writers, it could not better have succeeded. All the supporting evidence is bottom-rooted in front of television screens across the nation. (Fader, *Hooked on Books*, pp. 13-14.) [52]

32.   The article by Sidney Harris is on pages 297 and 298 of *Dimensions of the Future: Alternatives for Tomorrow*, edited by Maxwell H. Norman. [36]

32.   There seems, in fact, to be a direct relationship between awareness of occupational change and distance from the actual students in the classroom. Statements of objectives and OE guidelines are likely to describe awareness of change and the need for flexibility as major goals. Curriculum materials and nuts and bolts program descriptions are likely to contain only a pro forma discussion; and the vocational student is not even aware that the subject came up. See, for example (in sequence): John F. Thompson, *Foundations of Vocational Education: Social and Philosophical Concepts* [77]; Harry N. Drier, Jr., *et al., K-12 Guide for Integrating Career Development into Local Curriculum* [50]; James A. Rhodes, *Vocational Education and Guidance: A System for the 70's* [71]; your local vocational education curriculum packages; and any five students, selected at random, who have taken a vocational education or career education program in the last several years.

For a summary of the amount of occupational change which currently exists, see Toffler, *Future Shock*, pages 98 to 100. [40]

34.   The increase in interest and productivity that occurs among the subjects of an experiment is known as "the Hawthorne effect," after an early experiment:

In 1927 the Hawthorne plant of the Western Electric Company initiated a series of experiments to raise productivity and morale. A group of female workers engaged in wiring relays was placed in a separate room, and, in the tradition of efficiency experts Frederick W. Taylor and Frank B. Gilbreth, changes in working conditions were introduced which were calculated to improve efficiency — changes to piecework production, increased rest periods, hot meals, earlier quitting times, etc. — and with each change productivity increased. However, when all these improvements were removed, productivity rose still higher. (*The International Encyclopedia of the Social Sciences*, Vol. 6, p. 289.) [314]

35.   The passage by Jerry Farber occurs on pages 32 to 35 of *The Student as Nigger*. [53]

36.   The petition approach (to finding out whether people agree with the principles in the Bill of Rights) produces dramatic negative results, but the approach itself is rather biased, particularly in contrast with a more conventional opinion poll. Individuals may refuse to sign the whole thing because they disagree with one part, because they may be much more reluctant to sign their names than to give an anonymous verbal opinion, or because they may regard anyone who circulates a petition as being a "radical" of some sort. There has, however, been a carefully designed public opinion poll on the same subject. (See Chapter 1, "The Bill of Rights," in Robert Chandler, *Public Opinion: Changing Attitudes on Contemporary Issues*.) The results indicate that a majority of the public support some fundamental rights (e.g., trial by jury, separation of church and state) but reject others (e.g., free speech, free assembly, and protection from double jeopardy) — still a disturbing result.

36.   The Davis quotation is from "The Soft Sell," *Newsweek*, July 23, 1973, p. 11. [44]

38.   Toffler's encounter is paraphrased from a speech he gave in Anaheim, California on March 9, 1974.
    An even more graphic example of the same problem of disillusionment comes from *Time* magazine:

> A multicolored map of the U.S. appears on the television screen and slowly begins to burn from the center. As the flame widens, voice-over narration accompanies a dramatic juxtaposition of images and objects to conjure up for the viewer a reckless driver, an unconcerned citizen littering a street, a man confronted by a bottle-laden table who declares "One more won't hurt," and another man's gruff refusal to sign a petition to fight pollution. After the map is burned totally black, a wind begins to scatter the ashes and a deep, doom-ridden voice warns: "Great civilizations decay from within. But it's up to you. Will history repeat itself?"
> This apocalyptic message is not the handiwork of aging cynics gone sour on the American dream but of six

Naperville, Ill., teen-agers. Invited by A. Eicoff & Co.,
a Chicago advertising agency to dream up a 60-second
public service spot, the youngsters produced a stark,
unadorned outcry against what they conceived to be a
deadening decline in the quality of American life. When
agency professionals suggested that they coat their bitter
pill with a cartoon format or offer solutions to the problems they were portraying, the students flatly refused.
The commercial will be aired next week, and the agency
hopes to distribute it nationally. "They wouldn't put any
icing on the cake," says Carole Darr, the agency's creative director. "They figured nothing will ever change if
you give people an out." (*Time*, July 22, 1974, p. 8.) [83]

38.   The Muller quotation is from *Uses of the Future*, pages 53 to
54. [67]

38.   The Hopkins quotation is from "Towards an Ameliorated
World," in *The Futurist*, December, 1973, page 258. [58]

40.   Donald Michael believes that we will fail in our attempts to
bring the pro-change and the anti-change people to any real
accommodation with each other:

So, in tomorrow's world of rapid change, we will have,
at least at the ends of the continuum, two cultures: one
designed for those who enjoy and seek rapid change and
one designed for those who are made anxious and inadequate by such rapid change. The life ways of the two
cultures will be different, perhaps as different as those
that have characterized the affluent compared to the
poor. Perhaps, as with poverty in America, for a long
time we will pretend the difference doesn't exist or we will
rationalize its existence on some latter-day moral
grounds. But as with poverty, one way or another, the
difference in capacity to adapt will add new tasks for
those trying to evolve the whole society at minimum cost
to its parts. (Michael, *The Unprepared Society*,
pp. 26-27.) [34]

40.   For an extended (and elegant) discussion of the importance of a more tentative, less absolutist approach, see Bertrand Russell's essay, "Philosophy and Politics," in *Authority and the Individual*, pages 94 to 101. [177]

41.   The Sturgeon quote is from the story, "If All Men Were Brothers Would You Let One Marry Your Sister?" in *Dangerous Visions, Vol. 3* [215], edited by Harlan Ellison, page 44. It is unclear from the (distant future) context whether Sturgeon is quoting an actual contemporary person; the quotation may not be original with him.

PART II
Concepts and Methods

CHAPTER III
Ways of Thinking
About the Future

Concepts of Time

Concern with the future is a distinguishing and universal human characteristic. Efforts to predict the future and to control it occur in all societies and provide a basis for ritual in most religions. And every society teaches its children a distinctive set of concepts and attitudes about the future.

In our society, time is used in very complex ways. We *spend* it, *measure* it, *budget* it, and *waste* it; we use it to communicate subtle messages and blatant insults. Mastering this system in all its formal, informal, and technical details takes the child about twelve years (and some never do grasp it, even as adults). Mastering the use of time is a vital part of growing up, but adults are rarely of much help in explaining the system because most of us use it without understanding it.

Because we expect mastery, but give so little assistance, children tend to be very interested in the meanings and uses of time and to be more aware than adults of the complexities, contradictions, and incongruities of our time system. They delight in learning about the

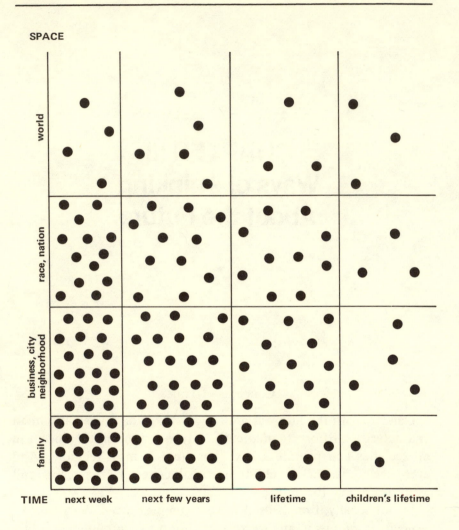

FIGURE 3–1

"PERSPECTIVES ON TIME AND SPACE"

Although the perspectives of the world's people vary in space and in time, every human concern falls somewhere on the space-time graph. The majority of the world's people are concerned with matters that affect only family or friends over a short period of time. Others look further ahead in time or over a larger area — a city or a nation. Only a very few people have a global perspective that extends far into the future. (From Meadows, *et al.*, *The Limits to Growth.* Reproduced with permission of D. H. Meadows.)

seemingly strange ways people from different cultures think about time and make use of it, and in tales of the sometimes funny and sometimes tragic encounters between people with different expectations about the use of time.

Learning about a people's concept of time is an important part of understanding how they think, why they behave as they do, and how their society functions, so this is a natural as well as entertaining component of normal social studies and history courses. The next step is to compare the time concepts of others with our own, and it is often easiest to understand our own culture by comparison with other ways of thinking.

EXERCISE 1: *Concepts of Time*

Procedure: Have the students arrange themselves in a circle (this works best with a discussion group of 5 to 9). Start by distributing copies of Figure 3-1, "Perspectives on Time and Space" and asking the students how much of their thinking is located in each part of the chart. Then broaden the topic to "people they know" and "most people in the U.S." At each point, ask if they think this distribution is desirable or appropriate. When discussion tapers off, distribute the "discussion focuser" from *The Silent Language* by Edward T. Hall (see box, page 62). Is Hall's description of American attitudes generally accurate? Is one of the three approaches "better" than the others? Why?

If the discussion is a lively one, it can then be led to consider the consequences of different ways of thinking about the future. For example, Americans are very adept at manipulating the near-term future. Sloppy as our procedures may seem to us while we are using them, the American habits of careful planning, tight scheduling, and punctuality have given us a technical efficiency equalled in only a few other countries. This efficiency (and a great deal of luck in having abundant resources) has made the U.S. both rich and powerful.

However, if the American genius is in manipulating the near-term future — anywhere from next Saturday's bake sale to a ten-year program to put a man on the moon — our twin failings are in our use of the present and our use of the more distant future.

DISCUSSION FOCUSER:

While we look to the future, our view of it is limited. The future to us is the foreseeable future, not the future of the South Asian that may involve centuries. Indeed our perspective is so short as to inhibit the operation of a good many practical projects, such as sixty- and one-hundred-year conservation works requiring public support and public funds. Anyone who has worked in industry or in the government of the United States has heard the following "Gentlemen, this is for the long term! Five or ten years."

For us a "long time" can be almost anything — ten or twenty years, two or three months, a few weeks, or even a couple of days. The South Asian, however, feels that it is perfectly realistic to think of a "long time" in terms of thousands of years or even an endless period. A colleague once described their conceptualization as follows: "Time is like a museum with endless corridors and alcoves. You, the viewer, are walking through the museum in the dark, holding a light to each scene as you pass it. God is the curator of the museum, and only He knows all that is in it. One lifetime represents one alcove." (pp 20 and 21, *The Silent Language*)

As has been pointed out, the white civilized Westerner has a shallow view of the future compared to the Oriental. Yet set beside the Navajo Indians of northern Arizona, he seems a model of long-term patience. The Navajo and the European-American have been trying to adjust their concepts of time for almost a hundred years. So far they have not done too well. To the old-time Navajo time is like space — only the here and now is quite real. The future has little reality to it.

An old friend of mine reared with the Navajo expressed it this way: "You know how the Navajo love horses and how much they love to gamble and bet on horse races. Well, if you were to say to a Navajo, 'My friend, you know my quarter horse that won all the races at Flagstaff last Fourth of July?' that Navajo would eagerly say 'Yes, yes,' he knew the horse; and if you were to say, 'In the fall I am going to give you that horse,' the Navajo's face would fall and he would turn around and walk away. On the other hand, if you were to say to him, 'Do you see that old bag of bones I just rode up on? That old hay-bellied mare with the knock-knees and pigeon toes, with the bridle that's falling apart and the saddle that's worn out? You can have that horse, my friend, it's yours. Take it, ride it away now.' Then the Navajo would beam and shake your hand and jump on his new horse and ride away. Of the two, only the immediate gift has reality; a promise of future benefits is not even worth thinking about." (pp 22 and 23, *The Silent Language*)

Many people whom Americans tend to regard as "lazy" or "inefficient" regard us as compulsive, clock-ridden, and unable to relax and enjoy ourselves. Many "successful" Americans do seem to feel that the pursuit of their goals should have permitted them more happiness than it has.

An increasing number of people believe that, as a nation, much of our short-term competence has been expended on goals that make little long-term sense. Our technical efficiency has allowed us to construct magnificent access highways — which have resulted in congested and polluted cities. We have struggled to keep our GNP growing ever larger, only to discover that a bigger GNP may mean more damage to the environment without necessarily improving the quality of life. And we have undertaken extensive military interventions, only to discover that our security, prestige, and influence have been reduced, rather than increased.

Over the years, Americans have had a staunch faith in "progress," in the idea that if we work hard, everything will automatically turn out all right: "Take care of today, and tomorrow will take care of itself." But we are now discovering that hard work invested toward a poorly chosen goal produces only frustration and bitter disappointment.

With older students, you may want to direct the discussion further to consider the role of the schools in teaching the attitude that competence in the project at hand is important, but consideration of long-term goals or problems is not. What other attitudes toward the future might be taught instead? How might this be done, and what would the consequences be? How can a student direct his own education to avoid the normal short-sighted perspective?

The Concept of the Future

One reason we may find it difficult to think about the future is that we have poor conceptual tools to think about it with. For instance, the basic concept of "the future" is very ambiguous in our culture and we are used to seeing different and conflicting meanings for it. Here is a simple exercise to illustrate the point.

EXERCISE 2: *Metaphors for "the Future"*

Procedure: Reproduce the four metaphors given below and hand them out to the class or discussion group. Give the students a few minutes to read through them and then ask for volunteers to read them aloud to the group. Then open up the discussion with some of the questions that follow.

1. The future is a great roller coaster on a moonless night. It exists, twisting ahead of us in the dark, although we can only see each part as we come to it. We can make estimates about where we are headed, and sometimes see around a bend to another section of track, but it doesn't do us any real good because the future is fixed and determined. We are locked in our seats, and nothing we may know or do will change the course that is laid out for us.

2. The future is a mighty river. The great force of history flows inexorably along, carrying us with it. Most of our attempts to change its course are mere pebbles thrown into the river: they cause a momentary splash and a few ripples, but they make no difference. The river's course *can* be changed, but only by natural disasters like earthquakes or landslides, or by massive, concerted human efforts on a similar scale. On the other hand, we are free as individuals to adapt to the course of history either well or poorly. By looking ahead, we can avoid sandbars and whirlpools and pick the best path through any rapids.

3. The future is a great ocean. There are many possible destinations, and many different paths to each destination. A good navigator takes advantage of the main currents of change, adapts his course to the capricious winds of chance, keeps a sharp lookout posted, and moves carefully in fog or uncharted waters. If he does these things, he will get safely to his destination (barring a typhoon or other disaster which he can neither predict nor avoid).

4. The future is entirely random, a colossal dice game. Every second, millions of things happen which could have happened another way and produced a different future. A bullet is deflected by a twig and kills one man instead of another. A scientist checks a spoiled culture and throws it away, or looks more closely at it and

discovers penicillin. A spy at the Watergate removes a piece of tape from a door and gets away safely, or he forgets to remove the tape and changes American political history. Since everything is chance, all we can do is play the game, pray to the gods of fortune, and enjoy what good luck comes our way.

Questions: Which metaphor best describes your idea of the future? Which description is the most "valid" or "realistic"? Is there any way you could prove that one description is "right" and the others are "wrong"? What would be the consequences for society of assuming the truth of one metaphor instead of the others? Would it be more *useful* to assume one of them, even if it were not more "correct" than the others?

Try to keep the discussion from degenerating into an argument over the validity of either the first or the fourth view. Each of the four dramatizes (and exaggerates) a useful observation about the future. The first says that much of what we do is determined by our conditioning and our circumstances and not by "free and rational" consideration. The second says that deliberate cultural change is an immensely difficult thing to achieve. The third says that with foresight, flexibility, and determination, we can choose and achieve the future we want. And the fourth reminds us that there is a strong element of chance in everything that happens and a wise person (or society) tries to insure against the bad breaks and take advantage of the good ones.

Most futurists seem to operate most of the time from a perspective that combines the "river" and the "ocean" metaphors. Over the next twenty or thirty years our range of choice is restricted by a set of severe problems which we *must* cope with, and by forces which have already been set in motion. (For example, a population continues to grow for about seventy years after a stabilized birth rate is reached.) If we survive the next thirty years in reasonably good shape, the range of choices and opportunities will open up considerably as the "river" reaches the "ocean."

A Forecast is Not a Prediction

Unfortunately, the public (especially the press) tends to think of the future as "That Which Will Happen," and this leads inevitably to misunderstandings. The most common misunderstanding is the confusion between a *forecast* and a *prediction*. Suppose that Professor Farsight of Crystal Ball University says that, if things continue the way they're going, the population of the U.S. will be 335 million by the year 2000. When that remark is reported in the Sunday Gossip, however, it comes out sounding different: "NOTED CRYSTAL-BALLER PREDICTS U.S. POPULATION UP BY ONE HALF AT END OF CENTURY!"

Note the fact that Professor Farsight made no prediction at all; instead he made a factual statement about the consequences of a trend continuing (see chapter four). He is almost certain to be aware that either chance events or deliberate decisions could alter the trend, and he may even have made the statement as part of an attempt to *change* the trend.

Professor Farsight's statement is called, in fancy language, a "primary forecast." A forecast is a statement about a future *possibility* (as opposed to a certainty), and forecasts come in many forms. Here are some examples: 'A' is a future possibility. The chances of 'A' happening are x% (as long as x is between zero and one hundred). If 'A' happens, 'B' will happen. If 'A' happens, the chances of 'B' happening are greatly increased (or decreased, or unchanged).

A *primary* forecast is one like Professor Farsight's — a statement of what will happen if things continue on the way they have been going. (For example: "If it continues its current course and speed, the hurricane will strike the coast north of Miami late tomorrow night.") A *secondary* forecast is a statement about any future possibility, including those which involve a change in the way things happen. ("It is also possible that the storm will become stationary, or that it will swing to the west striking Miami sometime tomorrow . . .") And a *tertiary* forecast is a statement about the most likely course of events, i.e., the secondary forecast with the highest probability of happening. (". . . but the experts agree that the storm is most likely to swing to the east, missing the coast entirely.") By contrast, a *prediction* is a statement about a 100% certainty, a situation where there are *no* other possible alternatives. ("Whatever happens, there will be strong seas and unusual tides along the entire Florida coast tomorrow.'')

A prediction can obviously be proven right or wrong, and one of the main uses of prediction is to test our understanding. If we understand a process completely, we should be able to predict its outcome under any circumstances; if the prediction is wrong, our understanding is incomplete. A forecast, on the other hand, cannot usually be proven or disproven by a single course of events. If you forecast a fifty percent chance of heads on a coin toss, your forecast is not proven wrong because the coin comes up tails; it is still true that the odds of getting heads *were* fifty percent.

Good Forecasts

But if a forecast cannot be proven or disproven, how can you tell a good forecast from a bad one? Robert Bundy, one of the pioneers in developing future-oriented education, has summarized the basis for evaluating forecasts as follows:

> Let us begin with the premise that having choice options and understanding our choice options are deeply rooted in the concept of human freedom. Let us also accept that understanding choice options implies some understanding of the probable future implications of these choice options. We can then say that without forecasting there is no freedom of choice, and if we wish to improve the process of decision making in the present we have to learn to improve the process by which we make forecasts. Forecasting, therefore, is a natural activity of the mind and an important activity because it serves to help us make more explicit the choice options we have in the present.
>
> However, for a forecast to be useful, i.e., for a forecast to help us to be more informed and make more explicit our choices in the present, it seems reasonable to argue that forecasts should not attempt to persuade merely on the basis of authority or the prestige or reputation of the forecaster. A forecast should be able to stand on its own; i.e., it should have two components: (1) a solid intellectual scaffolding on which (2) assertions about the future are based.

With this basis, Bundy derived a number of specific standards for judging the quality of forecasts, which have been condensed here to four essential characteristics: clarity, plausibility, imagination, and justification.

Clarity: A forecast should be *clear*. It should be stated with a minimum of ambiguity, with a specified time frame, and with assumptions which are clearly articulated. The idea is to make sure that the reader or listener is in no doubt as to what is being forecast, for what period, and why. Here, for example, is a forecast written by this writer in 1971:

> There is a good probability — at least 30% — that the U.S. will enter a severe depression by the early 1980's, based on five assumptions: a)The probability is high that American demand for energy will continue to grow at approximately current rates. b) The probability is relatively low that the U.S. will fund a crash program of energy research at a level considerably above the present before 1980. c) At this level of funding, the odds are poor of achieving a major breakthrough in energy technology. d) It is highly probable that the cost of recovery of crude oil will skyrocket by the early 1980's. e) It is probable that environmental interests can block the use of high-sulfur coal and extensive strip mining for 4 or 5 years.

(Note that, *if* this was a good forecast at the time it was made, the Arab oil boycott of 1973-1974 was a blessing in disguise because it partly invalidated assumption "b.")

Plausibility: A forecast should be *plausible*. It should be self-consistent, and if it contradicts current knowledge or beliefs about "reality," the basis for doing so should be carefully laid out. Note that a forecasted event can be quite unlikely and still be plausible. For example, a visit from an alien spaceship in the near future might be quite unlikely, but it is not — so far as we know — impossible. On the other hand, a forecast that the earth might stop turning tomorrow would require an extremely convincing argument before being accepted as even remotely plausible.

Imagination: A good forecast is *imaginative*. A forecast is a work of art that can be more or less accepted, but cannot be proven false. It should demonstrate insight in the selection of its component parts and the judgments about their interaction. Forecasts which alert us to a potential crisis or opportunity are the most useful because they can move us to action to avoid, adjust to, or minimize the crisis, or capitalize on the opportunity.

Justification: A good forecast should clearly reveal its justification, the basis on which it rests. Justification includes all of the above characteristics, but in addition a forecast should be built on as high an order of rational argument as possible. A forecast is most useful as a means for making our choice options more explicit and as a tool of persuasion if it is based on a high order of explanation, such as models, theories, laws, and empirical generalizations. However, it must be remembered that no matter how high or perfect a level of explanation is used, we are still not dealing with proof. We can never predict the future with certainty.

EXERCISE 3: *Understanding Forecasts*

Procedure: Begin by explaining to the students the difference between a forecast and a prediction, and the difference between the three kinds of forecasts (primary, secondary, and tertiary). When you have discussed these concepts and are satisfied that the students understand them, give them the following two-part assignment.

Part One: Prepare a set of forecasts on a subject which interests you. Include in the set a *primary* forecast (where things are currently headed), at least three *secondary* forecasts (alternative possibilities), and a tertiary forecast (the most likely outcome — may be the same as the primary forecast).

Part Two: Forecasts and predictions occur commonly in books, magazines, and newspapers. Find at least four forecasts and at least one prediction and bring them into class. Be sure to include the context in which each statement occurs.

Ask for volunteers to read their own sets of forecasts aloud. After each one, be sure to distinguish between understanding the terms and agreeing on the content of the forecasts themselves. As you proceed, the students should become adept at distinguishing between predictions and the three kinds of forecasts. It should also become obvious that some forecasts are in some sense *better* than others. When this point is reached, read aloud and discuss the two paragraphs on page 67 on the purpose of forecasting, and then describe the four criteria of *clarity, plausibility, imagination,* and *justification.*

Finally, go around the room asking the students to read both the items they found in print and the remainder of their forecasts. After each one, have the class evaluate it according to the four criteria. In the discussion of the students' own forecasts, try to bring out the strengths of each one and prevent arguments over which forecast is best or worst. Focus instead on how each forecast could be improved. Also, be especially supportive of imaginative but "far-out" forecasts: a good forecast need not be probable, merely possible.

Finally, following is a set of fifteen questions developed by Bundy, which can be used as a follow-up to the three preceding exercises. (As an alternative, you may wish to use this as both a pre- and post-course questionnaire if you are teaching a longer unit specifically about the future.)

EXERCISE 4: *Beliefs About the Future:*

Procedure: Distribute the questionnaire to the students and ask them to complete it. (Be sure to tell them it is *not* a quiz.) Then ask the students to compare their answers and discuss the differences between them. Be cautious about giving your own opinion, even if asked. Usually, it is best to reserve your views until near the end of the discussion of each point, and even then you should make it clear that yours is just another opinion and not the "right" answer. Otherwise the discussion tends to collapse into a session of guessing-what-teacher-thinks.

A word of warning: question six is a "trick" question — the answer is determined by how you read the question. If "knowledge" is taken to mean "absolute foreknowledge of events" most students will disagree (though some will mention "absolute certainties" such as the movements of the planets). Those who interpret "knowledge" to mean "useful knowledge about possibilities" (such as knowing the chances of filling an inside straight) will generally agree.

What Fundamental Beliefs About the Future Do You Hold?

Here are fifteen statements about the future. Please indicate your opinion of each statement by circling *one* of the numbers beneath it, according to the following key:

-3 = strongly disagree	3 = strongly agree
-2 = disagree	2 = agree
-1 = somewhat disagree	1 = somewhat agree
	0 = uncertain

1. From a broad historical viewpoint the human race is moving toward a more desirable future.

    -3   -2   -1   0   1   2   3

2. The future is largely predetermined, at least in all of its important aspects. Individuals, therefore, play out an historically necessary role, i.e., people are swept along by forces over which they have little control.

    -3   -2   -1   0   1   2   3

3. An array of alternative futures, both desirable and undesirable, are open to mankind at any point in time.

    -3   -2   -1   0   1   2   3

4. A prediction is not basically different from a forecast.

    -3   -2   -1   0   1   2   3

5. If one could completely dissect all the forces operating in the present, one could accurately predict the future.

    -3   -2   -1   0   1   2   3

6. It is possible to have knowledge of the future.

       -3   -2   -1   0   1   2   3

7. The most surprising future we can imagine is one in which there are no surprises. It is unreasonable to expect a future in which there are no surprises.

       -3   -2   -1   0   1   2   3

8. Today we can predict outcomes in the social order about as well as we can predict outcomes in the natural order.

       -3   -2   -1   0   1   2   3

9. Generally speaking, the future was more foreseeable for pre-modern man than it is for modern man.

       -3   -2   -1   0   1   2   3

10. Modern approaches to forecasting the future, i.e., attitudes, techniques and beliefs, don't differ basically from approaches used by pre-modern man.

       -3   -2   -1   0   1   2   3

11. The real purpose of futures forecasting is to help us to make better decisions in the present.

       -3   -2   -1   0   1   2   3

12. A useful side effect of futures forecasting is that it helps us to understand the present better.

       -3   -2   -1   0   1   2   3

13. Without forecasting there can be no freedom of choice.

       -3   -2   -1   0   1   2   3

14. How one thinks about the future is intimately connected with how one deals with social and interpersonal relationships.

       -3   -2   -1   0   1   2   3

15. The future 20 years from now is very likely to be completely different from the present.

       -3   -2   -1   0   1   2   3

WAYS OF THINKING ABOUT THE FUTURE:

ESSENTIAL POINTS

1. Different societies have different approaches to thinking about time and about the future.
2. Within our own society, individual perspectives differ greatly from one person to another.
3. There are at least four contradictory approaches to "the future" in our culture: complete determinism; broad social determinism, but with freedom to adapt; individual and societal self-determination, within the limits of reality; and complete randomness.
4. Futurists find it most useful to assume a future that is partly predetermined, partly determined by chance, and partly determined by our own free choice.
5. Our freedom of choice is lowest in the immediate future and grows larger as our planning horizon extends further into the future.
6. A forecast is a conditional or probabilistic statement about the future.
7. A primary forecast is a statement about what will happen if a current trend continues into the future.
8. A secondary forecast is a statement about any future possibility, including those possibilities in which current trends do not continue.
9. A tertiary forecast is a statement about the most likely course of events.
10. A prediction, in contrast to a forecast, is a statement about a 100% certainty, a situation in which no other outcome is possible.
11. Unlike a prediction, a forecast cannot usually be proven or disproven by the course of events.
12. The purpose of forecasting is to improve our ability to make wise choices in the present.
13. The quality of a forecast can be judged by four standards: clarity, plausibility, imagination, and justification.
14. When dealing with societies, absolute foreknowledge is impossible; the best we can do is to obtain useful knowledge about future possibilities.

NOTES

59. On the role of concern with the future in human nature, societies, and religion. Thomas Green has written:

> Man's desire to know the future may be among his most basic characteristics. The Church Fathers regarded it as evidence of man's sinful nature, and the ancient Hebrews had a great deal to say about the human disposition to want to live in knowledge of the future rather than in faith. It is not likely that men shall outlive the desire to know the future. (Hostrop, *Foundations of Futurology in Education*, p. 163.) [60]

See also Edward Norbeck, *Religion in Primitive Societies*, particularly pages 52 to 70. [309]

59. On the formal, informal, and technical uses of time, see Chapter 4, pages 63 to 91, of *The Silent Language*, by Edward T. Hall. [55]

60. Figure 3-1, "Perspectives on Time and Space," is from *The Limits to Growth*, by Donella Meadows, *et al.*, p. 19. [105]

62. The first half of the page is from pages 20 and 21 and the second half is from pages 22 and 23 of *The Silent Language*, by Edward T. Hall. [55]

63. Einstein put it succinctly: "Perfection of means and confusion of goals characterize our age." (*Saturday Review/World*, August 10, 1974, p. 87).

65. On the basic working assumptions of most futurists, see Appendix A, particularly the Tugewll quote in the notes.

66. The treatment accorded to our hypothetical Professor Farsight is neither hypothetical nor uncommon. At times, the treatment of forecasts by the media has gone beyond misinterpretation and misquotation to vitriolic denunciations. A classic example is an article by John Crosby, which appeared in *Newsday* in 1971, entitled "Demagogic Demographers?":

> The arrest and probable decline of American population shocked and dismayed demographers who had predicted exactly the opposite. The huge war baby generation did not product children "as abundantly as had

been expected, mainly because of developments in contraception and changing attitudes toward the size of the family."

Why hadn't demographers foreseen developments in contraception? Everyone else did. Why didn't they foresee and take into their calculations "changing attitudes toward the size of the family"? Didn't it ever occur to anyone that population explosion headlines might cause some change in family thinking?

One of the most startling changes in population patterns in Western Europe — totally unforeseen by the demographers, as usual — was the use of contraceptives by Catholic women. Why couldn't demographers foresee this? Another was the lowering of the size of lower-class families. This too, could have been predicted and allowed for. It wasn't.

The fact is, all population experts are nuts, every last one, since the first one, Thomas Malthus; if there has ever been an accurate population prediction, I have never encountered it . . .

You mustn't lose any sleep about the population explosion; if demographers predict that it will happen, it won't. Nothing the population nuts have predicted has been right and generally when they predict something, exactly the opposite happens. (Polhman, *Population: A Clash of Prophets*, p. 78). [143]

Crosby appears to be projecting his own demagogic tendencies onto those he criticizes. He begins with a flat misrepresentation of fact: the American population has not been "arrested" and, barring a nuclear war, or similar disaster, its "decline" below present levels at any time during the next 50 years is wildly improbable; even if the near-replacement birth rates of the last few years turn out not to be temporary, population in the U.S. will increase by about 50% in the next 70 years. What has dropped is the birth rate, which is a very different thing from the population.

The lack of attribution or context for the quote in the first paragraph makes it a convenient straw man for Crosby to knock down in the second. There are direct errors of fact in the remainder of the passage, but what is important is that Crosby is treating every population forecast (or "projection") as a prediction. This allows him to mock the demographers with the 20/20 vision of hindsight. ("This too, could have been predicted and allowed for." Could it? Crosby has a touching faith in the predictability of changing social values.)

In a way, Crosby pays his victims a fine compliment. If every "prediction" about adverse population trends has been "wrong," it seems at least somewhat likely that the "predictions" had something to do with the reversal of the trend — which is precisely what they were intended to do. Crosby asks, "Didn't it every occur to anyone that population explosion headlines might cause some change in family thinking?" A more sensible question would be, Didn't it ever occur to Crosby that that was precisely the purpose of the headlines? If it did not, it is no fault of the demographers. Here, for example, is a fairly representative statement by Philip M. Hauser, a leading "population nut," from testimony before a special Senate subcommittee in 1971:

> I have on a number of occasions stated that anyone who claims to be able to predict future population is either a fool or a charlatan. I reaffirm this statement, well documented by experience.
>
> However, although neither the demographer nor anyone else can predict future population, he can make projections which indicate the possible courses of events. Such projections are based on varying assumptions about the future levels of fertility, mortality and migration, assumptions about which there is no certainty. Moreover, the very publication of projections invites public reaction which may well operate to nullify the assumptions. (Polhman, *Population: A Clash of Prophets*, p. 84). [143]

67.   The passage quoted and the precis which follows it are taken from a mimeograph handout prepared by Robert Bundy in 1971, entitled "Purposes and Characteristics of Forecasts." [4] The material appears to have been derived originally from Bertrand de Jouvenal's *The Art of Conjecture*. [6]

71.   The questionnaire is a slightly modified version of another Bundy handout from 1971, "What Fundamental Beliefs About the Future Do You Hold?" [4] Three questions from the original have been dropped and two of the remainder have been slightly altered to eliminate ambiguities.

CHAPTER IV
Trends

The Concept of a Trend

There are many observable patterns and regularities in the social and physical world around us. Often we have good, even detailed, knowledge about a pattern while having only the vaguest, if any, idea as to the reasons for the pattern. When this is true, we can usually make a better forecast by simply assuming that the pattern will continue into the future than by trying to "reason out" a most plausible sequence of events. Our assumption in doing so is that patterns have causes, even if we don't understand them, and that patterns which recur over extended periods of time have causes with considerable internal stability and persistence.

The extension of patterns from the past and present into the future (trend extrapolation) is one of the oldest and most pervasive ways of thinking about the future. This is both good and bad, since trend extrapolation is enormously valuable if used wisely and very misleading if used thoughtlessly, as it frequently is. In this chapter, we will be exploring ways of identifying and understanding different kinds of trends, as well as their uses and the limits of their usefulness.

The first thing to consider in planning your teaching about trends is that it is linked with teaching math and mathematical thinking. The idea of a trend is the idea of change (or stability) over time, and this is one of the most fundamental concepts in math. With very young children, teaching about trends is a basic way of preparing them for the idea of a function, even though you may be using the concept of a trend in a purely intuitive way, without numbers or arithmetic.

With older children, teaching about trends should be intermixed with teaching about graphs, functions, equations, and even basic physics (velocity and acceleration) and biology (population dynamics and ecology). The math they are learning helps them understand the discussion of trends, while the trends they are looking at help them to understand why they are studying the math and what it is good for.

The exercises that follow have been geared primarily to the middle grades (5-8), relying on the individual teacher to adapt or extend them as necessary. In most cases this is not difficult; despite the obvious differences in age and preparedness, we have found it possible to teach at least the most basic concepts in all grades.

EXERCISE 5: *Some Simple Basic Trends*

Materials: You may make copies of page 79, if you prefer, or you can simply put the figures on the board as you come to them.

Procedure: First make sure that the students understand the idea of a trend and the idea of a graph. Then explain each graph on page 79 and the trend associated with it, using the following discussion as an approximate guide. Then have the students identify the type of trend associated with the trends listed and with the trends which they think up.

Discussion: The simplest trend of all is the assumption that nothing is changing, that the thing we are thinking about has remained the same in the past and will continue to do so in the future. During much of man's history, the rate of change was so slow that the average man was unlikely, in one lifetime, to see a major change in his society, his way of making a living, or his way of thinking about the world. So this assumption of no change was the basic assumption about both past and future in a traditional society: " . . . as it was in the beginning, is now, and ever shall be." In our

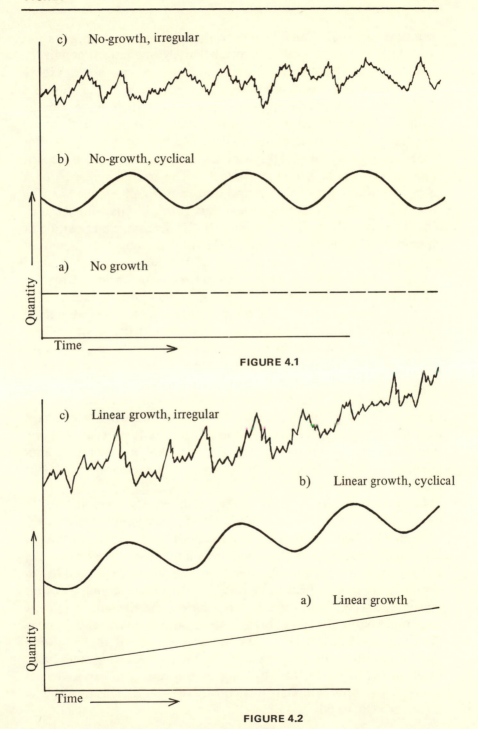

c)   No-growth, irregular

b)   No-growth, cyclical

a)   No growth

Quantity

Time

FIGURE 4.1

c)   Linear growth, irregular

b)   Linear growth, cyclical

a)   Linear growth

Quantity

Time

FIGURE 4.2

own times of rapid change, however, there is almost nothing that we can count on as continuing in an absolutely unchanged condition.

A variation of the straight-line no-change situation (see Figure 4.1) is the pattern which oscillates up and down on either side of a straight line without providing any long term change in the average situation. Such patterns are called cyclical trends, and many cyclical trends dominate the natural environment of man. For instance, the amount of light or heat varies from noon to midnight and back again in a regular pattern. The overall distance of a planet from the sun varies around a norm throughout the year, as do the daily average temperatures, thus providing us with seasons. The tides vary in a cyclical pattern with the distance and position of the moon. This pattern is imposed on another, longer cycle caused again by the distance and position of the sun.

All of these external cycles are reflected in various ways by internal cycles in the bodies of all animals, including ourselves. For example, most people's body temperature, height, and weight all vary in regular daily patterns. Of course, one of the most obvious cyclical patterns is that of blood pressure, which swings up with each beat of the heart and down again in between beats, in the cycle we call the pulse.

The next basic kind of trend is that of simple linear growth, sometimes called arithmetic growth. This occurs when a constant amount of something is being added to the basic quantity in each interval of time. For instance, if you put a nickel in your piggy bank every week, the amount of money saved will increase in a linear fashion.

Linear trends also need not grow in an exactly straight line, as long as the central *tendency* of the trend can be represented by a straight line (see Figure 4.2). For instance, you might put fifteen cents in that piggy bank this week, take a nickel out the next week, put fifteen cents in the week after that, and so on. This would be a combination of a cyclical trend and a linear growth trend. For that matter, the type of variation does not have to be regular, as long as it averages out to the same thing. You could put seven cents in your bank this week, three cents next week, none at all the following week, eight cents the next week, five cents the following week, and so on in that fashion, and as long as the average over a typical interval was approximately constant, we would consider this a linear growth trend.

(We've been talking about linear trends as "growth" trends. It should be pointed out that "growth" can be negative. That is, you can have a trend that slants downward, as well as a trend which slants upward. All of these variations can be applied to any of the trends that we look at. They can go up and down in a smooth cycle; they can go up and down in a random, jagged pattern around a central tendency; or they can go downward instead of upward. For simplicity, however, we normally talk about the basic types of trends as if they were always smooth upward lines or curves.)

Here are four examples of trends. Identify each one by the type it belongs to:

- Your age (linear growth, smooth; Figure 4.2a)
- The speed of light (no growth, smooth; Figure 4.1a)
- The total number of students who have graduated from this school (linear growth, irregular; Figure 4.1c)
- The number of children in this classroom (no growth, cyclical, and irregular; Figure 4.1b and 4.1c)

If students at this point volunteer trends of their own, help them to clarify in their own minds the kind of trend, being careful to point out that their suggestions may not fit into the two general categories we have just discussed. In particular, if a trend is suggested to you which clearly falls into the category of exponential growth, say something like, "Well, that trend isn't one of the ones we've been talking about, but it's a kind of trend which is especially interesting," and write down the name of the trend, such as "growth in number of automobiles," on the chalkboard well off to one side so you can refer to it during the discussion after the next set of exercises.

Exponential Growth

Many of the achievements and most of the problems of this century are intimately related to an *exponential growth* trend of some sort, whether it is the use of pesticides and fertilizers, the amount of scientific knowledge, the number and power of our weapons, the size of world population, the amount of pollution, or any of the large number of other key growth trends.

The question of growth will be one of the most crucial policy issues for at least the next fifty years. Unless your students understand growth and how it works, they will be unable to cope intelligently with the many growth-related issues facing them. The purpose of the next three exercises is to familiarize your students with the basic idea of exponential growth, to make them comfortable with the notion, and to enable them to interpret figures concerning it in a meaningful way.

EXERCISE 6: *The Hero's Reward*

Materials: You will need four 2-lb boxes of ordinary uncooked rice (you can get by with only two), seventeen plastic bags, and seventeen rubber bands or twist-ties for sealing the bags.

Preparation: Open one box of rice and measure it out into the seventeen bags as follows:

Bag #1 — 1 grain of rice	Bag #10 — 2 scant teaspoons
#2 — 2 grains	#11 — 4 scant teaspoons
#3 — 4 grains	#12 — 8 scant teaspoons
#4 — 8 grains	#13 — 16 scant teaspoons
#5 — 16 grains	#14 — 1/3 cup
#6 — 32 grains	#15 — 2/3 cup
#7 — 64 grains	#16 — 1-1/3 cup
#8 — 1/2 scant teaspoon	#17 — 1/2 box
#9 — 1 scant teaspoon	

These should almost exactly finish off the box. (If you don't have enough for the last bag, you have probably put too much in the three or four next largest ones.) Tie the bags off tightly and put them into a box or paper bag, *with the heaviest bag on the bottom and the lightest one on top* so that you can remove them in order. (If you use twist-ties, it helps to write the bag numbers on the ties.)

Procedure: Announce that you're going to tell the class a story, which goes as follows:

"A long time ago there lived in China a King who was very, very rich and had a very beautiful daughter. One day this daughter was carried off by an evil fire-breathing dragon. (Everybody hiss.) As the

dragon was carrying the beautiful princess off to its cave, it
encountered a handsome young man on his way to the city to earn
his fortune. The handsome young man promptly killed the fire-
breathing dragon and rescued the princess. (Everybody cheer.) The
hero then restored the beautiful princess to her grief-stricken
father, who, as is customary in fairy tales, asked him, 'What reward
would you like? A sack of gold? My daughter's hand in marriage?'

"Instead, the young man surprised them. He went over to the
King's chessboard and cleared away the pieces and said that what
he wanted for a reward was to come to the palace once a day for 64
days — one day for each square on the chessboard — and pick up a
certain amount of rice each day. The first day, for the first square of
the chessboard, he would get one grain of rice. The second day he
would get two. The third day he would get four, and the fourth day
eight, and so on, doubling the number of grains of rice each day
and for each square on the chessboard." (Go to the chalkboard and
draw a large chessboard, eight squares by eight squares.) "The
King of course agreed, though he thought the hero was a most
peculiar young man to want so paltry a reward.

"But the proper instructions were given and the next day the
young man came to the palace and went away with one grain of
rice." (At this point take out the first plastic bag and put it on the
right front corner of your desk. Then turn to the chalkboard and
put the number 1 in the first large square on the chessboard.) "On
the second day, the young man came back to the palace and this
time went away with two grains of rice." (Place the second bag
beside the first one and mark the number 2 in the second box of the
chessboard.)

Continue in the same fashion through the first seventeen squares,
asking the students to do the multiplication. When you come to
square 18, explain that, by careful analysis, you have discovered
that there are exactly 131,072 grains of rice in an ordinary box of
rice. Take an unopened box and put it on the desk just to the left of
the line of bags. In addition to writing 131,072 in the square of the
chessboard, put "1 Box" underneath it.

Continue as before " . . . and on the nineteenth day, the young
man returned to the palace and received 262,144 grains of rice,"
meanwhile placing the two remaining boxes of rice together on the
desk a little distance to the left of the first box. At this point, you
should switch from recording the number of grains in the

chessboard squares to recording the number of boxes. Abbreviate
the narration from now on, asking the class to call out the number
of boxes to go in each square of the chessboard, and just fill in the
squares, until you reach 1,024 boxes of rice on the 28th day. Here,
remark to the class that this much rice would cover the entire floor
of the classroom to the depth of one inch (assuming approximately
500 square feet of floor space). Write "1 inch" underneath "1,024
Boxes" on the blackboard. Fill in the next six squares with the
approximate number of inches, illustrating as you go along the
approximate height. (An adult desk is about 28 inches tall. And 64
inches, of course, is the height of a 5'4" student or teacher.)

When you reach square number 35, put in "128 Inches or 1 Classroom," explaining that, on the 35th day, the amount of rice would
have filled this entire classroom, wall-to-wall, floor-to-ceiling. Now
resume the story: "For the first few weeks when all this was going on,
all the people at the court thought this was very silly and made fun of
the young man, although the Princess was sad to think that such a
strong and handsome hero was a little bit touched in the head. But
along about the 35th day, the King began to get worried about this
line of carts pulling away from his storehouse. So he called in his
finest mathematician and asked just how much rice this was going to
involve by the time they got to the last square on the chessboard.

"Now the King was not exactly what you would call a whiz at
math, so it took the royal mathematician some time to convince the
King that the answer he received was correct. But when the King
finally understood the answer, he took immediate action. And on
the 36th day, when the young man showed up with a string of carts
to get his rice, he was set upon instead by soldiers, who dragged him
away and executed him.

"If this seems harsh to you, you should know what it was that the
royal mathematician told the King. He said that at the end of the 64
days, the King would have owed the young man all of the rice in the
entire Kingdom, and all the rice that the Kingdom would produce
for the next ten thousand years. (And, as the King said, 'It's not
that I'm ungrateful, it's just that I can't stand a wise guy.')"

Quite conveniently, that one inch layer of rice we have on the
floor of the classroom on the 28th day would weigh just about one
ton, so you can switch from inches to tons,. Instead of filling in all
the remaining squares in the chessboard, you can simply fill in the
following days with the following amounts:

38 days = 1,000 tons
48 days = 1,000,000 tons
58 days = 1 billion tons
64 days = 64 billion tons

(By comparison, the total annual rice harvest of the world these days amounts to less than 350 million tons.)

When you have finished filling in the squares on the chalkboard (see Figure 4.3) and putting the total amounts in perspective for the students in the class, you should explain that they have been looking at the effects of what is called an exponential (or "geometric") growth curve. With students who have had algebra, you can put the equation ($y = 2^{x-1}$) on the board, and ask one of your eager beavers to draw a graph that shows the curve. The student will quickly discover that it is impossible to create a scale for the vertical margin of the graph which permits plotting the whole curve in a way that makes any sense at all. If, for example, you draw it with one inch per grain of rice, so that you can tell the first day from the second day, the height of the vertical axis would be a million times greater than the distance from the earth to the sun. If, on the other hand, you put it at one inch per billion tons of rice, you will be able to see a nice curve for the end of the graph, but the first 54 days will be represented by an absolutely straight line that is apparently identical with zero. (If you are doing this in conjunction with a math class, this would be a good time to introduce semi-logarithmic graph paper.)

With younger students, simply ask them if they noticed how slowly things started off and how, all of a sudden, they started to get really big. It is worth emphasizing this by recapitulating some sequences. Remind them that after ten whole days the young man had received only four teaspoons-full of rice (gather up the first ten bags and hold them up), and that on the 30th day he had received 4 *tons* of rice. For further emphasis, point to the plastic bags lined up in order on the desk or table, and remind them that it took 18 days to get from one grain of rice to one box of rice, but only 17 additional days to get from 1 box to an entire room-full of rice.

One useful point that may come up during the discussion of the story is that a curve like this obviously has to run out of room somewhere. In other words, exponential growth goes on indefinitely *only* in the world of theoretical mathematics. In the real world, an

The Hero's Reward

1 1 grain	2 2	3 4	4 8	5 16	6 32	7 64	8 128
9 256	10 512	11 1,024	12 2,048	13 4,096	14 8,192	15 16,384	16 32,768
17 65,536	18 131,072 = 1 box	19 2 boxes	20 4	21 8	22 16	23 32	24 64
25 128	26 256	27 512	28 1,024 boxes = 1 in.	29 2 inches	30 4	31 8	32 16
33 32	34 64	35 128 inches = 1 room	36	37	38 1,000 tons	39	40
41	42	43	44	45	46	47	48 1 million tons
49	50	51	52	53	54	55	56
57	58 1 billion tons	59	60	61	62	63	64 64 billion tons

Total amount of rice equals 128 billion tons.

FIGURE 4.3
Your chalkboard should look something like this
at the end of the story in Exercise 6.

exponential growth curve *always* comes up against a limit sooner or later, and if the growth rate is fairly rapid, that limit will be reached sooner rather than later. What makes exponential growth situations especially troublesome is the way in which they approach their limits. They go along at apparently harmless levels for such a long time that they lull people into a sense of security, but when they are approaching their limit, they do so extremely rapidly. The next two exercises are designed to illustrate this problem.

EXERCISE 7: *The Riddle of the Pond*

Materials: This is a brief and simple exercise. The only materials required are graph paper and a pencil. The graph paper should preferably be four-to-the-inch, although the exercise can be done on paper with smaller squares.

Procedure: Start by asking the students this riddle (from *The Limits to Growth*): Farmer Jones has a pond, and the pond contains a lily plant which doubles in size each day. It will take the plant thirty days to completely fill up the pond, and Farmer Jones doesn't want that, because the lily plant will choke the pond and die and rot and make a big mess. The farmer wants to cut the plant back before that happens, so his question is, "On what day will the lily plant fill half the pond?"

If you get a correct answer (the 29th day) fairly quickly, you will almost certainly have a majority response of "I don't understand" from the rest of the class. Have the student who gives the right answer explain it to the rest. If, as is more likely, the students toss out several numbers, simply as guesses, pick one of them (e.g., 15) and ask the student, "Well, if the pond is half full on the 15th day, and the plant doubles in size each day, how full will the pond be on the sixteenth day?" This will usually be sufficient.

The next step is to distribute graph paper and have each student mark off a big square with 32 of the small squares on each side. This 32 x 32 area represents the pond in which the lily plant is growing. Now the question for the students is, if the lily plant would have completely filled this pond on the 30th day, how many of the small squares did it occupy on the 20th day? (Ask for guesstimates before actually figuring it out with them.)

The simplest way of arriving at a solution is to work backwards, like a time-lapse movie run in reverse. First divide the pond in half and label one half '30'. This is the portion that was *added* on the thirtieth day. Then divide the remaining half in half again and label one portion of that '29'. Continue in the same fashion, dividing the unlabelled half of each segment in half again until you reach the number 21. The remaining portion will be a single small square, the total size of the plant on the 20th day.

After working this out with the class, compare it with their initial guesses. Now, ask them if the farmer, after watching the plant grow for twenty days and seeing it fill only one insignificant little corner of the pond, would be likely to think that he could take a ten day vacation without worrying about the pond becoming overgrown. The point again remains the same: that the suddenness with which exponential curves reach their limits plays tricks on human psychology unless we are trained and aware of the effects of these kinds of situations.

EXERCISE 8: *Percentages and Doubling Times*

Objectives: The purpose of this exercise is to familiarize students with percentage growth rates and enable them to interpret the meanings of growth rates much more easily. For example, demographers can get very excited because the population growth rate of such and such a country drops from 3.3 to 2.6 percent per year and the response of the average person is "So what?" Our objective here is to give students a very quick and easy way of making those kinds of figures meaningful.

Materials: A one page mimeograph sheet for the exercises is a convenience, but they can be done on the chalkboard if you prefer.

Procedure: First point out that, in both of the two preceding exercises, we were talking about quantities that doubled in one day, whether the amount of rice or the size of the lily plant. Now, it happens that one absolutely basic characteristic of exponential growth is that it has a constant doubling time. If it is an exponential curve which happens to take ten years to double the first time, it will take ten years to double again, and ten years for each successive doubling. It also happens that the length of the doubling time is related in a very specific and simple way to the amount of increase per year (or per whatever time period you're talking about). This is important because most growth situations are quoted to us in terms of the percentage of growth each year, and for those figures to be meaningful to us, we need to convert them into the doubling time that they represent.

Let's look at some examples. It happens that the population of the United States is growing at approximately one percent per year. *If* it continues to grow at this rate, it will take about 70 years to double in size. Meanwhile, the population of the whole world is growing at approximately 2 percent per year. Since this is twice as fast as the American growth rate, it seems reasonable that it should take the world only half as long to double its population, and in fact this is true. It will take only 35 years to double the size of humanity if the current rate of growth continues.

We can use a similar procedure for converting any (small) percentage growth rate into an *approximate* doubling time: simply divide the percentage into 70.[1] The process also works backwards: if you know the doubling time, you can divide it into 70 and get the percentage growth rate.

If your students are at the age level where drill in long division is appropriate, give these examples as a handout. Otherwise, just read them off or put them on the chalkboard and have the students call out the answers. (The answers are given in parentheses for your convenience.)

- If you put $100 in the bank at 5% interest, how long do you have to wait before you can get $200 back? (14 years)
- During the 1960's, the gross national product of Japan was growing at 10% per year. How long did it take to double? (7 years)
- The population of Mexico is doubling every 20 years. What is the percentage growth rate? (3.5%)
- If you buy a bond for $1,000 that increases in value at the rate of 7% per year, how long will it take to double in value? (10 years) How much will it be worth in 20 years? ($4,000)
- The table on the following page gives either the population growth rate or the population doubling time, and either the economic growth rate or the economic doubling time for each of the listed countries. Fill in the blanks.

Are the countries listed in the table getting richer or poorer? What about countries like Uruguay, Haiti, or Guyana, where the table indicates that the population is growing faster than the economy? What does it mean in practical terms when the population of a country doubles in twenty years? (They must build twice as many schools, hospitals, stores, houses, and roads; train

---

[1]This is a handy rule of thumb up to about 35% (2 years), but the discrepancies start getting larger as you go up. Obviously, something growing at 70% per year takes *more* than one year to double. Though the error is "only" a few months, the size of the error in comparison to the answer has increased.

| Country | POPULATION | | ECONOMY | |
	Growth Rate	Doubling Time	Growth Rate	Doubling Time
Finland	.4%	(175) years	5.0%	(14) years
Denmark	(.5%)	140 years	(4.7%)	15 years
Italy	(.7%)	100 years	6.1%	(11.5) years
Uruguay	1.2%	(58) years	1.0%	(70) years
Guyana	2.8%	(25) years	(1.5%)	47 years
S. Korea	(2.0%)	35 years	12.2%	(6) years
Ghana*	3.0%	(23) years	2.3%	(30) years
Haiti*	2.5%	(28) years	(1.0%)	70 years
Iran	(2.8%)	25 years	(10.0%)	7 years
Chile	(2.3%)	30 years	(3.5%)	20 years
Sweden*	.5%	(140) years	4.0%	(17.5) years
India	(2.5%)	28 years	4.7%	(15) years
Erehwon[1]	14.0%	(5) years	(7.0%)	10 years
Zambia*	(3.0%)	23 years	(10.0%)	7 years
Libya	3.1%	(23) years	(17.5%)	4 years
Venezuela	3.4%	(21) years	(4.0%)	17.5 years

(Economic data from 1972 U.N. Statistical Yearbook; population data from the 1972 World Population Data Sheet, except (*) which are from 1971 World Population Data Sheet.)

twice as many teachers, doctors, administrators, judges, engineers, etc.; grow twice as much food; and earn twice as much foreign exchange *just to break even*. To make matters worse, in a population growing that fast, half of the population is made up of children, which puts a terrible burden on the other half.)

The Use and Misuse of Trends

We have now had a look at some of the more basic kinds of trends, including an extensive look at the most important kind for our immediate future — the exponential growth curve. Some additional sorts of trends are described in Figure 4.4 As with the types of curves we have already discussed, these are "pure" types which will generally occur in real life in combination with others or disguised by oscillations or random patterns.

Students by now should be adept at identifying and understanding patterns in the past, but of course our purpose in learning about trends is to help us understand better about our own

---

[1]Read it backwards; why couldn't it be a real country?

future. How can we go from one to the other? In two words, the answer is: "Very carefully!"

The popular idea of using a trend, of course, is to extend the trend out into the future as a prediction. This is hazardous for two reasons. First, you must be sure that you have identified the trend correctly. Second, you must be sure that nothing will change the causes of the trend. Since we can rarely, if ever, be sure of either of these, it is very hazardous to attempt to use trends for prediction.

As we discussed in the preceding chapter, there is an important difference between a prediction and a forecast. The purpose of a forecast, if you remember, is not to *know* the future, but to gain information about the future that will help us make better decisions in the present, and trend extrapolation is the source of a very important starting point in forecasting — the *primary* forecast.

As we defined it earlier, a primary forecast is a statement of what will happen *if* things continue on in the future as they have been going. This saves us from the second problem of using trend extrapolation for prediction, because we have side-stepped the question of the continuation of the causes of the trend by making this a condition of the forecast. We still have the first problem, however: correctly identifying the nature of the trend. Often, our choice among the possibilities for the primary forecast depends not so much on "reality" — the real conditions "out there" — as on the sophistication of our knowledge and understanding of the trend.

Consider the problem posed by a simple exponential growth curve. We can look behind us into the past and see the curve stretching out with its characteristic exponential pattern. If, to the best of our knowledge, we are not approaching a limit on that curve, we can simply extend the curve into the future, and this will constitute our primary forecast. (The fact that a simple continuation is not impossible does not, of course, mean that it *will* happen. It might even be quite unlikely, but as long as it is possible and would not require a fundamental change in the basic causal mechanism, it would be considered the primary forecast.)

On the other hand, let us suppose that we do know that the curve we are on is approaching some external limit, like the lily plant filling up the entire pond. Is there any way that we can tell how it will behave (see Figure 4.4) when it reaches that limit? Not very easily. About the best we can do in choosing a primary forecast is to try to pick the course of events that is most likely to occur *if* there is

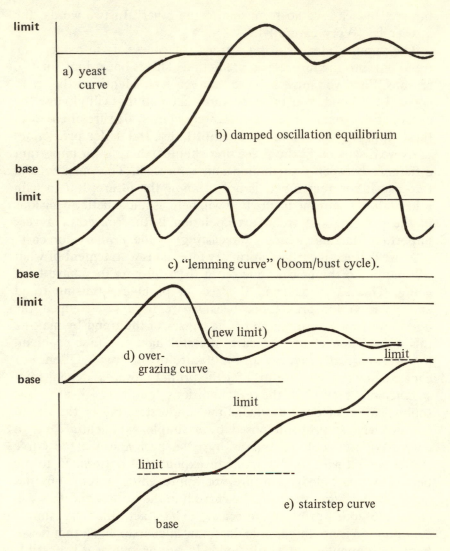

FIGURE 4.4
EXPONENTIAL GROWTH APPROACHING A LIMIT

a) Population cannot exceed limit or damage environment
b) Population cannot damage environment; can exceed limit, causing die-back of more
   than excess; each successive swing is shorter.
c) Same as b), except that each new burst of growth exceeds the limit as much as the
   first one.
d) Population can exceed limit, can damage environment.
e) Population approaches and circumvents a succession of limits.

("Population" is used as a reference because these are common population growth patterns in nature, but the curves can describe any growing quantity. "Limit" refers to the
long-term capacity of the environment, not the short-term maximum quantity.)

no deliberate human intervention aimed at changing from one pattern to another.

To make matters even more difficult, the experts will often disagree at virtually every point. In fact, the source of many major disagreements among policy makers is a difference in belief about "the status quo extended" — what will happen if we do nothing. If you believe, for instance, that the population can just keep on growing (or that it will taper off in a nice smooth S-curve pattern), then population is obviously a very low priority on your agenda. If, on the other hand, you believe that continued population growth will result in a massive die-off in population, as many experts suggest, then measures for controlling population would be very high on your priority list.

If trends are so difficult to use well, why is it so important for students (and, indeed, everybody) to understand them? In the first place, trend extrapolations are all around us. Our fundamental guiding image of "the future" is very much a combination of many primary forecasts into an intuitive and rather hazy notion of "where we are headed." In the second place, the media are constantly bombarding us with trend extrapolations and "predictions" which are very naive or badly done, and we need to know when to be skeptical of what we read and hear, even from "the experts."

In the third place, and possibly most important, trend extrapolation is the key to a vital question: "What are the important issues?" Often we speak of trend extrapolation as if it were a first step in looking at a problem. On the contrary, its most important use is in deciding what issues *are* the problems. If we are confident that a trend will continue (providing we don't interfere) and we consider the continuation desirable, then this is a subject we can push to one side. We can thereby save our attention and other resources for those areas where the continuation of the trend is either unlikely or undesirable. In other words, if you either don't *know* where you are headed, or don't *like* where you are headed, you need to pay much closer attention to the different possibilities open to you.

TRENDS: ESSENTIAL POINTS

1. A trend is a regular pattern of events in the past and present.
2. Trend extrapolation is the extension of a trend into the future.

3. When we do not understand why events are happening as they are, trend extrapolations may provide the best (or least bad) forecasts about the future.
4. Unless there is reason to be certain that underlying causes will not change, reliance on trend extrapolation can be misleading and dangerous.
5. Two of the simplest trends are "no-growth," and "linear" (or "arithmetic") growth.
6. Cyclical and/or random patterns may be superimposed upon any basic trend.
7. "Exponential growth" is one of the most important kinds of trends to understand in dealing with the problems that society faces.
8. A quantity which is growing exponentially has a constant doubling time.
9. When the doubling time is divided into the number 70, the result is the percentage growth rate (and vice versa).
10. A quantity growing exponentially within a limited environment appears to grow very slowly at first, and then to "explode" toward the limit; this creates a problem because it is contrary to normal intuition and creates a false sense of security until the limit has very nearly been reached.
11. An exponential curve approaching a limit may behave in a number of radically different ways, depending upon the nature of the limit and the vulnerability of the environment.
12. Trend extrapolation is a risky basis for planning, but a valuable guide for further forecasting.

NOTES

77.   For more about the background and basic assumptions of trend extrapolation, see "The Current Methods of Futures Research," by Theodore J. Gordon, particularly pages 167 to 169, in *The Futurists*, edited by Alvin Toffler. [14]

78.   Isaac Asimov has described the static nature of life during most of history as follows:

> Until the middle of the eighteenth century, the domi-
> nant factor in human history was stasis. Empires rose and

empires fell. Conquerors flashed across the world stage. Barbarians thundered in from the steppes. To the peasant on his farm, generally speaking, it all meant nothing. The generations went on.

The "changes" that seem so impressive in the history books, the rise of this city or that, the fall of this empire or that, are really not changes to the average man. A given individual might have the current of his life turned awry if a war band clattered through his patch of farming ground, or if pestilence struck or famine ground him. If he survived, however, he was back in the old place, and if in a large city a hundred miles away, a new king reigned, he heard it only by rumor and it meant nothing. (Dick Allen, *Science Fiction: The Future*, p. 265.) [289]

81.   On the key role of exponential growth trends, see John McHale, *World Facts and Trends*. McHale's book is an indispensible resource for teaching about trends. [32]

82.   The chessboard story is described on page 29 of *The Limits to Growth* [105] as an old Persian legend. The locale of this version was switched to China because rice was the only grain handy when the exercise was designed.

85.   Figures on the annual world rice harvest come from the *United Nations Statistical Yearbook, 1972*. [315]

85.   In *World Dynamics*, Jay Forrester gives a very clear explanation of the relationships between the scales on a chart, the eventual limits to exponential growth, and the apparent shape of an exponential growth curve. [102]

87.   The riddle of the pond appears in *The Limits to Growth*, by Donella Meadows, *et al.*, on page 29. It is described there as a riddle which is popular among French children. [105]

88.   The constant doubling time and the procedure for computing doubling times and percentage growth rates are discussed on pages 29 and 30 of *The Limits to Growth*. [105]

91.   Robert Ayres quotes Ralph Lenz on the dangers of blind extrapolation, which "errs by extending short-term trends, ignoring long-term trends, and forgetting common sense." The quote occurs on page 100 of *Technical Forecasting and Long Range Planning*, in a very thorough and interesting chapter on "extrapolation of trends." [1]

91.   For further information on growth curves approaching a limit, see *The Limits to Growth* [105], pages 91 to 92, and *Technological Forecasting and Long Range Planning*, pages 101 to 109. [1]

CHAPTER V
Group Opinion

Another of the oldest approaches to social forecasting, and still one of the most common, is to identify an "expert" and ask him what he thinks will happen. This is known as "genius forecasting," and in practice it tends to be like the little girl in the nursery rhyme: when it is good, it is very, very good; and when it is bad, it is horrid. The problem, of course, is in telling which is which while one still has time to make use of the forecast. Even if one has identified a genius (and this is hard to define, much less establish), there will usually be considerable unevenness of quality among that individual's forecasts, some being brilliant and others overlooking essential points.

One popular way to smooth out the unevenness of individual intuition is to assemble a committee or commission of experts and ask them to arrive at some consensus on the subject at hand. The advantage of this approach is the extensive debate and rigorous scrutiny that each idea gets as it competes for acceptance before a group of informed, articulate, and skeptical judges. The disadvantage is that the results of the debate and scrutiny are usually influenced as much by the prestige and persuasiveness of the various members as by the relative merits of the ideas.

An alternative to the committee approach is the poll or survey, in which the experts are asked to answer questions about the likelihood, probable timing, desirability, and/or likely impact of a variety of possible future events. The results are tabulated and averaged to obtain a crude estimate of the opinion of the group. A poll is thus a way to successfully minimize the principal disadvantage of the committee: the excessive influence of personality. At the same time, the principal advantage of the committee is also eliminated: the face-to-face interchange of ideas and opinions, which is so important when dealing with subjects (like the future of whole societies!) which require information and expertise from many different disciplines. Another disadvantage to the poll is that it requires many more participants and gives much smaller rewards (in terms of ego-satisfaction and educational opportunity) to each, thus diluting the effects of the best minds and ensuring that answers will be given without the extensive consideration normal in the committee or commission process.

Several attempts have been made to combine the best features of the commission and the opinion poll, while minimizing their drawbacks. These range from conferences with provision for anonymous polling (or even anonymous debate) to repetitions of an opinion poll with provision between rounds for telling each panelist what the group's responses were on the previous round (the "Delphi" method).

When used properly, each of these three methods — the commission, the poll, and the combinations such as Delphi — can be a source of valuable insights into the future. Like trend extrapolation, however, each of them is easily misused (particularly the poll and the Delphi) and can be persuasively misleading.

The exercises that follow are designed to give students first hand experience with each method and some insight into their potential for use and misuse. The exercises have also been designed so that they can be used separately to explore several different issues or in sequence to explore one issue in great depth, beginning with a simple poll, developing from that a more elaborate Delphi, and using the results of the Delphi as an input to a Commission proceedings. An exercise is also included on "brainstorming," a procedure which may be helpful at several different stages in the group processes described in this chapter and in the next chapter on alternative futures.

The exercises have not been tied to any particular topic or topics, so that you may adapt them to the content you need or wish to cover. It may be useful, however, to suggest some of the many topics that could be used:

Transportation	Population
Energy	Cities
Genetic Engineering	Life Styles
Food Production	Occupations
Environmental Protection	Education
Space Travel	Race Relations
Privacy	International Relations

Polls

There are several reasons for exploring polls in the classroom. Public opinion polls that tell us what we think, who we like, how we're going to vote, and so forth, are an increasingly important influence on our lives. In addition, polls are one of the simplest means for gathering expert opinion. And finally, polling can be a valuable educational technique both outside and inside the classroom.

There are four basic approaches to the use of polls in the classroom. First there is the simple verbal poll or hand vote, done in class with the students. Second, there is the more formal in-class type of questionnaire, generally written out and answered in writing (see Exercise 4, pages 70 - 72). Third, there is the analysis and discussion of polls prepared by others. And finally, there is the preparation by the students of a poll or questionnaire to be administered by them to a subject population outside of the classroom. The exercise that follows combines all four of these approaches, but any of the four portions can be used separately.

EXERCISE 9: *Questions, Questions*

Procedure: Your first task is to select a topic area. This exercise combines quite naturally with Exercise 11, with the information gained from these polling activities used as an input to the Commission proceedings, providing always that the topic you choose is amenable to both a commission and a questionnaire type of approach. In this exercise, however, you have one further requirement: you will need a poll conducted by researchers or

**TYPES OF QUESTIONS TO ASK
ABOUT POSSIBLE FUTURE EVENTS**

- What is the earliest year by which you think this is likely to have happened?
- What is the earliest year by which this has a 20% chance of occurring?
- In what year do you think it is most likely to occur?
- What do you think is the probability that it will occur in the next 30 years?
- Which of these several alternatives do you think is most likely to occur?
- Which is least likely?
- Which is most desirable?
- If the first event occurred, would it increase or decrease the likelihood of the second event occurring?
  How much? In what way?

And so on.

GUIDELINES FOR GOOD QUESTIONS

- The questions should be completely unambiguous. (If different people are actually answering completely different questions, you can't very well make sense of an average of their answers.)
- The method for answering should be completely unambiguous. (As above.)
- Avoid mixing two questions together. ("Do you think A and B will happen?")
- Avoid leading questions and unconditional assumptions. ("Will you have stopped beating your wife by the year 1990?")
- Avoid questions that will produce a lot of "never" answers on time-lines. ("When will anti-gravity be invented?")
- In general, be sure to make provision for the whole range of possible answers. (Nothing will annoy your respondents more than wanting to say "none of the above" when there is no such choice.)
- Keep it as brief as possible.

professional pollsters in the general area that you wish to discuss. (You will generally find journals and news magazines to be better sources than books, as timeliness is important.)

Introduce the topic that you have chosen into general discussion in the class. Gradually ease into a pattern of questions directed to the class, beginning with such questions as, "Does anyone know anything more about that, which they can share with the class?" Move to simple yes or no questions which can be answered by a show of hands — "How many of you think that that is likely to happen in the next ten years?" Don't try to hurry this initial lead-in period. Keep the discussion low-key and informal, and encourage the students to explain their views if they wish and to discuss conflicting views. Your intent is as much to allow the students to get into the subject as to focus attention on questions which draw out their own opinions.

Eventually, you will find yourself asking the same question several times in slightly altered forms (e.g., "Do you think this is likely to happen within the next ten years? . . . Within the next fifteen years? . . . The next 20 years?") At this point introduce them to the idea of a *time line* by putting a line on the board marked off in five or ten year units from the present date to a fairly distant future date:

| : : : | : : : : | : : : : |
1975   2000   2025   2050+ Never

Now, ask the same question in a different form: "What do you think is the earliest date by which this is likely to occur?" Be sure the students understand exactly what the question asks. You don't want them to guess the year in which it will happen: instead, you want them to estimate the year *by which* they think the event is as likely to have happened as not to have happened.

The simplest way to record the answers is to make a short vertical line at the date of an answer and put the initials of the student giving it directly above the line. (Where the line gets crowded, you may have to use arrows.) When you have finished discussing the results of this question, ask several more questions in the same vein, putting a new time-line up for each one.

When you have done this several times, ask the students what other kinds of questions you might ask about the future (see page 100). As you explore some of these variations and alternatives,

SCORING PROCEDURES

- With yes/no, or true/false, or multiple choice, compute the percentage for each answer.

- With time-lines and probabilities, and other linear ranges, the usual response is simply to give the average, but this means that two sets of scores-- one bunched tightly in the middle and the other scattered across the whole range -- will be represented in the same way. So some people prefer to give the bottom, average, and top scores. Unfortunately, this can be thrown off quite a distance by one freak score at either end, so a more effective solution is the "interquartile range" (the middle 50%) accompanied by the average, a procedure known as "making a house":

First find the average and make a tall line at that point, then put the scores in rank order from highest down to lowest. Count the number of scores and divide by 4. If it comes out even, with no fractions, count that number up from the bottom and find the value that would be half way between that score and the next one above it. Do the same thing counting from the top down. If it comes out with a fraction, *round the number up* and count up from the bottom to that exact score; do the same thing counting from the top down. The two values you have found are approximations of the first and third quartile points. Record them on the horizontal line with two vertical marks half as high as the mark indicating the average, and join the tops of the three marks together.

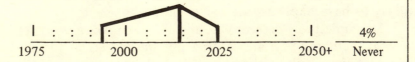

1975   2000   2025   2050+   Never

In the example above, the middle 50% of the answers (other than never) ranged from 1993 to 2025, and the average of all the answers was 2014. Four percent of the panelists (e.g., 1 out of 25, or 2 out of 50) answered "never."

suggest that the students draw up a poll or questionnaire for the class on the subject you've been discussing. You may wish to share the guidelines on preparing good questions with them immediately, or you may prefer to elicit the guidelines from them as they go along. However you go about it, try to help the students draw up good questions without dominating the process of deciding which questions to ask.

When the students have finished drawing up a list of questions, have them print the questions directly on a ditto master. Run these off and distribute them at your next class session. When the students have finished answering the questions, collect the sheets and immediately, before discussing the answers to their own questionnaire, distribute the copies (which you have already prepared) of the *questions* from the professional poll.

After these have been answered and collected, explain the scoring procedure. Arrange a sequence so that the students score the questions themselves. When the scoring is done, return the students' own answer sheets and put a summary of the class answers up on the board, along with the "expert" answers to those questions.

Now go through the questions one by one, giving the class ample time to discuss them. Ask the students why they gave the answers they did. Were they surprised by the class answer? Was everyone actually answering the same question? Was it a useful question the way it was asked? (This is especially important with the questions from the outside poll.) Would you answer it differently now that you've found out how the class answered it? What about the "experts'" answers? These and similar questions will help you keep the discussion moving without degenerating into an argument over who was right and who was wrong. (Emphasize strongly that the "experts" are often wrong.)

When you have finished going through the individual questions, ask the students for a general comparison between the questions they drew up and the questions from the prepared poll. Why did the poll's authors choose the questions they did? Do you get different results by asking the same question in a different way? Is there a "neutral" or "objective" way to ask a question?

When they've had a chance to discuss the different problems involved in constructing a valid questionnaire, ask them if they would like to try creating a questionnaire out of the best questions from the two previous polls (and any additional ones which they might wish to add) to be given to some group outside of the classroom, such as the teachers in your school or the students' parents. If the class is interested, help them to prepare the questionnaire in a way that is neat and easy to understand, and decide on a procedure for administering it. Be careful on one point: if there are "sensitive" questions in the poll, especially ones relating to personal values, make sure that you can promise to keep the answers anonymous. This can simply mean including an envelope and the appropriate instructions with the poll. You will get more honest answers this way, and you will also avoid student anxieties about how their parents' answers will seem to the rest of the class.

You then score the answer sheets in the same way as before, but separately for each group of respondents, so that the pattern of answers from one group to the other can be compared. For instance, if the students administered the questionnaire to the other teachers in the school and their own parents, you would then have a three- or four-way comparison: the students themselves, the teachers, the parents, and — for those questions borrowed straight off the outside poll — the "experts."

If no pattern is found to the differences among the groups, there is nothing much that can be said except that this is an issue which all of the groups see in much the same way. If on the other hand, as is quite common, there is a distinctive pattern of differences in the answers given by the different groups, you have some very fruitful leads for discussion as to why those groups tend to see this particular subject in the different ways that they do.

Combination Strategies

There have been quite a few attempts to devise combinations of the poll and the commission approaches, preserving the advantages of each, while minimizing the disadvantages. These have ranged from "maximal" combinations on the one hand — taking a poll among a large group of experts and using it as an input to a commission made up of a smaller group of experts — to augmented polls with some provision for exchange of ideas and feedback on results on the other hand. One of the latter, called the Delphi technique, has become the single most widespread (and notorious) of the forecasting tools developed since World War II.

The idea behind Delphi is quite simple. Unless a person is completely certain of his own opinion, he will generally tend to take the opinions of other people into account in making up his own mind. The less certain he is, the more he will let the opinions of others influence his judgment. This is especially true if he is allowed time to forget his original estimate before being told the opinions of other "experts" and asked to estimate again. Delphi exploits this pattern to create a convergence of opinions toward a group consensus, a consensus which is also "weighted" to reflect the different degrees of conviction among the members of the group.

In the decade following its development at the RAND Corporation in the early 1960's, Delphi became highly popular among many would-be forecasters, who often treated it as a universal method for predicting the future and misused it severely in the process. (The guidelines for good questions on page 100, were largely derived from the horrible examples in several bad Delphi studies.) This pattern of misuse makes it necessary for us to take a hard look at just what a Delphi is good for and what it is not.

In the first place, the purpose of a Delphi — or any poll — is to identify a consensus, a best opinion of the group. The Delphi is simply windowdressing if the consensus can be determined more easily by other means, such as a review of books or journals in the field. The Delphi is also the wrong technique to use in the middle of a controversy when no consensus exists; intense scientific or scholarly debates are not settled by putting the issue to a vote, nor will convergence of opinions occur when each side has clearly thought out and well articulated reasons for its divergent view.

Even compared with the two methods it combines, polls and commissions, Delphi has some special disadvantages. These are especially related to the percentage of the selected group of experts who simply refuse to respond. (This is a major headache in any statistical procedure because the "dropouts" may be decidedly nonrandom, thus distorting your results.) In most cases the Delphi offers the response group no greater rewards than a one-shot poll would have offered, but demands three times the amount of time and effort from them.

Against all this, it must be pointed out that where a poll is appropriate, the Delphi is usually a much superior form of poll;

where a commission is appropriate, a Delphi may do essentially the same thing with much less expense and much less danger of domination by prestige or personality. (In this case, of course, we are speaking of forecasting procedures; the commission has a substantial advantage as a procedure for generating policy recommendations and creative solutions to problems.) The place where Delphi shines most, however, may be as an educational device and as an intragroup communication device.

EXERCISE 10: *Delphi*

Background: You can use the procedure that follows instead of the simple polls in the previous exercise. It can be used to replace either the written poll given to the class or the poll which the students prepare and administer to an outside group, or both. Alternatively, it can be used as a continuation of the preceding exercise or entirely on its own.

Procedure: Prepare your questions as you would for an ordinary poll, except that you must restrict yourself to questions whose answers cover a continuous range and make sense when averaged together, such as dates and probabilities. (I.e., no true/false or multiple choice questions.)

ROUND ONE: Distribute the first round of the poll to the panel, explaining the answering procedure and the three-round format of the poll. Collect the answer sheets and compute the average and the interquartile range for each question. (See box on scoring procedures, page 102.)

ROUND TWO: Mark the group's responses — the average and the interquartile range — on the new answer sheets for round two and distribute these sheets to the panelists with an explanation of the method used to represent the group's first-round responses. Instruct the panelists to answer the questions again and, where they have strongly felt reasons for an answer, to state those reasons as concisely as possible. Collect the answer sheets and compute the group scores as before.

ROUND THREE: Mark the group responses to round two on the answer sheets for this final round; where a distinct contrast of views exists, add a representative sample of the comments supporting the divergent viewpoints. Distribute the final round of answer sheets, asking the panelists to answer the questions again, taking the group response and the quoted justifications into consideration. (Panelists need not provide new justifications on this round.) Score the answer sheets as before.

CONCLUSION: Your analysis will of course depend on the kinds of questions you asked and the kinds of answers you got. Often, it will be useful to rearrange the questions so that questions with similar answers are grouped together. For example, "The panelists gave the innovations in the first group a 50% or greater chance of occurring within the next decade, those in the second group a 40-50% chance, those in the third group a 30-40% chance . . ." and so on.

When the class or task force has finished the analysis and written up the results of the poll, make *sure* that the panelists each get a copy of the results. This is very important and easy to overlook. They have each contributed a good deal of time and thought to make the study possible and they will naturally be curious about the results.

Classroom Commissions

One of the valid criticisms levelled at our educational system is that our schools generally teach a solitary approach to work and learning. Our young people spend 12 to 16 years in competitive and very individualistic effort in the classroom; then as adults they will be engaged in work which is largely cooperative and group-related. This is not a question of whether competition is better than cooperation, or vice-versa. It is rather a question of whether individuals who will spend much of their adult life in business organizations, government agencies, staffs, administrations, committees, and task forces, would benefit from at least some exposure to the special problems and requirements of group research and decision making.

The blame for this situation probably lies with the grading system. It is difficult to give grades fairly to participants in a team project. So, since we generally have to give grades, we tend to avoid group assignments. For the most part, however, these problems can be circumvented if the teacher believes that there is an important reason for doing so.

The exercise that follows has a three-fold purpose: to provide students a chance to work in a task-force-type situation, to give students an understanding of the advantages and shortcomings of the commission approach to making policy recommendations, and finally, to give students an in-depth understanding of one important and complex issue.

EXERCISE 11: *The President's Select Commission*

Background: The basic procedure here is to choose a potential problem and to select a date, preferably within the next ten or fifteen years, when that problem will culminate in a crisis. Your students are then asked to be participants in a Presidential Commission, called together at the time of the crisis to recommend effective solutions.

The students will have to enter into two bits of make-believe. The first is that they are in fact important members of a prestigious Presidential Commission. The second is that "the present" is the future year that you have specified. To do this easily, they need some help from you in creating a persuasive and believable context for their role-playing effort.

The basic instrument for doing this is the scenario, or "future history."[1] This is a simple description of a plausible sequence of events leading up to the crisis which you have postulated. If the crisis occurs in 1990, for example, then the scenario is written in the past tense as if describing the history of the problem to someone living in 1990. At minimum, your scenario should cover the events between the real present and the fictitious "present." However, the most important characteristic of the scenario is that it be a rich and interesting sequence, full enough of detail and imagination so that the students have no trouble slipping into their roles and sustaining their make-believe situation.

---

[1]See Appendix B for a sample scenario and commission exercise.

Procedure: Begin by selecting a problem. Ideally, it should be a real possibility, in an area in which your students are interested, with enough complexity so that the underlying issues are just within the students' grasp. It should be neither too simple to sustain interest and debate, nor so technical that the students cannot really cover all of the basic parts of the dilemma (but in general it is safer to over-estimate their capacity). Once you have selected a topic, you should prepare a scenario, leading up to and including the establishment of the commission and their appointment as members. Conclude the scenario with a detailed statement of the roles that they are to play (who they are) and of the task which they are being asked to perform as commissioners.

Explain the procedure to the students and distribute copies of the scenario and the instructions. The number of students on the commission will depend partly on the topic you choose, partly on the age level of the students, and partly on whether or not you intend to do this exercise again with another topic. If you are planning to run the exercise with the whole class, your first step (after giving the students a chance to read the scenario) should be to convene the commission as a whole, with yourself as chairperson, and divide the commission up into subcommittees or task forces. Each task force is responsible for researching a specific area or representing a specific constituency. It should be made up of three to six students and it should report back to the commission as a group (although minority reports are allowed if persistent disagreements occur).

The students should select their own task forces, with some encouragement from you to get things to come out even. Once the task forces are set up, create a specific role and identity for each student, based as far as possible on the particular student's own aspirations. Thus, "Chrissie Smith" becomes "Dr. Christina G. Smith, world famous physiologist" and "Jack Kelley" becomes "the Honorable John R. Kelley, Mayor of Chicago." Encourage students to use the names and titles associated with the commission membership while involved in the exercise. The easiest way to do this is for you to always address them formally in their role identities: "Excuse me, Dr. Smith, I believe Mayor Kelley has the floor," instead of "Chrissie, don't interrupt."

When the subcommittees and individual identities have been established, set a time for the next meeting of the whole commission and make sure that each subcommittee knows what will be required of it at the next meeting. Tell them that you will be available to the subcommittees if they wish, as a resource person for factual information, legal opinions, etc. Then allow the class to split up into subcommittees so that each group can discuss how best to approach its task.

When you reconvene the entire commission to receive the subcommittee progress reports, physically arrange the room so that members of the same subcommittee sit together and the different subcommittees face each other across the room. If you have chosen your topic well, the debate will be well under way by the time the subcommittees have finished their reports, and your principal task will be to act as moderator and stay out of the discussion. After this meeting, allow the students, insofar as possible, to organize the remainder of the project: how many more meetings to have, when to have them, and what should be covered by them.

As the project progresses, you will probably have to remind the class that these are not just study or discussion sessions: the commission's *task* is to produce a set of specific recommendations for action to cope with a specific problem facing society. When the group has finally reached a consensus (or decided instead on a majority report with dissenting opinions), you should ask them to consider a concluding question: If this problem could have been anticipated 'x' years ago, what actions would you have recommended in 19___ to have prevented or ameliorated the problem? ('X' is the difference in years between the fictional present and the real present, and 19___, of course, is the real present year.)

Appendix B contains an example of a scenario which has been successfully used in workshops on the future of education. No "general-purpose" scenario has been included for you to use directly for two reasons. The first is that scenarios need to have a lot of plausible detail in the interval between now and then. This provides "realism," but it also insures that they become outdated very quickly — just as the one in the appendix will undoubtedly be outdated by the time you read it. (For several years — up through 1973 — this writer used a very successful scenario dealing with an energy crisis in the year 1977. Unfortunately, events overtook us four years ahead of schedule.)

The second reason is that there would be a definite tendency to "use the one in the book," and we have found that the scenarios are quite sensitive to grade level. What works for high school probably won't work well for junior high. What works for junior high seldom will work well for 4th grade. Furthermore, you will want to select topics which enable you to kill several birds with one stone. This is a long exercise, but if you choose carefully, you can incorporate into it a considerable amount of content for nearly any subject, from energy or population to American government or the future of the arts.

Follow-up: After the exercise is finished, the students may be curious about real commissions, how they work, and how *well* they work. It happens that the findings of two important Presidential Commissions are available on film as well as in book form. These are the President's Commission on "Population and the American Future," and the Kerner Commission on "Violence in the United States." (See Appendix C for ordering information.) The population film is an official filmed report from the commission, and it is an interesting exercise in making necessary political compromises among divergent viewpoints, while still presenting some fairly forthright conclusions. The Kerner Commission film is a powerful documentary about the findings of the Commission, rather than an official report by the Commission.

Group Process

Quite a number of procedures have been devised for helping people work together better, ranging from sensitivity training to Robert's Rules of Order. One of the simplest and most effective of these procedures is known as "brainstorming." In the previous exercises, your students may come up against a situation where, instead of looking for a "right" answer which will yield to facts and analysis, they are looking for a creative *new* solution; this is where brainstorming can help. It is a method for increasing the ability of a group to produce unusual or creative solutions, based on the simple but somewhat surprising observation that good ideas tend to be "sparked off" by other ideas, regardless of whether the other ideas are good or bad. If this is true, then it follows that the volume of ideas is more important, at least initially, than the quality when the object is creativity.

EXERCISE 12: *Brainstorming*

Materials: At least two and preferably four or five large pads of newsprint or poster paper; an equal number of bright marking pens or crayons.

Procedure: Carefully state the exact task to which a solution is being sought. Post the pads of newsprint around the room where everybody in the class can see them. Take a marking pen yourself and stand in front of one of the pads; assign the other pads and pens to students who can write clearly and rapidly. Explain that they are going to try a procedure called brainstorming, and that the first step has three very simple rules:

1. Everybody calls out ideas as fast as they can, no matter how silly, crazy, or stupid they may sound.
2. The recorders write down every idea, writing as fast as possible.
3. *Absolutely NO criticism,* by word or expression or gesture, is permitted. On the contrary, off-beat ideas should be encouraged.

The third rule is the key. The object is to produce a huge outpouring of ideas, with no regard for quality. It is especially important for the teacher not to convey the slightest disapproval of any idea, no matter how eccentric. (That's one reason for keeping you busy as a recorder.) As sheets are filled up, tear them off the pads and tape or tack them up around the room where everyone can read them. If the flow of suggestions runs dry, recommend that students look at the different pages and try out combinations or variations of ideas that are already up.

Only after suggestions have dried up with some finality should you tell the class to shift to the second half of the process — the evaluation. Now the students bring back the critical judgment which you asked them to deliberately suspend during the brainstorming part. They should carefully go through the suggestions, one at a time, trying to find ways that they could be applied or made to work and eliminating those which could not be effective solutions to the stated problem. The idea sounds so simple — think first, criticize later — that it is hard to believe how effective it can be. You will find that it is a rare brainstorming session that does not produce at least one truly creative or off-beat solution to a problem.

GROUP OPINION: ESSENTIAL POINTS

1. Intuitive forecasting by a single expert is called "genius forecasting"; it is one of the oldest methods of forecasting, but the results tend to be uneven and hard to validate.
2. Expert commissions "smooth out" the unevenness of intuitive forecasting and provide intensive research and debate, but may be excessively influenced by the prestige and persuasiveness of some of the members.
3. A poll is less expensive than a commission and minimizes the excessive influence of personality, but it also eliminates any exchange of ideas and opinions.
4. Numerous attempts have been made to combine the advantages of both the commission and the poll; the most successful and widely used of these combination methods is the Delphi.
5. The Delphi is a poll which is repeated several times; before being asked their opinions again, the experts are told the results of the previous round.
6. The way a question is asked greatly influences the answers; meaningful answers depend upon well-framed questions.
7. The ability of a group to produce creative solutions can be enhanced by brainstorming, a technique which depends upon the initial suspension of critical judgment to get the maximum number of ideas, both good and bad.

NOTES

97. In the first two chapters of *Profiles of the Future*, Arthur C. Clarke presented the classic discussion of intuitive forecasting, and why it so frequently goes wrong. The two chapters are reprinted as one essay, called "Hazards of Prophecy," on pages 133 to 150 of

The Futurists, edited by Toffler. Theodore J. Gordon's essay on "The Current Methods of Futures Research," is also reprinted in *The Futurists*, pages 164 to 189; it has a good discussion on the problems of the commission approach and an excellent, straightforward description and evaluation of the Delphi technique. [14]

99. The impact of public opinion polls on modern life is discussed in many places; one of the best sources on the impact of polls on politics is *Polls, Television, and the New Politics*, by Harold Mendelssohn and Irving Crespi.

100-103. An invaluable aid in the process of preparing and analysing polls is Stanley L. Payne's little book, *The Art of Asking Questions*. [311]

105. Timothy Weaver's chapter on "The Delphi Forecasting Method," (pages 43 to 59 of Hostrop, *Foundations of Futurology in Education*) gives you a good general history and evaluation of the technique. [60]

106. Weaver's comments on the educational uses of the Delphi are pertinent:

> To sum up quickly, although Delphi was originally intended as a forecasting tool, its more promising educational applications seem to be in the following areas: (a) a method for studying the process of thinking about the future, (b) a pedagogical tool or teaching tool which forces people to think about the future in a more complex way than they ordinarily would, and (c) a planning tool which may aid in probing priorities held by members and constituencies of an organization. (Hostrop, *Foundations of Futurology in Education*, p. 59.) [60]

112. There is a good, concise description of brainstorming on page 145 of *Technological Forecasting and Long Range Planning*, by Robert Ayres. [1]

Chapter VI
Alternatives and Imagination

At several points in the two preceding chapters there have been cautionary comments about the dangers inherent in trend extrapolation and expert consensus techniques. Although the methods themselves present pitfalls, the greater danger lies in the tendency to search for a *single* forecast (either primary or tertiary) and then to focus on it to the exclusion of other alternative possibilities. In this chapter we are going to look at reasons why it is important to consider other alternatives, and ways in which students can learn to do so more effectively.

How Likely is "Most Likely"?

Consider this situation. You are about to choose a card at random from a well-shuffled deck. There are 52 cards, each with the same very low chance of being chosen. Whichever one you choose, an improbable event will have come about.

Most of the time when we are talking about the future of society, or of any moderately complicated portion of society, we are confronted with a situation which is analogous to that deck of cards. We are unable to say, "This is going to happen," or even, "This is probably what's going to happen." We are usually faced instead with a wide range of alternative possibilities, any one of which is improbable in itself.

Unlike cards in a deck, however, these alternative possibilities are not equally improbable; some are more likely (or less unlikely) than others. This creates a danger for the unwary. There is a temptation to try to discover the one course of events which is most likely to occur, and then — consciously or unconsciously — to plan on the assumption that the most likely course of events will occur. It is easy to fall into this trap even when the "most likely" outcome is merely the "least unlikely" of many unlikely alternatives.

Suppose you add an extra ace of hearts to that deck of cards. The card you draw is now much more likely to be an ace of hearts than any other specific card in the deck; would you therefore make your plans on the assumption that you will draw an ace of hearts? It would be the sensible thing to do only if you had to pin *all* of your hopes on a single card. In most social situations, however, we do *not* have to "bet" on one single future, so there is no reason to rely on the "least unlikely" forecast. Instead, we can (and should) examine the whole range of alternatives and try to make our plans so they will make sense in as many different alternative futures as possible.

Assuming No Change

The other common kind of "single-future" fallacy is to rely too much on the primary forecast, the assumption that the future will be a simple extension of the present. A particular policy or program may make excellent sense in the present and in a future which remains unchanged from the present in its essential features. But the future which actually occurs will usually be different in many important respects from the present. That same policy or program may produce quite unexpected results or fail completely in such an unanticipated environment.

An individual is most likely to fall into this trap when he is aware of potential changes within his own particular field, but tacitly assumes that the rest of society will continue to be "the same, only more so," i.e., that essential features will be retained and present trends will continue, but these trends will produce only changes in degree, not changes in kind.

For instance, an educational planner will almost certainly take into account many recent innovations and proposals — e.g., vouchers, computer-assisted instruction, performance contracting — which could transform the educational system, but he is much less likely to consider equally plausible changes in the economic or political areas, which might equally well transform education, its environment, and the expectations placed on it. A case can be made, for example, that the U.S. faces a significant risk of a major depression by the early 1980's. Such an event would have a very considerable effect on education, so that even if it is judged to be relatively unlikely — perhaps one chance in five or even one chance in ten — it would still be prudent to take the possibility into consideration. Yet is is quite unlikely that an educational planner would do so, since he is (usually) not an expert economist.

Alternatives and Imagination

It is unreasonable to expect any person to be familiar with all possible developments in all areas of society. One solution to this problem is to prepare *sets* of plausible alternative future histories of society as a whole, each one differing from the others in several major respects. This makes it possible to "test" a policy against a number of (hopefully representative) future contexts and provides a reminder of how different the many possibilities for the future can be.

The ways that have been devised to generate and analyze these sets of alternative future histories include some of the most exotic and complicated methods in all of long-range forecasting. Yet what most of us need is not an elaborate methodology but simply better imagination. Even if we *know* that tomorrow is going to be very different, it is all too easy to assume unconsciously that it will be "like today, only more so," because we never stop to imagine the many different forms that tomorrow might take.

This failure of imagination is probably the single most common mistake in thinking about the future. The exercises that follow are therefore primarily "head-stretching" exercises — ways to use history, creative writing, scenarios, and science fiction to improve our thinking about the wide range of possibilities facing us as a society and facing each of us as individuals.

A good place to start is with a simple procedure for finding out how inhibited your students are in their imagination about the future.

EXERCISE 13: *Story Completion*[1]

Materials: Mimeograph two one-page handouts; you will need enough of each handout for half of the class. Both handouts are mostly blank except for a brief heading at the very top. On the first sheet the heading should read:

Instructions: Read the sentences below. Then, using the situation they describe as a starting point, continue the story, telling what you imagine happened next.

* * *

"Dr. and Mrs. Hamilton live in a suburban neighborhood with their adopted Korean daughter Karen. Karen is five years old. One afternoon, not too long ago, Dr. Hamilton heard some loud yelling outside the house. He went to the door to investigate, and saw Karen and a group of other children in the front yard. Karen was sobbing and her dress was torn. The other children stood near her, looking at her. Dr. Hamilton ran down the front steps and . . .

The second handout is identical except that the tense is changed:

Instructions: Read the sentences below. Then, using the situation they describe as a starting point, continue the story, telling what you imagine will happen next.

* * *

"Dr. and Mrs. Hamilton live in a suburban neighborhood with their adopted Korean daughter Karen. Karen is five years old. One afternoon, in the near future, Dr. Hamilton will hear some loud yelling outside the house. He will go to the door to investigate, and will see Karen and a group of other children in the front yard. Karen will be sobbing and her dress will be torn. The other children will be standing near her, looking at her. Dr. Hamilton will run down the front steps and . . .

---

[1]The original version of this exercise was an experiment designed by Professor John Condry, as described by Toffler in *Future Shock*.

Procedure: Distribute the sheets and tell the class that this is a creative writing exercise. Don't draw their attention to the fact that there are two separate versions, and avoid quoting the instructions on the page. (Also try to prevent students from asking questions which will accomplish the same thing.) Tell the class that this is the beginning of a story and each student is to complete it in whatever way his imagination indicates.

When the students are finished, ask them to exchange papers and count the number of words on the papers they receive. Explain about the difference in the papers (for those who haven't already noticed), and be sure to tell them that this is *not* a test and that the number of words has nothing to do with a grade. Then ask each student in turn to call out "past" or "future," and the total number of words added to the story starter. Put the numbers on the board in two columns, one for past and one for future. When you have all the numbers on the board, total and average each column separately.

From here on you must play it by ear according to the results. The "normal" result is to get a batch of long, richly detailed stories written in the past tense, contrasting with a few sketchy sentences for the future tense stories. In other words, for most people the mere fact of phrasing something in the future tense inhibits their imagination.

The impression so far — and there has not been enough experience with this exercise to be more than tentative — is that the tense of the story makes less difference with young children than with high school students and adults. The implication is that, somewhere approximately between ages six and twelve, society (education?) *conditions* people not to be imaginative about the future.

History and the Future

One aspect of teaching people to be *un*imaginative about the future may be, ironically, our approach to history. We invest so much effort in discovering and explaining "why" things happen, that we almost always convey the impression when we have finished that no other history was possible, that the causal forces we have just identified were so overwhelming that the results were inevitable (e.g., the Civil War, or the break-up of feudalism). We rarely hear a teacher (or an historian, for that matter) say, "Well, the way that turned out was mostly a matter of chance; we can find 'explanations' for it in the preceding events, but we could find equally good 'explanations' for many other outcomes."

The first consequence of this is that the most wildly implausible sequences of events are treated as mundane, normal, inevitable, provided they actually happened. The second consequence is that we teach the logical corollary of inevitable history: that there is a single *future* which flows out of this present. As a result, the past tense can be as imaginative as we like — after all it "happened" — while the future tense must be an attempt at *predicting* what will happen. But when there are only "least unlikely" alternatives, prediction is a losing game, *so most people learn not to play it*.

The next two exercises are examples of ways to use history to achieve the opposite effect. (They also make history more interesting to students, which is a valuable bonus.)

EXERCISE 14: *Improbable Histories*

This exercise can be done at any time, but it is a special favorite of students nearing the end of a history course. Give them as an assignment the task of writing an outrageous prediction that came true. The first step is for each student to select an historical sequence of events which seems to him to be highly improbable. He then makes a summary of the situation as known to the people living at the time the sequence began. Finally, he summarizes the actual historical events in the form of a *prediction* written just before the beginning of the sequence of events. The prediction should be in the future tense, of course, and should be strictly factual, with no interpretation or explanation.

In the next class, ask each student to read his "prediction" aloud, giving first the date when he is speaking, then the summary of the situation as of that date, and finally the prediction itself. As an example, here is a favorite "improbable history" — a ten year prediction about the future of the American presidency:

"Today is November 1st, 1963. John Kennedy is the popular, liberal Democrat president of the United States, Lyndon Johnson is his Texas Dixiecrat vice-president. Richard Nixon is a former vice-president who made his reputation as a virulent anti-Communist and was narrowly defeated by John Kennedy three years ago. He has just lost the election for governor of California and has retired from politics with an angry public tantrum. Robert Kennedy is attorney general and Eugene McCarthy, Hubert Humphrey, Barry Goldwater, and George McGovern are all Senators of the United States. With this as background, I am going to make some predictions.

"I predict that John Kennedy will be assassinated within a month and Lyndon Johnson will become president, where he will be a strong advocate of integration and civil rights. Barry Goldwater will run against him in 1964. Goldwater will lose largely because he will advocate sending stronger forces into Vietnam. After his landslide victory over Goldwater (with Hubert Humphrey as his Vice-President), Johnson will do precisely as Goldwater recommended. Then, despite being a popular president, Johnson will refuse to run for re-election in 1968.

"Robert Kennedy (who at this point will be a Senator — not from Massachusetts, but from New York!) will move ahead of early starter Eugene McCarthy for the Democratic nomination, but will be assassinated during the primaries. Hubert Humphrey will win the nomination, but he will lose the election to anti-Communist Richard Nixon, who will campaign on a promise to end the war in Vietnam. During the next four years, he will not do so, but will instead have tea with Mao-Tse-Tung in Peking and trade bear-hugs with Brezhnev in Moscow and Washington.

"In 1972, Democrat George McGovern will campaign for president on a promise to withdraw from Vietnam. Nixon will defeat him by the largest vote margin in history and immediately gain considerable additional support by withdrawing from Vietnam. He will then suffer within a year the biggest and fastest loss of popularity of any American President. By November of 1973 — ten years from today — many of his staff will be in jail or under indictment, his fiery law-and-order vice-president will have been convicted of a felony, and he himself will be facing impeachment."

The result as you can see is an accurate "prediction" which would have been dismissed out of hand as foolishly implausible if it had actually been made in 1963. Encourage the students to "ham it up" when reading their predictions, using mock-serious expressions and mysterioso tones. The more implausible the examples, the more the basic point will sink in: *unlikely things happen* — history is full of extraordinary surprises and the future will be too.

The students by now should be losing their conditioning (or becoming innoculated against acquiring it). The next step is to give them some active practice at seeing history as just one of a number of possible outcomes that could have occurred.

EXERCISE 15: *Historical "What If's"*

Procedure: Choose, or ask your students to choose, one historical incident which greatly altered the flow of history. Then ask each student to write out an imaginary but plausible history in which the chosen event does *not* occur. For instance, to use the same subject used above, "Write an imaginative but plausible history of the U.S. in the 1960's assuming that John Kennedy had not been assassinated." Emphasize that they should try to make the alternative histories as *different* as they can from the actual past while still being able to go back and "explain" the reasons for the events in their history.

When you get the papers in, go through them and select several that are especially inventive. Ask the authors to read them aloud to the class. Where possible, point out for special praise the invention of plausible but completely fictional surprises in the different papers. All of the class papers together constitute a set of alternative histories for the indicated period, a set which should show considerable diversity. You may wish to put these up on the bulletin board or along the wall with a heading such as "Alternative Histories of the U.S., 1960-1970," for the students to look at further. (Also post — without comment — a copy of Robert Frost's poem "The Road Not Taken.")

If you ask students to compare the response to this exercise with the response to the previous exercise, they may be surprised to find that their own invented histories sound tamer in general than the real histories. At this point, if not before, someone is likely to comment, "Well, you know what they say — fact is stranger than fiction." Reply that this is actually backwards thinking: it's not that fact is stranger than fiction, it's that fiction is seldom as strange as fact, because we refuse to regard the fiction as being "believeable" if it is anywhere near as strange as reality often is.

The students should now have a good grasp of the concept of "alternative histories." The next step is to involve them in preparing "alternative *future* histories," or scenarios. This is simply an extension of the preceding exercise into the future. It can be done on an individual basis, as an exercise in forecasting and creative writing, or it can be done as a group project by a number of students or the whole class. (The latter version is described in the next exercise.)

EXERCISE 16: *Scenario Writing*

Background: Your emphasis in preparing the class for this exercise should depend primarily on the quality of background that your students already have. If the students tend to be relatively unaware of the world around them, you will need to acquaint them with some of the range of forecasts about potential crises and opportunities facing us, and possible scientific breakthroughs and important technological innovations. (See Appendix C for a good sampling of sources.) On the other hand, if your students are fairly sophisticated about the future possibilities which are now receiving serious consideration, your task will not be to give them more information, but to convince them to use their imaginations freely and not be limited by what they know to be "reputable" speculation.

The students should understand that a scenario is a fictionalized forecast, written from the point of view of a specific future date, looking back over the period between now and then as if it had already happened. If you have already done the "President's Commission" exercise from chapter five, you can use your own scenario as an example. Appendix B contains a scenario on education; nine additional scenarios on education can be found in *Education . . . beyond tomorrow*, (Hostrop, ed.); another scenario that is widely available is Paul Ehrlich's essay, "Eco-Catastrophe." It might also be useful to review the section on "Good Forecasts" in chapter three (pages 67-69).

Procedure: Explain to the students that the class is going to undertake a joint project to create a coordinated set of alternative scenarios for the future of the United States and the world. The first step is a brainstorming session (see chapter five) during which the students list all of the possible events which they think might occur to our society in the next fifty years. You may find it helpful to break this down into a large number of topic categories — such as biology, education, politics, life-style, transportation, environment, international affairs, and so forth.

As soon as the group stalls on one subject, switch to another, and continue through the whole cycle of categories three or four times or until all suggestions dry up. Be sure to include an "open" category for "wild-card" possibilities that don't fit in the other categories. Encourage students to relate possible events in one category with spin-offs they might produce which would affect other categories. If you notice any major possibilities which they have omitted, contribute them yourself as unobtrusively as possible.

The next step is to organize the class into 8 to 10 teams of approximately 3 students each and to divide the future possibilities among the teams. Begin by going through the lists of possibilities and grouping together items that would almost certainly go together. (For instance, elaborate moving sidewalk systems imply that automobiles are not permitted in cities.)

When you have finished this "lumping" process, start going through the lists of possibilities and assigning them on a rotation basis to the different teams. For instance, you might start off with transportation: "Team #1, you get slidewalks and car-free cities; Team #2, you get matter transmitters and teleport booths; Team #3, you get the very-high-speed national rail system; Team #4, electric cars; Team #5, automatic highways; Team #6, . . ." Of course your lists won't come out even, so if you end up one list with Team 3, assign the first item on the next list to Team 4, and so on.

As you assign the items to the teams, you should put the team numbers right alongside the items on the big lists. Meanwhile, each team should be keeping a separate list of the items that have been assigned to that team. Eventually, you will assign an item to a team which seems to conflict directly with the items that have already been assigned to it (in that category or in previous categories). When this happens, the team involved should ask you to go on to the next item instead. Give the item that was skipped to the next team, and continue in this fashion until you have parcelled out all of the items on the brainstorming sheets.

The third major step is for each team to create a scenario utilizing the possibilities that have been assigned to it. There are 5 basic rules:

- All the scenarios should be written looking backward from the perspective of the same future year (designated by you or selected by the class).
- Any two groups can agree to exchange items from the same category or from different categories, on a one-for-one basis.
- If a team feels that it absolutely *has* to have an item being used by another team, they can ask you for a "special dispensation"; this should be granted (if they have a good argument), with the stipulation that they must introduce the item during a different decade from the one in which the other team introduces it.
- At least 50% of all of the items assigned to a team (after all trading and special dispensations) must be woven into the scenario in some fashion.
- A team may introduce completely new items provided they clear them with you and add them to the brainstorming sheets.

Within these rules, the object for each team is to make its scenario sound as plausible as possible.

The final step parallels the preceding exercise. Collect all of the scenarios and post them in a suitable location with a general heading such as "Alternative Future Histories of the U.S., 1975-2025 A.D." (If it is appropriate to your classroom, you might also suggest that the students create art work to illustrate the worlds which they have described.) If possible, mimeograph enough copies of all the scenarios for each student, but in any case be sure that every student has a chance to read all of the scenarios.

The follow-up discussion should need little prodding from you. Some of the relevant questions are:

"Which of these scenarios do you think are the most plausible?"

"Which do you think are the most unlikely?"

"Do any of these scenarios fit the image of the future that you had before doing this exercise?"

"What are your own personal plans for the future?"

"How well do those plans fit into each of these different scenarios?"

These last two questions are especially important, as experience has shown that students will fail to connect the forecasts that they have made with their own personal lives unless they are specifically encouraged to do so.

Science Fiction

The theme throughout this chapter has been the development of imaginative thinking about alternative future possibilities. One of the basic and necessary elements in developing such imagination is a familiarity with the literature of serious speculation about the future, a literature which is somewhat inappropriately called "science fiction." In *Profiles of the Future*, one of the first modern books on the art of forecasting, Arthur Clarke described the educational importance of science fiction:

> Over the last thirty years, tens of thousands of stories have explored all the conceivable, and most of the inconceivable, possibilities of the future; there are few things that *can* happen that have not been described somewhere, in books or magazines. A critical — the adjective is important — reading of science fiction is essential training for anyone wishing to look more than ten years ahead. The facts of the future can hardly be imagined *ab initio* by those who are unfamiliar with the fantasies of the past.
>
> This claim may produce indignation, especially among those second-rate scientists who sometimes make fun of science fiction (I have never known a first-rate one to do

so — and I know several who write it). But the simple fact is that anyone with sufficient imagination to assess the future realistically would, inevitably, be attracted to this form of literature. I do not for a moment suggest that more than 1 percent of science fiction readers would be reliable prophets; but I do suggest that almost 100 percent of reliable prophets will be science fiction readers — or writers.

To Clarke's case, we need only add that our task is not (primarily) to produce "reliable prophets," but to educate prospective citizens to be more future-oriented and more imaginative about possible changes. Alvin Toffler's warnings about the dangers of "future shock" are widely known; however, future shock is not an inevitable product of rapid change, but a product of *unanticipated* change. Since science fiction deals with so many different possibilities, there is probably no better innoculation against future shock than a youthful addiction to reading it.

What *is* science fiction? The question is difficult because science fiction has changed drastically over the last fifty years, and because readers and writers of science fiction take great delight in disagreeing, loudly and cogently, with anyone who attempts to define it. To avoid such hazards, here are *two* definitions which, between them, may bracket the "truth." The broad definition is: *Science fiction is fiction based on a plausible-sounding setting which is different from the real world of the present or the known past.* The narrow definition is: *Science fiction is fiction which is concerned with the impact of possible social, technological, and environmental changes upon human beings and human societies.* Both definitions would exclude allegory, mythology, and fantasy, where there is no attempt to make the plot and the setting seem plausible. Despite the literal meaning of the phrase "science fiction," both definitions would also exclude stories about science or scientists in the actual past or present.

The gray area between the broad and narrow definitions is inhabited by three questionable genres: social fiction, gadget science fiction, and adventure science fiction or "space opera." Social fiction, according to Isaac Asimov, "is that branch of litera-ture which moralizes about a current society through the device of dealing with a fictitious society"; it includes most utopias and dystopias. Gadget science fiction is devoted to describing the invention of some technological process or device, ranging from wacky implausibilities to hard-headed and nearly patentable extrapolations from current science (e.g., Arthur Clarke's "invention" of ComSat in the 1940's). And adventure science fiction is slam-bang action fiction, often an adaptation of the Western or "horse opera," with spaceships instead of horses, ray guns instead of pistols, and bug-eyed monsters or cosmic baddies instead of Indians or rustlers.

If you are not a regular reader of science fiction, you may be surprised to find these three kinds of stories classified as marginal categories of science fiction. The general public, when it thinks about science fiction at all, thinks first of Flash Gordon and Buck Rogers, second of the eccentric scientist in his laboratory, and third of *1984* and *Brave New World*. Aren't these the essence of science fiction?

The answer is no. Although science fiction contains strong elements of adventure, science, and moral warnings about the present, the *essence* of science fiction is an exploration of the effect on believeable human beings and human societies of circumstances which are different in some important way from the world we know in the past and present. Isaac Asimov calls this kind of fiction "social science fiction," and maintains that it is the only socially significant kind of science fiction. Having already disposed of social fiction in his essay on "Social Science Fiction" — one of the best discussions of science fiction available — Asimov presents an effective illustration of the differences between gadget science fiction, adventure science fiction, and social science fiction:

> Let us suppose it is 1880 and we have a series of three writers who are each interested in writing a story of the future about an imaginary vehicle that can move without horses by some internal source of power; a horseless carriage, in other words. We might even make up a word and call it an automobile.
>
> Writer X spends most of his time describing how the machine would run, explaining the workings of an internal-combustion engine, painting a word-picture of the struggles of the inventor, who after numerous failures, comes up with a successful model. The climax of the yarn is the drama of the machine, chugging its way along at the gigantic speed of twenty miles an hour between a double crowd of cheering admirers, possibly beating a horse and

carriage which have been challenged to a race. This is gadget science fiction.

Writer Y invents the automobile in a hurry, but now there is a gang of ruthless crooks intent on stealing this valuable invention. First they steal the inventor's beautiful daughter, whom they threaten with every dire eventuality but rape (in these adventure stories, girls exist to be rescued and have no other uses). The inventor's young assistant goes to the rescue. He can accomplish his purpose only by the use of the newly perfected automobile. He dashes into the desert at an unheard of speed of twenty miles an hour to pick up the girl who otherwise would have died of thirst if he had relied on a horse, however rapid and sustained the horse's gallop. This is adventure science fiction.

Writer Z has the automobile already perfected. A society exists in which it is already a problem. Because of the automobile, a gigantic oil industry has grown up, highways have been paved across the nation, America has become a land of travelers, cities have spread into suburbs, and — what do we do about automobile accidents? Men, women, and children are being killed by automobiles faster than by artillery shells or airplane bombs. What can be done? What is the solution? This is social science fiction.

I leave it to the reader to decide which is the most mature and which (this is 1880, remember) is the most socially significant. Keep in mind the fact that social science fiction is not easy to write. It is easy to predict an automobile in 1880; it is very hard to predict a traffic problem. The former is really only an extrapolation of the railroad. The latter is something completely novel and unexpected.

The stimulus for a social science fiction story may be technological (as in Asimov's example), or social (perhaps a new religion, or contact with alien species), or environmental (such as an abrupt change in the Earth's climate, or a radically different form of biology on a newly colonized planet). The novel situation may be fascinating in itself, but the emphasis is on the *meaning* of that situation in human terms for the people who must cope with it. In this way social science fiction serves as an invaluable source of vicarious experience which helps the reader to anticipate the social impacts of the rapidly increasing tide of change and innovation which dominates our daily lives.

In discussions with teachers about science fiction, one objection has been frequently voiced, an objection which can be paraphrased somewhat like this: "You're talking about a fairly mature and sophisticated kind of science fiction, the kind that deals with values and social issues, but I don't think my kids are up to that. All they're interested in is ray guns and space pirates." There are three answers to this objection. First, "ray guns and space pirates" can lead a student into the more sophisticated kinds of science fiction. Second, there is no rule that says that social science fiction can't be just as full of adventure and excitement as its less sophisticated counterparts; some of the most exciting science fiction ever written for young adolescents has been written by Robert Heinlein, one of the great masters (and co-inventors) of social science fiction. And third, the young people who read science fiction do not, in practice, regard social science fiction as something "difficult" or "sophisticated"; they read it because it is enjoyable, and acquire some sophistication about the social issues as a result.

Toffler's *Learning for Tomorrow* provides some confirmation from another teacher in this regard. In that book, Priscilla Griffith describes a high-school future studies course which she taught in the mid 1960's. At one point, while describing the reactions of her students to a set of provocative readings about future possibilities, she comments:

> It was, incidentally, quickly possible to identify the science-fiction buffs in the class because, with a few exceptions, they had already learned from their reading to think more in terms of the social and ethical problems of the future than simply the gadgetry.

Considering the importance of the social and ethical problems we face, this is not an insignificant educational accomplishment.

Some students find their own way to science fiction, of course, while others may need some encouragement. One of the simplest ways to provide this encouragement is through reading assignments, but this is an approach which should be used sparingly and with some caution. The attitude of many young people today is still that anything connected with schooling, particularly homework, must be unpleasant. Even in a normal classroom environment, the anxieties created by examinations, papers, and intensely analytical class discussions can translate easily into a dislike of the materials on which the anxiety is focused, so it is well to keep in mind that your objective is to create interest and a desire to read more, rather than to insure that students have "understood" a particular assignment.

One of your first steps should be to check on what is available in your school and community libraries and to request additional titles if that seems necessary. The section on science fiction in the bibliography contains a number of suggested titles; there are also recommendations in Appendix C for books with which to introduce yourself to the field, in case you are unfamiliar with it.

Perhaps the safest way to assign a science fiction book or story is to make it one of several alternative resources for a class project which has already been assigned on a related topic. It may even be sufficient just to indicate to students that science fiction has your approval as source material under appropriate circumstances. Moreover, students are not confined merely to reading science fiction; writing it can be ot as much educational value, if not more. Exercise 16, on scenario writing, can be used as a starting point. In effect, each of the alternative future histories which the students prepare provides a setting for one or more science fiction stories, requiring only the addition of characters and plot.

Another related kind of project is the future autobiography. The student is asked to write a contrasting set of three imaginative auto-biographies looking backwards from a point 50 years in the future. Each autobiography should be keyed to a different scenario for society as a whole and should reflect some of the student's own personal interests and ambitions. (A shorter but sometimes more threatening variation on the future autobiography is to ask each student to write three obituaries for himself, each one tied to a particular scenario).

No detailed exercises for using either science fiction or creative writing have been included here because their use will depend greatly on your particular classroom situation. Work them in wherever they seem to fit naturally, and the imaginative horizons of your students will open up considerably. But perhaps the most important factor in teaching students to be imaginative in considering future alternatives is your own example. If you demonstrate your interest in exploring alternatives and your willingness to speculate and to reward imagination, your students will quickly follow your lead, to their considerable future advantage. Furthermore, anything else you can do — whether related to the future or not — which enhances their creative and imaginative skills is desirable. Paradoxical as it may sound, the most hardheaded and realistic approach to the future is a highly imaginative one.

ALTERNATIVES AND IMAGINATION: ESSENTIAL POINTS

1. A common mistake in thinking about the future is to rely too heavily on a single forecast — either the extension of the status quo or the "most likely" course of events.
2. In dealing with social and institutional change, it is important to think in terms of a wide range of alternative possibilities.
3. The most effective way to avoid the "single-future" trap is to train ourselves to be imaginative about future alternatives.
4. Most people seem to be very inhibited in their use of imagination about the future.
5. One way we teach people to be unimaginative about the future may be the false determinism implied in the way we teach history.
6. One way to undo this unintentional lesson is to help students recognize the unlikely events that have occurred and the many alternative possibilities which might have occurred, but did not. This process can then be extended to thinking about alternative future possibilities.
7. Reading widely in science fiction is an essential part of learning to be imaginative about the future and preparing psychologically to cope with change.
8. A broad definition of science fiction: fiction based on a plausible-sounding setting which is different from the real world of the present or the known past.
9. A narrow definition of science fiction: fiction which is concerned with the impact of possible social, technological, and environmental changes upon human beings and human societies.

10. A desirable result of reading science fiction is that students learn "to think more in terms of the social and ethical problems of the future than simply the gadgetry."
11. It is more important for students to enjoy science fiction and become motivated to read more on their own than it is for them to have a detailed and analytical understanding of each story.
12. The most important element in teaching your students to be more imaginative about the future may be your own example, especially your willingness to speculate and to reward them for doing so.

NOTES

117. Herman Kahn, the dean of hard-nosed social forecasting, has been quoted as estimating that the chances of a depression between 1974 and 1980 are one out of three. ("Thinking About Depression," editorial in *The Wall Street Journal*, July 22, 1974.) [110] See also page 68.

117. The method referred to as the most exotic technique in forecasting is the Field Anomaly Relaxation (FAR) method for generating comprehensive sets of alternative future histories, originally developed by Johnson Research Associates and the Educational Policy Research Center, Stanford Research Institute. A good starting point for educators is Harman, Markley, and Rhyne, "The Forecasting of Plausible Alternative Future Histories: Methods, Results, and Educational Policy Implications." [7]

117. For a thoughtful discussion of the importance of imagination in forecasting, along with a number of very entertaining examples of forecasts that went wrong because of a lack of imagination, see Chapter 1, "The Failure of Imagination," of Arthur C. Clarke's *Profiles of the Future*. [5]

118. The origins of the story used in Exercise 13 are perhaps worth recounting. In *Future Shock*, Alvin Toffler describes in very general terms an experiment conducted by John Condry. The passage caught my interest, and in devising an exercise to test it out, I followed Toffler's description with a depressing lack of originality:

In separate studies at Cornell and UCLA, Condry gave groups of students the opening paragraph of a story. The paragraph described a fictional "Professor Hoffman," his wife and their adopted Korean daughter. The daughter is found crying, her clothes torn, a group of other children staring at her. The students were asked to complete the story.

What the subjects did not know is that they had previously been divided into two groups. In the case of one group, the opening paragraph was set in the past. The characters "heard," "saw" or "ran." The students were asked to "Tell what Mr. and Mrs. Hoffman did and what was said by the children." For the second group, the paragraph was set entirely in the future tense. They were asked to "Tell what Mr. and Mrs. Hoffman will do and what will be said by the children." Apart from this shift of tense, both paragraphs and instructions were identical. (*Future Shock*, pp. 374-375.) [40]

The only deliberate change was from Hoffman to Hamilton (because of possible confusion with my own name), yet I have no idea whether the story in Exercise 13 actually resembles the story used by Professor Condry. Our results, however, have paralleled his almost exactly:

The results of the experiment were sharply etched. One group wrote comparatively rich and interesting story-endings, peopling their accounts with many characters, creatively introducing new situations and dialogue. The other produced extremely sketchy endings, thin, unreal and forced. The past was richly conceived; the future empty. "It is," Professor Condry commented, "as if we find it easier to talk about the past than the future." (*Future Shock*, p. 375.) [40]

Aside from its resemblance to Condry's original, there is, of course, no particular reason for keeping to the version of the story presented in Exercise 13. Several teachers have devised their own story-starters with good results. Kathleen Weinmann has had excellent success in combining this exercise with Exercise 15 by asking her third-graders to write alternative endings for fairy tales and children's stories.

119. If the story about Dr. Hamilton and Karen is a deliberate imitation of something never seen, the first two paragraphs under "History and the Future" are a striking example of the possibilities for unintentional duplication. Several months after writing them, I came across the following passage in an article by Robert Bickner:

> We look to history — the art or the science — not only to report history, but to explain it. This dual task the historians perform very well — too well. We know that a war took place, or a revolution succeeded, or a new political alliance was formed; and we set ourselves to the task of explaining it. We succeed, more or less. Why shouldn't we?
>
> But in haste we forget something, and we delude ourselves. We forget that if the war had not occurred; or if the revolution had failed, or if the new political alliance had fizzled, we could just as well have explained that too! Because we can generate plausible explanations of whatever happened, we think we really understand history. We begin to believe that had we been living at a time preceding any turning point in history, we would have recognized this inevitable outcome. This is the myth we are taught, unintentionally, over and over again in our history courses. And on this myth, this illusion that history is well understood, we build exaggerated hopes about our ability to forecast the future course of history: the future.

The correspondence between the two passages — mine and Bickner's — is so close that it seems that it almost has to be a case of unconscious plagiarism, yet I am almost certain I had never previously encountered the Bickner article. (The quoted passage appears on page 60 of Hirsch, *Inventing Education for the Future.*) [56]

124. "Eco-Catastrophe" — the scenario by Paul Ehrlich — is anthologized in both *The Futurists* (edited by Toffler) [14] and *Search for Alternatives* (edited by Tugwell) [15], as well as in several ecology books.

126. In *Learning for Tomorrow*, Alvin Toffler comments on the failure to connect forecasts about the outside world with the students' own personal lives.

> I asked respondents to draw up two lists. First, I asked in a general way for a list of future events. When not a single personal reference turned up, I asked for a separate list of events that would happen to them personally. It was then easy to compare each personal future with the larger, public or social future in which it would unfold. The results were dramatic. One could not help but be struck by the disconnectedness between the two sets of forecasts. One fifteen-year-old girl, for example, after picturing a U.S.-U.S.S.R. alliance against China, a cancer cure, test-tube babies, an accidental nuclear explosion, the spread of anarchism over large parts of the world, and robot computers holding political office in the United States, offered the following personal forecast:
>
> Moving into my own apartment
> Interior-designing school
> Driver's license
> Getting a dog
> Marriage
> Having children
> Death
>
> The world in upheaval would leave her untouched. (pp. 10-11.) [78]

126. The passage by Arthur C. Clarke is from page xv of the introduction to *Profiles of the Future*. [5]

127. The Asimov quotation is on page 264 of *Science Fiction: The Future*, edited by Dick Allen. Pages 127 through 129 draw heavily on this essay. [289]

128. Arthur Clarke gives an account of the ComSat story, along with a thoughtful discussion of the social implications of communication satellites, in Chapter 16 of *Profiles of the Future*. [5]

128. The Asimov quotation is from pages 272 and 273 of *Science Fiction: The Future*, edited by Dick Allen. [289]

130. The Griffiths quotation is from page 204 of *Learning For Tomorrow*, edited by Alvin Toffler. [78]

131. On the effect of classroom anxieties on reading enjoyment, see Farrell, *Deciding the Future* [54], pp. 140-144; Fader, *Hooked on Books* [52]; and Farber, "The Student as Nigger," in the book of the same title [53].

CHAPTER VII
Models That Help Us Think

Introducing the Idea of a Model

An aircraft designer can't build a plane to test out every configuration he thinks might work. It would cost too much in time, money, and lives. Instead, he builds models and manipulates them in a wind tunnel to simulate actual aircraft behaviour under different conditions. A person trying to understand a society is under even more severe limitations. Society-sized experiments can seldom be run in the real world and can never be truly repeated. The solution to the dilemma is the same as for aircraft design, but this time the "models" are constructed of ideas or equations instead of balsa wood or steel.

The idea of a mental model bothers some people at first, but in fact we all use mental models frequently. You have a model in your head, for instance, of the U.S. form of government which helps you make sense of the behavior of the actual thing. Your model is made up of a great many bits and pieces — people voting, writing congressmen, donating money; seniority rules in Congress, civil-service rules in the Executive, lifetime appointments for judges; lobbyists wining and dining, reporters hunting headlines; budgets, pork-barrel bills, and vetoes; and so on — bits and pieces which are certainly incomplete, but which add up to a working picture of how the whole complicated structure hangs together and why it works the way it does. In this sense, a model is a simplified or incomplete representation of a thing or a process, a representation which is nevertheless useful in explaining the features of the different parts, their relationship to each other, and the character of the whole.

Because *some* models and simulations are complex, many people assume that the subject is suitable only for advanced levels. This is not necessarily the case, although it does seem to be more difficult to design methods to teach these concepts successfully to a younger group. For this reason, the exercises that follow (and those in chapter eight) have been geared to the youngest ages that seem able to handle them, relying on teachers of older students to "upgrade" them appropriately.

For example, the next three exercises are aimed at grades 1-4. The first two provide an explanation of the concept "model" while the third involves the students in the direct use of a model, thus reinforcing the more abstract concept. This process can be streamlined and simplified for each successive grade level up through high school, where a brief general definition of "model" would probably suffice.

EXERCISE 17: *Models*

Procedure: Paraphrase the following introduction to the students, then ask them to suggest additional kinds of models. Discuss with the class whether each suggestion really fits the definition of a model.

"A model is something we use to take the place of something else. The model looks like the real thing or is similar to it in some important way. The model is also different from it in some important way. Usually, the model is enough like the real thing so that we can learn something about it from the model, but the model is cheaper, or smaller, or lighter, or safer, or easier to use. Here are three examples of models we often see around us:

"Dolls are models. A doll of a baby allows you to play at being parents. But if you drop it on its head or leave it out in the rain, it won't be harmed in the way a real baby would.

"A picture can be a model. If you have a dog and you want to show the class what your dog looks like, it is much easier to bring a picture into class than it is to bring your dog. (Sometimes we *have* to use models because the real thing doesn't exist anymore. If you want to show the class what your dog looked like *when he was a little puppy*, you will have to show them a picture.)

"A slot-car track is a model of a real race-track. You can play with it and learn something about driving cars and being a race driver. On the slot-car track it doesn't matter if you have an accident. If you were learning to drive a real car, an accident could hurt you or kill you and do a lot of damage to the car."

Because many toys are models, younger children may assume that all models are toys, and vice versa. If they have been introduced to maps or bar graphs, these can be suggested as variations of pictures. Other non-toy models might include science exhibits around the classroom, an architect's model of a building, and a model plane in a wind tunnel. Another way to make the distinction is to point out that tinker toys and erector sets are not models, but they can be used to *make* models of many things. As soon as the students grasp the idea, move on to the next exercise.

EXERCISE 18: *Mental Models*

Procedure: Paraphrase the following text and present it to the students, then once again ask for suggestions for additional kinds of models.

"Not all models are things you can touch or see. Some models are imaginary. These are called mental models and they exist only inside our heads. A mental model is a description of something or an explanation of how it works. If it is a good model, it lets us do things we've never done or seen and understand things we have never experienced. Here are some examples.

"You each have a mental model of this school building. Think about how to get from this room to [name a point in another part of the building that the students all know]. Can you think of a way to get there that you've never used? (It might mean doing something silly like going upstairs and then back down again, or out one door and around the building and back in another door.) How do you know you can get there that way? You can do it because you have a mental model of the building that you can use to try out different paths. [Note: avoid this example with younger children during the first weeks of school.]

"You also have a model of the English language in your head. This model tells you how to say things that other people will understand.[1] We all say brand new things all the time. Nobody has told us that these things we say are correct. You expect your friend to understand what you say because both of you have the same mental model of how to speak. (If he speaks a different language, he won't understand you because he has a different model of how to speak.)"

Other examples of mental models include songs or melodies, how you expect a close friend to act, ways to behave that will make the teacher mad, the solar system, how a car engine works, and so on.

The exercises above should convey the concepts of a physical model and of a mental model. Next are two examples of the use of physical models to stimulate futures thinking.

EXERCISE 19: *Future Body Board*[2]

Materials: A flannel board and a large stock (50-100) of images of separate parts of the human body, of animals, of fish, of birds, and of machines, including arms, legs, heads, torsos, wings, tails, wheels, gears, antennae, and so forth. These can be drawn on paper or cloth, or cut from magazines.

Procedure: Ask the children to experiment by selecting different parts and placing them on the flannel board in different positions, until each child has discovered an arrangement which represents

---

[1]"As Noam Chomsky has suggested, most people find it easy to identify one of the following sentences as grammatical although the reason for the distinction is not at all clear:
   Colorless green ideas sleep furiously.
   Furiously sleep ideas green colorless."
Both are nonsense, but only one fits our model of the language we speak.

[2]Developed by Patricia Guild, U. Mass. / School of Education.

the body he would most like to have in the future if such inter-
changeability became possible. Ask each student to explain the
features he has selected, the functions they would perform, and his
reasons for desiring them. Discussion between students of which
features would be most desirable should need little encouragement
from you.

After the discussion has had a chance to develop for a while,
encourage students to consider: the use of tools and machines to
modify and extend our physical abilities; the use of optical,
mechanical, and electronic devices to enhance our sensory
capabilities; and the use of information storage, retrieval, and
manipulation devices (ranging from a daily attendance book to an
adding machine to a complex computer) to enhance our mental
capabilities. Contrast some of the external devices with their
corresponding built-in body parts, asking, for instance, whether it
is better to have built-in wheels or a car one can get into and out of,
and whether it is better to have built-in antennae or a portable
radio.

Without pushing it too hard, you may wish to ask the students
whether a particular adaptation might be useful for a specialized
purpose, but a nuisance the rest of the time. The students are most
likely to agree to this with respect to essentially external types of
gadgets and with respect to very specialized changes in limb
functions, such as a fish-tail instead of feet. Three very common
changes, however, tend to be staunchly defended: an extra pair of
arms, an extra pair of legs (a centaur shape), and a monkey- or
cat-like tail.

In a long-term sense, the exercise serves to alert students to some
of the possibilities and some of the problems associated with man's
adaptation of himself to different tasks and different environments.
In a more immediate sense, it alerts students to the possibility for
bodily change in themselves and, in particular, provides a starting
point for a discussion of human growth and maturation, the very
substantial changes which they are beginning to experience.

With older students, you may wish to initiate the discussion with
science fiction stories such as McCaffrey's *The Ship Who Sang*,
Niven's "The Jigsaw Man" (in *All the Myriad Ways*), or Heinlein's
The Moon is a Harsh Mistress. These raise, in a direct and fairly
serious way, some of the issues involved in organ transplants, body
restructuring, artificial intelligence, and cyborgs (human brains

linked directly to a computer), some or all of which are considered to be real possibilities within the next half century, or so.)

The next exercise uses a model to turn outward and consider the possibilities for change in the community around us.

EXERCISE 20: *Designing Your Own Community*

Materials: Marking pens, colored pencils, or crayons in different colors, mostly light colors plus black; a very large sheet of cardboard or heavy paper and enough space to spread it out; several large-scale maps of your town or neighborhood (available from the library, city hall, zoning board, or planning commission) at different periods (such as 1880, 1930, 1955 and the present). An alternative approach is to use grease-pencils or "china-markers" and clear plastic overlay sheets.

Procedure: Part I: Have the students lay out a grid in light pencil on the big sheet and then have them transfer the maps to it, starting with the oldest. Begin with the lightest color and use a different color for each successive map. Outline major landmarks, old or important buildings, key arteries, the school, and each student's home in black, and key them to a numbered list in the margin. Also have them make a color key for the different map dates.

Part II: When the map is completed, expose the students to whatever of the community's history is available and appropriate. Arrange field trips if possible to see the area first-hand. Invite an old-time resident to come talk about the town and answer questions. (A retired police chief or fire captain is ideal.) Finally, arrange a field trip to the planning commission or zoning board to hear about future plans and planning problems.

Part III: Have the students design their ideal future community, using the map as a base and paper cutouts that can be shifted around. When a final design is agreed on, it is traced onto the map in a contrasting color. The students then prepare a report on what they have done, explaining why they chose their ideal future arrangement. Finally, put the map up in the foyer of the school or the public library, or in a shopping plaza, with the pages of the report arranged as a frame around it. Or call the mayor's office and arrange for the mayor to meet the class and have the map and report displayed in the lobby of town hall.

Depending on the grade level, this project can tie together a wide range of curriculum topics, from math, geography, and general science, to history, sociology, English, and civics. It helps students become aware of their community environment, with a sense of its historical background and future potential. They also gain an understanding of the practical, political, and social problems in planning and social change, as well as a sense of what it means to participate in the process as citizens. This is especially important in disadvantaged or environmentally precarious communities, where enlightened citizen participation is an urgent necessity.

A note of caution: If the scales of the maps don't match, be sure that the grid from the map is *correctly* scaled up or down and transferred to each of the source maps.

The Uses of Models

Models themselves can be invaluable for explaining concepts to others; we would understand little about many social processes if we had to see every step of a process first hand to know how it works. But the real importance of models for forecasting is when they can be brought to life in some fashion and made to *simulate* the response of the real thing to a variety of different policies or interventions.

The first way devised to "activate" a model was in the form of a game. In fact, the two oldest and most intellectually challenging games in the world (Go and Chess) are both simulations of combat. Like the elaborate mock-battles or "war games" which are their modern equivalent, they permit experimentation with a great many different tactics and strategies under different circumstances without risking the high cost of failure in real life. Modern simulation-type games range from feeble (Monopoly as a simulation of real estate) to elaborate and quite realistic week-long games used for training business executives.

The development of modern digital computers has brought another type of simulation to the fore. If each of the relationships in a model can be expressed in terms of numbers, then it can be converted to a mathematical model. Such models are very useful for their precision and flexibility, but until recently their use was restricted to very simple forms because the sheer quantity of arithmetic is overwhelming for even a moderately complicated model. Now, a properly programmed computer can print out in minutes the results of an elaborate simulation covering a hundred years, results which would take a mathematician the whole hundred years to calculate by hand. This speed and capacity allows the researcher to try out many alterations in the basic structure of the model, corresponding to possible alternative policies in the real world. Insofar as the model is an accurate representation of reality, it allows a social planner for the first time to run controlled, repeatable experiments, and to compare the consequences of two or more policies under otherwise identical circumstances.

Unfortunately, there are two major limitations on the use of such simulations. The first has to do with the quantitative nature of the model. A clever model builder can make his model describe basically non-quantitative relationships surprisingly well, but even the best simulation is skating on thin ice when it attempts to simulate the actions of discrete individuals, or of groups acting as individual units. The computer may be able to simulate very accurately the decisions which 100,000 rush-hour drivers will make tomorrow morning, but if you want to know what John Doe is going to do, you would be better off asking Mrs. Doe than asking the computer.

The other limitation has to do with reality testing. The aircraft designer will eventually scale up his most successful models into full-sized aircraft and can then study in detail the discrepancies, if any, between the behavior of the model and the behavior of the full-sized reality. But suppose a social simulation is designed to cover a period 50 years into the future. Must we then wait 25 or 50 years in order to compare it with actuality? Aside from the fact that the simulation would be worthless to us now, we would still gain very little. We would learn only whether the simulation *was* accurate for *one* possible set of policies and circumstances. We would still not know how accurate the simulation was for all of the other policies and circumstances which might have been possible, nor would we know that the simulation would continue to be a faithful representation of society — only that it had been.

The best and, ultimately, the only useful test of large-scale models is whether, piece-by-piece, they reflect the best knowledge available. Is the relationship between life expectancy and the birth rate *actually* the way the model describes it? Does supply and demand *really* function that way in peasant economies? If each of the pieces accords with our best understanding of social reality, then *at the very least*, the simulation is a powerful device for discovering the implications of our beliefs about how the world functions.

In the next chapter we will look closely at the concept of a "system" (and the related idea of "feedback") because it is by far the most important type of mental model for futures thinking. It is also the key to understanding, developing, and using classroom simulations and simulation-games.

MODELS THAT HELP US THINK: ESSENTIAL POINTS

1. A model is an incomplete replica which is more available for our use than the thing it models.
2. Models can be either physical or mental.
3. A model is better than a collection of separate facts in helping us to understand something, because the model presents a holistic representation; a picture enables us to recognize a stranger at a glance, but a verbal description — even if quite detailed — usually does not.
4. When we use a model to simulate the behavior of the thing it models, we can discover information about the real thing which we did not know when we created the model.
5. A very old, and still effective, way to activate a model is in the form of a simulation-game, in which human players take different roles and compete within a framework of rules.
6. A second kind of simulation is the mechanical analog; this is most useful when simulating a complex physical process, such as the flow of air past an airplane.
7. The most important kind of simulation in modern forecasting is the high speed computer simulation based on a mathematical model.

NOTES

139. For a further discussion of mental models in the elementary classroom, see John Holt's book of activities and curriculum suggestions, *What Do I Do Monday?* [57]

141. The quotation contained within the footnote is on page 115 of *Culture, Man, and Nature,* by Marvin Harris. [308]

141. Patricia Guild describes the future body board exercise in the Spring 1971 issue of *Trend* Magazine, in a short article called, "Designing Your Future Body: A Futuristic Project for Elementary School Children."

143. Map board exercises are quite old, and there are a number of simulations and simulation games of this form available commercially today, so it is impossible to give credit to any one person as the "inventor" of this procedure. Nevertheless, I would like to thank Ronda Brenner, whose undergraduate paper on a similar exercise inspired this present version.

144. "Go" is generally considered to be the oldest board game still in widespread current use; it originated in China in prehistoric times and reached its full modern development in Japan, where it is considered the national game. Many who play both Chess and Go consider the latter to be superior, for several reasons:
- Go is much easier to learn; all of the strategy and tactics are implied in five simple rules.
- Closely fought and enjoyable games are possible between players of unequal ability because Go includes a sensitive, graduated handicapping system which does not drastically alter the game.
- Go is ultimately more complex than Chess, and much less likely to be turned into a long drawn-out defensive battle by a careless early move.

If you are interested in learning the game, the best introductory source is *How to Play Go,* by Shukaku Takagawa. It is available for $3.00 from: The Nihon ki-in, 14-23 Takanawa 2-Chome, Minato-ku, Tokyo 108, Japan.

144. For a good history and description of modern simulation-games, see *Simulation and Society: An Exploration of Scientific Gaming,* by John R. Raser. [88]

145. For more information on mathematical models and computer simulation, see Section IV (Simulations/Games), Section V (The Systems Perspective), and Section VI (Economics and Environment: the Growth Debate) of the bibliography.

CHAPTER VIII
Systems and Simulations
In the Classroom

"Systems thinking" is probably the most important advance in this century in *how to think* and how to understand the world around us. Without the fields which are based on it — e.g., cybernetics, information theory, computer science, systems analysis — much of our present science, technology, business, and government would grind to a shuddering halt. But, despite the importance and complexity of the fields it has spawned, systems thinking is based on three remarkably simple concepts: the idea of a "system," the idea of "feedback," and a way of thinking about cause and effect called "non-linear" causality.

Systems and Stability

A "system" is a set or arrangement of things so interrelated as to function as a unit or a whole. Whether the set of items is viewed as a system or as a part ("sub-system") of a larger system often depends only on our perspective at the moment. Thus, the radiator, fan, hoses, thermostat, water pump, and water jacket in a car make up the *cooling system*, which is also a *subsystem* of the engine, which is a subsystem of the car, which is in turn a subsystem of our whole transportation system.

A system is not confined to a collection of machines. It can also be purely physical (like the solar system), biological (an ecosystem, or your circulatory system), intellectual (your value system), social (like the governmental system discussed at the beginning of chapter seven), or any combination of these.

One of the characteristics of a system is that it has some kind of stability over time built into it, that it is not just a random and transient interaction of unrelated parts. A system is normally stable in one of two ways. First, it can be *statically* stable, operating in a constant way because that is the only possible result of the way its particular components were put together. Second, it can be *dynamically* stable, varying in its actions but capable of self-correction and always tending toward a central norm of behavior.

An example of the difference, again drawn from the field of transportation, would be a driverless train going around a single circle of track and, nearby, a car being driven around a circular road. The track forces the train to follow exactly the same path with each circuit. The driver, on the other hand, guides the car in circles that are always slightly changing, because he is continually observing the position of the car, comparing it with where it "ought" to be, making corrections in the car's path, and repeating the process.

The train-track system has *static stability* and it would seem to be preferable in a number of ways to the car-driver system. It is more precise, less complex, and more reliable — as long as conditions remain unchanged. The great advantage of a *dynamic system*, on the other hand, is its ability to cope with changes in its environment. To illustrate, imagine a boulder plunked down in the middle of each of the two circular paths. The driver can easily detour around it and continue on, while the train can only stop or run smack into it.

Dynamic systems are much more common than static ones in biology and in human affairs and institutions. As Kenneth Boulding has put it,

> If all environments were stable, the well-adapted would simply take over the earth and the evolutionary process would stop. In a period of environmental change, however, it is the adaptable not the well-adapted who survive.

Many of man's early efforts to design better societies were in the form of static utopias, "perfect" societies which, once installed, would remain unchanged. Because we know that we are facing a fairly long period of rapid change in our environment, current attempts to improve society are usually attempts to build better, more flexible, and more foresightful mechanisms for dynamic stability into our social and personal systems. So when we speak of "systems" we will primarily be referring to (and be interested in) *dynamic* systems. Dynamic systems appear all around us and we need to understand them in order to understand the functioning of our environment. Indeed, our very survival may depend on designing good ones for ourselves.

The basic unit of a dynamic system is the "feedback loop." The process the driver uses to steer the car, in the example above, is a feedback loop. Another example would be the process by which a thermostat and furnace work together to keep a house at

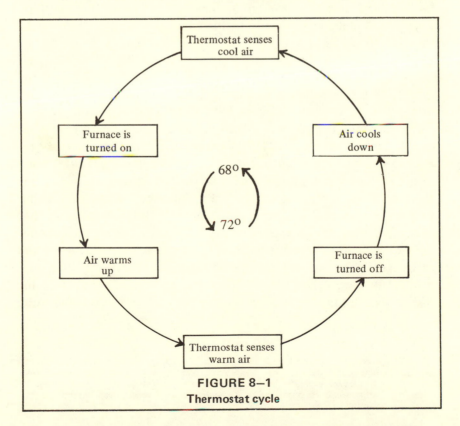

FIGURE 8–1

Thermostat cycle

approximately constant temperature, despite changing outside temperatures. Let's say we set the thermostat for 70°. The thermostat measures the temperature of the air, compares it with what the temperature is supposed to be (70°), and turns the furnace on if the real temperature is more than a degree or two below the temperature it was set for. The heat from the furnace causes the house to gradually warm up. Eventually the thermostat "notices" that the house temperature is again too far from what it should be (this time on the high side) and shuts off the furnace, causing the house to cool down until the cycle starts all over again.

All self-stabilizing (or "negative") feedback systems are basically like these two, the furnace-thermostat and the car-driver.[1] They have an element which measures the actual "output" of the system, compares it with a "reference," and alters the behavior of the system in response. This description is a valuable model of a process which is basic to things as varied as the population of rabbits in Minnesota, the American system of government (with its checks and balances), and an automated lathe.

Non-Linear Causality

Despite the prevalence and importance of feedback systems all around us, most of us find it hard to think in those terms because we have been trained in, and are used to thinking in terms of, simple cause and effect ("linear" logic). But it is not so easy to determine what is cause and what is effect in a feedback loop: where is the beginning of a circle, and where is its end? Using the thermostat example (Figure 8-1), we can ask, "What caused the furnace to shut off?" In an immediate sense, the thermostat did so because the house was warm, and the house was warm because the furnace was on, so the furnace being on caused the furnace to be turned off. Or, we can continue further around the loop and arbitrarily assign the "cause" wherever we choose — even to the previous time that the furnace was turned off. A more meaningful

---

[1]These are called "negative" feedback loops because they try to *reduce* the distance between the output and the reference. A system produces "positive" feedback when each time around the loop *increases* the distance (and the rate of increase of the distance) from the reference. Positive feedback produces the distinctive pattern called "exponential growth" which was examined in chapter four.

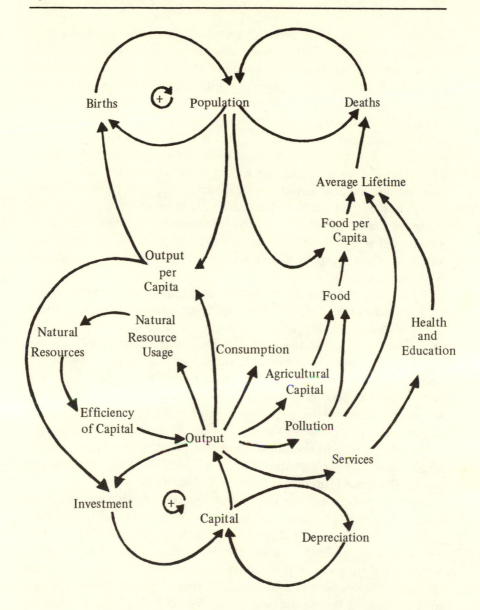

FIGURE 8–2

Basic Interactions Between Population Growth and Capital Accumulation. (From Randers and Meadows, "The Carrying Capacity of the Globe," *Sloan Management Review*, Winter 1972.)

Reproduced with permission of D.H. Meadows.

answer would be, "Because the *system as a whole* functions that way and interacts with its environment to produce that result."

Basic cause and effect logic becomes even less applicable in most real life situations, where we deal with systems containing many feedback loops combined. Then we have not only many causes "one-behind-another," but also many causes "side-by-side" for the same event. For example, Figure 8-2 is a greatly simplified flowchart of a model of our economic and environmental system. The arrows show some of the linkages between population, food production, natural resources, industrial capital, pollution, and health and education. (Read an arrow from one item to another as meaning that the first item "helps to determine" the second item.) The model is made up of a combination of two positive feedback loops (marked by plus signs) and a larger number of negative feedback loops.

The two positive loops are births and capital investment. Each creates sustained pressure for rapid exponential growth unless damped down by one or more negative feedback loops. Other things being equal, in the case of population, more people means more babies, which means still more people, and so on at an accelerating pace. But, other things being equal, it is also true that more people means more deaths, which means fewer people, so the actual behavior of the population level will depend on which is larger — the birth rate or the death rate. If the birth rate is larger than the death rate, the population will grow; if the death rate is larger than the birth rate, population will decline; and if the two are equal, the population will remain stable. (The same is true of industrial capital, taking investment as the "birth rate" of new machines and depreciation as the "death rate" of old machines.)

The birth and death rates which determine the population level are in turn determined by a multitude of other influences, some of which are shown in the flow chart. Each of these other influences has its own set of direct and indirect "causes," many of which are in turn influenced by population level, thus creating closed loops of varying length and complexity. As in the case of our simple furnace-thermostat system, the behavior of any one element in this more complex system depends not on one immediate cause, but on the structure of the system as a whole.

We have gone into the ideas of systems, feedback, non-linear thinking, and multiple causality at some length because schools have traditionally taught only simple, linear, cause-and-effect thinking, and because students must learn to understand and *be able to anticipate* the behavior of systems all around them. But how do we best get these concepts across to them? Examples and diagrams, such as the ones just used to explain these concepts, are useful to some extent. Experience has shown, however, that most students are best able to understand the workings of non-linear systems if they have the chance to experience these workings first-hand for themselves. This brings us to the subject of classroom simulations.

As was discussed in chapter seven, a simulation is just a model of a system where the model is "activated" in some fashion. One of the easiest ways to "activate" a simulation for actual classroom use is the "role-play," where students act out the behavior of the different parts of the system as if in a drama. The next exercise uses this device to dramatize the feedback cycle just examined.

EXERCISE 21: *The Thermostat*

Materials: One poster-sized Temperature Change Chart (see Figure 8-3).

Procedure: Begin by making sure that the students know what is meant by a "thermostat" and a "furnace." Tell them that they are going to help you demonstrate how a thermostat and furnace work to control the temperature in a house or a room, by *simulating* the process for the class to study.

Begin by asking for three volunteers to help you. The first volunteer is the Thermostat; if there is an actual thermostat in the room, station him next to it. The second volunteer is the Furnace; have him sit in a chair across the room from the Thermostat, near a radiator or a heating duct if possible. The third student is the Recorder, who is stationed at a large chalkboard. (With younger students you may want to play this role yourself.) Draw a blank graph on the chalkboard with the left margin marked off in degrees from 64° to 75°, and with the bottom margin marked off in hours from 7 a.m. to 7 a.m. (see Figure 8-4). Place the Temperature Change Chart where the class can read it. Finally, explain the instructions to the students, take a trial run to make sure they understand, and begin.

FIGURE 8–3
Temperature Change Chart

TIME	OUTDOOR TEMP.	AMOUNT INDOOR TEMP. CHANGES	
		IF FURNACE IS ON	IF FURNACE IS OFF
7 AM	40°	+1	−3
8	42°	+2	−3
9	45°	+2	−2
10	47°	+2	−2
11	50°	+2	−2
12 NOON	52°	+3	−1
1	55°	+3	−1
2	57°	+3	−1
3	60°	+3	0
4	58°	+3	0
5	56°	+3	−1
6 PM	54°	+3	−1
7	52°	+3	−1
8	50°	+2	−2
9	48°	+2	−2
10	46°	+2	−2
11	44°	+2	−2
12 MIDNIGHT	42°	+2	−3
1	40°	+1	−3
2	38°	+1	−3
3	36°	+1	−4
4	35°	+1	−4
5	36°	+1	−4
6	38°	+1	−3
7 AM	40°	+1	−3

Instructions:

1. "Set" the room temperature by drawing an arrow beside one of the numbers on the left edge of the board (70° is a good place to start). Then draw a bracket around the five numbers centered on the target temperature (e.g., 68° - 72°).

2. The simulation begins at 7 a.m. with the outside temperature at 40°; the inside temperature is at the value at which you set the thermostat and the furnace is "off" (sitting down).

3. Select a student from the remainder of the class to be Air for the first *simulated hour* (one round).

4. Air walks over to Furnace and peers melodramatically and nearsightedly at him to see if he is on or off (see rule 7).

5. Air then goes to the temperature chart, chooses one of the two columns according to the condition of the furnace and finds the correct increase or decrease in his temperature.

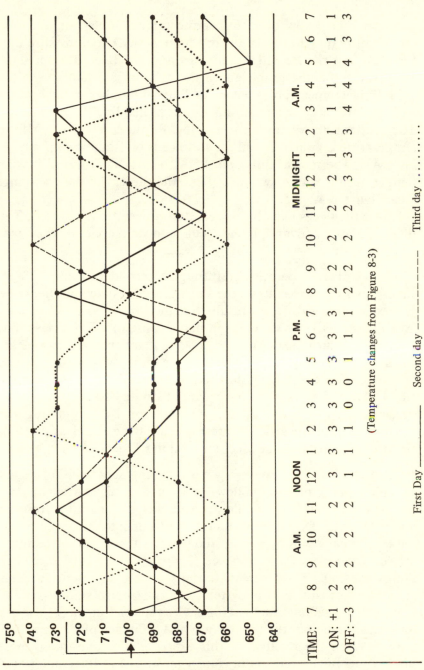

FIGURE 8—4

Indoor Temperature During Three Simulated Days

6. Air then walks over to Thermostat and tells him the new temperature (for the *end* of the one hour period), making sure that the class and the Recorder can hear, and the Recorder notes the temperature on the graph above the appropriate hour.

7. If the temperature is below the bottom number in the bracket and the furnace is off (sitting down pretending to be asleep), Thermostat calls over to Furnace "Hey, Furnace! Wake up!" If the temperature is "too hot" and the furnace is on (standing up waving his arms), Thermostat calls over, "OK, hot stuff, sit down!" If the temperature is within two degrees of the target, he does nothing. (See Figure 8-1, page 151.)

8. Air then goes back to his seat and a new Air is selected. The time of day is advanced one hour and the cycle is repeated, starting with step 4.

Variations: If time permits, go through a second and third "day," superimposing the results on the same graph to show that the same process produces different results but the same *pattern* of results. (See Figure 8-4.) For variety, you may choose to tell the class that many people turn the thermostat down at night or have thermostats which automatically drop 5° between 1 a.m. and 5 a.m. (or tell this only to the student playing the thermostat and let him surprise the class). After the students have caught on to the feedback-loop process, you can speed up the investigation by eliminating the physical roles of Air and Thermostat and having the class perform these computational and decision-making functions.

Follow-Up: End the exercise while students are still interested enough to participate in a follow-up discussion. The basic objective for the discussion is to enable the students to generalize from an understanding of the furnace-thermostat system to other systems of the same type. Begin by asking students to suggest other examples, offering examples of your own (see next page) where needed to keep things moving. Then direct the discussion to the particular advantages of this kind of system (e.g., long-term stability in the face of an unpredictably changing environment). You might also ask for conjecture about the importance and influence of the one hour time cycle on the realities of this exercise. (For one thing, most thermostats function instantaneously instead of at intervals, which would eliminate the "overshoot" of temperature outside the bracket). What would be the result of a change from one hour to

OTHER COMMON FEEDBACK LOOPS

Balance: Whether you are dancing, standing on your head, riding a unicycle, or just standing up, it is a pretty intricate feedback system that keeps you from falling down. If you try standing on one foot for 60 seconds, you can feel the process very clearly. The brain takes in messages from the eyes, the balance tubes in the inner ear, and the kinesthetic nerves that tell you where the parts of your body are located. This information is compared with the desired condition – staying upright! -- and if there is a discrepancy, the corrective action is immediately commanded, all without thinking about it.

Hunger: There are other determinants of hunger, such as the habit of being hungry at a certain time, but a basic influence is the feedback loop based on the amount of sugar in the blood. Your blood sugar is used up as you metabolize it for energy, until an internal sensor detects a condition of low blood sugar, which it signals by making you feel hungry. The digestion of food (especially carbohydrates) sends the level back up, which triggers the release of insulin, which is used to metabolize the sugar, thus bringing it back down and making you hungry again.

Hand-eye coordination: All types involve the basic feedback cycle of **observe, compare,** and **correct.** Some students say they don't do this. They claim that, when hitting a baseball for instance, they decide where the bat should go and then just swing it; there's no time to make corrections along the way. Suggest that they try shutting their eyes as soon as they start to swing the bat. (The coach tells you to keep your eye on the ball for a very good reason.) Even as short a motion as a hammer stroke receives numerous mid-course corrections.

Elections: You evaluate the candidates, compare their positions with your mental ideal, and choose the one that is closest. If a politician strays too far from what the public wants, he gets replaced by another who at least seems closer.

Prices: If people want more widgets than currently are being made, they bid against each other for the limited supply. This drives prices up, which makes it more profitable to make widgets, which makes more people want to get into the widget business. Pretty soon all these widget-makers are making too many widgets, which causes the price to drop. This makes widgets less profitable, so some people stop making them, which causes a widget shortage, which is where we started.

half an hour per cycle? (Reduce the overshoot). What if you made it two hours? . . . Four hours? . . . 12 hours? (The curve swings wider and wider until it goes out of control.)

Stability and Delay

Among the feedback systems discussed in the box of examples in the preceding exercise are those involving the coordination of sense perception and muscular movement, such as driving, riding a bike, threading a needle, or balancing a baseball bat on one's fingers. The latter — balancing a baseball bat — is the source, several times removed, of the following simulation.

Unlike the preceding exercise, this is a pencil and paper simulation for either one or two participants. Stripped down to its basic elements, as it is here, it is a good simulation of a fundamental choice process faced by sailors, pilots, businessmen, and many others: how to reach the best compromise between resources invested in achieving a goal and resources invested in preventing possible disaster — i.e., the proper mixture of offense and defense, or speed and safety. However, the primary educational objective of this simulation is to demonstrate the importance of delay times on determining the behavior and stability of feedback systems.

The very act of writing directions for a simulation provides an excellent example of the value of feedback in communication. A ten-year-old can be taught a complex game like Monopoly in a short period of time, yet the rule book for Monopoly is extremely long and detailed and even an adult can be expected to make mistakes if required to learn the game solely from the rule book. The difference is that a live instructor demonstrates the game and then needs to correct only the misunderstandings that actually arise, while the rule book has to try to cover every possible misinterpretation because there can be no feedback between learner and teacher.

Each version of the simulation in the exercise below takes only four or five minutes to teach to a group of students (who can then teach the remaining students). Nevertheless, it takes a considerable amount of space to describe and may appear somewhat formidable.

If you will keep some sheets of graph paper, a dice cube, and a pencil beside you as you read through it, and actually work through the instructions in each version, you will find that it is much simpler and more straightforward than it seems in print.

EXERCISE 22: *Channels*

Materials: For each pair of students: graph paper (the kind with 1/6" squares is best), a pen or colored pencil, a regular pencil with an eraser, and a dice cube or spinner card or other source of random numbers. Use the pen or colored pencil to draw a line down the center line of the graph paper and another line to each side of the center and 12½ squares away, as illustrated on page 164.

Background: At some point prior to the exercise, introduce the class to some of the games involving a conflict between balance and progress toward a destination. Balancing a baseball bat is fine if you have recess or Physical Education out of doors with the class. Indoors, substitute a long, skinny mailing tube or wooden dowel. (Four feet of 1/4 inch dowel costs 15¢ at the lumber yard; for safety tape a ball of cotton over the top end.) Or have the students place a marble on the cover of a book held flat on one hand at shoulder height (like a waiter carrying a tray) and try to walk a specified path around the classroom as fast as possible without dropping the marble.

Whatever object you use, get the class to observe the overall pattern. You can move forward as long as the object is centered. As soon as it gets unbalanced, however, you must change course to compensate, or stop altogether until you have brought it back into the "safety zone." Only then can you continue toward your goal.

Also ask the students what the effects would be of making the permissible path narrower and narrower. (Could you walk the edge of a 2 x 4 and balance a baseball bat on your finger at the same time? How fast could you move if you tried it?) Finally, have them consider the relationship of reaction-time to stability and smooth progress. (A good way to do this with the book-and-marble is to blindfold one student, give him the book and the marble, and have another student try to guide him in keeping the marble balanced, using only verbal commands.)

Procedure: One student can do this simulation alone, but you will get more reliable results if a second student rolls the die and records the moves for him. There are three versions of the simulation, and they should be played in sequence.

Before you begin, tell the students that they are going to try out a simulation and explain that a simulation is like a game but has a different result. The object of a game is to win, but the object of this kind of simulation is to figure out the best strategy. (When you do this to a game, it stops being any fun — like Tic-tac-toe when both people know how to play.)

First Version

This simulation is called "Channels" because the object is to get an imaginary point (represented by a sequence of dots) from one end of a channel to the other without being pushed out of bounds to either side. It is basically a solitaire, with "the Player" alternating moves with "the die." If two students play, the second one rolls the die and kibbitzes but has no active decision-making role. (The two should switch positions after each run.)

To start, a large dot is placed at the very center of the starting line. Then the die is rolled and the point is moved that many spaces to either the left or the right (it doesn't matter which). For example, if a three is rolled, a new dot is placed on the bottom line three spaces from the starting point.

The Player then selects his first move and places a new dot accordingly. To be a legal move, the point must go at least one space forward, and be a total of 7 spaces away from its previous location, measuring along the horizontal and vertical lines. In Figure 8-5 below, all of the alternative moves open to the Player are indicated (after an intial move of three to the left by the die). The move actually selected is six squares forward and one square to the right, abbreviated 0-6-1.

After the Player has moved, the die is rolled again. The die moves the point only *sideways* in its turns. Once it starts off moving in one direction, it continues to move the point in that direction on each of its successive turns (regardless of what the Player does) until a "one" is rolled. The role of a "one" reverses the direction in which the die moves the point, but it does not count as a turn in itself, so the die is immediately rolled again. (However, a second "one" in a

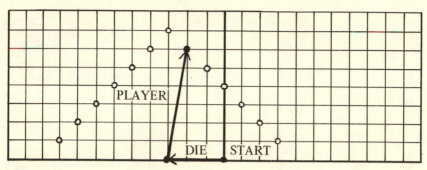

**FIGURE
8–5**

row on the same turn is treated as a move; it does not reverse the direction of travel a second time.)

Proceed in this fashion, alternating rolls of the die and moves by the Player, until the point either goes out of bounds or reaches the finish line in safety. See Figure 8-6 for a step by step illustration of one "run" of the simulation.

When the students have had a chance to learn the procedures, tell them that there is an "optimum strategy" — in this case, a rule which enables you to reach the other end in complete safety in the minimum number of turns. (Use the smallest sideways motion that will keep the point *no less* than 6 spaces from the nearest edge.) Some of the students will discover the rule more quickly than the rest, so have those who figure it out first explain it to the others. When all have grasped the idea, tell them to save the sheets for all their trial runs.

Second Version

Now we are going to introduce one change in the rules — a delay of one turn between the time the Player decides how to move and the time the move is actually made. Here are the instructions:

1. Make an opening move with the die.
2. *Write-down* your own next move (e.g., "4L" or "4-3-0" for "four left and three forward").
3. Make another move with the die.
4. *Make* the move you wrote down, cross it off, and write down your next move.
5. Repeat steps 3 and 4 alternately until you go out of bounds or reach the far end. (See Figure 8-7.)

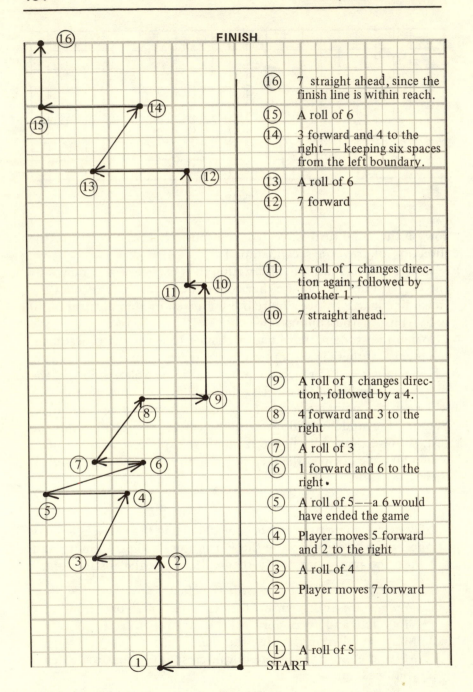

(16) 7 straight ahead, since the finish line is within reach.

(15) A roll of 6

(14) 3 forward and 4 to the right—— keeping six spaces from the left boundary.

(13) A roll of 6

(12) 7 forward

(11) A roll of 1 changes direction again, followed by another 1.

(10) 7 straight ahead.

(9) A roll of 1 changes direction, followed by a 4.

(8) 4 forward and 3 to the right

(7) A roll of 3

(6) 1 forward and 6 to the right •

(5) A roll of 5——a 6 would have ended the game

(4) Player moves 5 forward and 2 to the right

(3) A roll of 4

(2) Player moves 7 forward

(1) A roll of 5

FIGURE 8–6

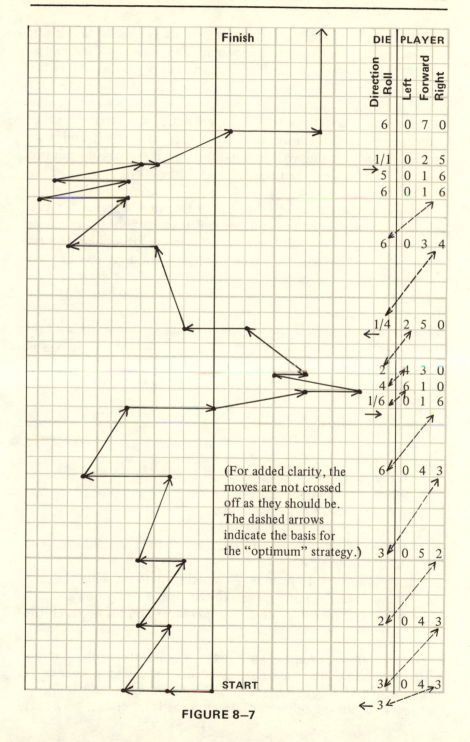

	DIE	PLAYER		
Direction Roll		Left	Forward	Right
6		0	7	0
1/1		0	2	5
5		0	1	6
6		0	1	6
6		0	3	4
1/4		2	5	0
2		4	3	0
4		6	1	0
1/6		0	1	6
6		0	4	3
3		0	5	2
2		0	4	3
3		0	4	3
3				

Finish

(For added clarity, the
moves are not crossed
off as they should be.
The dashed arrows
indicate the basis for
the "optimum" strategy.)

START

FIGURE 8–7

This time there is only one strategy that always works, and it will take most students longer to discover it. The "safe zone" down the middle has vanished, so the Player must always play to nullify the moves of the die. The rule is this: always write down the move that would put the dot exactly on the center line if the die weren't going to move first. In other words, if the dot is three spaces to the right of the center line, your move must be "three to the left and four forward." Any other move goes out of bounds if you should roll two sixes in a row (or a one-and-six and a six, if the "drift" is *toward* the center line.)

Some questions to ask: If we made this into a game for two players — a race to get to the other end first, without going out of bounds — would the completely "safe" strategy (above) be the best strategy? Compare trials of this version with the first version; did more of them go out of bounds this time? Why? Of the ones that made it to the finish line, did those from one version generally take longer — more turns — than those from the other? Why? What would be the effect of widening the "channel" — moving each of the sidelines out one square? What about moving them *in* one square?

Third Version

Now we are going to increase the *delay* from one turn to two. Here are the new rules:

1. Roll the die and move accordingly.
2. Write down your first move.
3. Make a second move with the die.
4. Write down your second move.
5. Make another move with the die.
6. *Make* your first move and cross it off, then write down your third move.
7. Continue in this fashion — making a move with the die, making the "oldest" move on your list, writing down a new move, and repeat — until you go out of bounds or reach the end.

Here are some questions to ask twice — right after explaining the instructions and again after the students have had a chance to experiment with them: Is there a "perfect" strategy that will always get you safely to the other end? If so, what is it? If not, why not?

(For one thing, if the first three rolls are sixes, you're dead before you even get started.) Is there a "best" strategy? Two suggestions: Move seven squares straight ahead every turn and hope for low rolls, especially for "ones" when you get close to the edge. Or move three spaces forward and four toward the center (to counteract the "average" roll) each turn, but treat yourself to a sprint — seven squares forward — if you roll a one while approaching an edge. Which one works best? Would there be a "perfect" safe strategy if you widened the channel from 24 to 35 squares? (No. Why not?) How about 36 squares? (Yes. Why? You are three moves "behind" the die, three times six is 18, so you need 18 squares of room in each direction. The test of any strategy is whether you can survive a run of sixes in either direction at any time.)

Conclusion: The manner in which this exercise is handled is important. The exercise does not work well if approached as a test or competition. It is not a question of who can perform best under certain rules, but rather a question of whether the class or group can together find out the *relationship* between the rules and the results. Frequently ask "Why?" and "What would happen if we made such-and-such a change in the rules?" Students are used to thinking as players or performers under arbitrary rules. Here, you must draw them out of that perspective and get them to think as *designers*.

The objective of the exercise is to have each student come away with at least a hazy, intuitive feeling for the following proposition: The stability of a dynamic system depends on the relationship between five factors —

- The maximum size of the outside forces pushing it off balance (in this case, the biggest number on the die).
- The maximum permissible latitude (the width of the "channel").
- The total delay time in getting information, calculating the correct response, and putting the correction into effect. (How many moves "behind" the die are we?)
- The accuracy of the information and of the calculations of correct responses. (Many of our tries went out of bounds because we didn't know the best strategy.)
- The "power" of our possible responses. (Suppose we could only move 5 squares sideways each turn?)

One of the best ways to establish this understanding is to relate the simulation back again to the "real world." Find a fairly smooth "successful" trial from the first version and label it — in big, bright letters — "Sober." Find a successful but erratic — lots of fives and sixes — run from the second version and label it "Tipsy." Find a wildly unsuccessful run of the third version and label it "Drunk." Stick these up or pass them around, explaining that one reason that drunk drivers are dangerous is that alcohol slows down a person's reaction time. (It also distorts your perception and reduces the accuracy as well as the speed of your responses. Ask the students if they can figure out a way to simulate these additional handicaps.)

Next, find a fairly erratic but just barely successful run of the third version, turn it sideways, write "Recession" in what was the left margin, label the center line "Prosperity," and write "Inflation" in the right margin. Then suggest to the class that running the U.S. economy is a lot like trying to drive "under the influence": you don't know where you are, you have only a distorted idea of where you've been, you aren't sure what corrections to make, and the corrections you do make seem to take forever to take effect.

In many "version-three" situations in the real world, the "random" pressures (represented by the dice) are not completely random. One strategy for coping with these situations is to attempt to *forecast* the future behavior of these "winds of change." If we had some way of knowing in advance when a roll of a "one" would occur, we could construct a "safe" strategy (after the first three moves) for version three of the simulation. Similarly, if we had prior knowledge of when the economy was going to "turn around" we could do a much better job of stabilizing its actions, and so a great deal of money and effort is spent on attempts at economic forecasting.

Other examples of this type are common in government, business, our personal lives, even in sports — hitting a baseball is a problem for the feedback loop of eye, brain, and muscles, but the accuracy of the feedback process is greatly enhanced if you happen to know that the next pitch will be a fastball, high and outside. We can derive from these observations a general principle: the stability of a dynamic feedback process is enhanced in proportion to the accuracy and extent of forecasts of future behavior of the system environment. Or, more simply: "Forewarned forearmed!"

We have discussed the basic elements of systems thinking, using some simple classroom simulations to explore these ideas in considerable depth. In effect, each exercise teaches about systems thinking in two different ways: both subject matter and process. Simulations (and simulation-games — see Appendix C) are fundamentally a systems approach to teaching about any subject. Compared with non-participatory forms of learning, they can provide a more vivid and holistic understanding of a complex problem or situation. So even when a simulation is used to teach about the past, it is also teaching an outlook, an approach to thinking about problems, that will help the student to better understand and cope with his own future.

The exercises in this chapter were designed to teach an understanding of the basic feedback process and the effects of delay times on system stability. They were, therefore, restricted to fairly simple, one-loop systems. In the real world, however, all natural systems and all but the most elementary man-made systems are built up of a great many feedback loops in combination, as in Figure 8-2 on page 153. The next two chapters describe ways to help students bring a general systems perspective to bear on some more complex situations, specifically the problems threatening human survival and the problem of lack of foresight in our own society.

SYSTEMS AND SIMULATIONS: ESSENTIAL POINTS

1. Systems thinking is the most important advance in this century in how to think and how to understand the world around us; in the last few decades, it has radically transformed our science, technology, business, and government.
2. A system is a set or arrangement of things so interrelated as to function as a unit or a whole.
3. A system may be physical, mechanical, biological, intellectual, or social, or any combination of these.
4. A system normally has some kind of stability built into it.
5. Dynamically stable systems are less precise than static systems in an unchanging environment, but possess the very important ability to adapt to a changing environment.
6. Negative feedback is the basic ingredient in all dynamically stable systems; it is the process by which the system continually

attempts to reduce the discrepancy between the desired condition and the actual condition of the system.

7. Simple cause and effect has little meaning in a dynamic system; the behavior of system components is determined by the structure of the system as a whole.

8. Positive feedback loops in a system produce exponential growth and instability unless balanced by negative feedback loops.

9. The amount of delay in the negative feedback loop(s) is a key element in determining the stability of a dynamic system.

NOTES

149. A good general introduction to system thinking is *The Systems View of the World*, by Ervin Laszlo. See also the section on systems and simulations in the bibliography. [92]

150. The Boulding quote is from page 23 of *The Meaning of the Twentieth Century*. [19]

151. The most famous of the static utopias is Plato's *Republic* [174]; see Russell's essay "Philosophy and Politics," in *Authority and the Individual*, for a cogent discussion. [177]

153. Figure 8-2 is from "The Carrying Capacity of the Globe," by Jørgen Randers and Donella Meadows (*Sloan Management Review*, Winter, 1972, p. 16). [108]

161. The simulation is described in terms of a dice cube, and has worked well in that form for the classes which have played it. Gerald Zaltman, however, has noted that alternatives to dice (such as cards or spinners) may be desirable with low-income students:

> The use of dice as a means of introducing environmental responses into the game posed no problem among students from middle and upper class families. However, in testing the game among adolescents from economically depressed inner-city areas this aspect of the game was found particularly disruptive, especially among female players. It became evident that this was due to the use of

dice which had an unacceptable gambling connotation among these players. The problem was overcome by substituting chance cards for dice. (Inbar and Stoll, *Simulation and Gaming in Social Science*, p. 142.) [86]

When using a spinner, divide the card into seven sections, labelling the first six with the numbers 1-6 and the seventh with the legend, "Change direction and spin again."

168. For a discussion of the delay and accuracy problem in running a national economy, see pages 181 to 186 of *Scarcity Challenged: An Introduction to Economics*, by Heinz Kohler, or see almost any introductory economics text. [103]

169. As discussed at the end of chapter seven, simulations are also important for research and for forecasting purposes. The most important forecasting simulations use computers to manipulate elaborate mathematical models. A book entitled *The Limits to Growth*, by Donella Meadows, *et al.*, describes the most controversial and influential of these computer simulations in non-technical language suitable for advanced high school students. (See page 251.) [105]

PART III
Special Topics

CHAPTER IX
Global Survival

In this chapter we are concerned with problems which seriously threaten the survival of human civilization, or even life itself, on this planet. Specifically, we will examine an organizing framework for dealing with the six survival problems which many observers believe are the most urgent and the most potentially dangerous:

- The unchecked exponential growth of world population.
- Our increasing inability to feed the world's people and the increasing danger of catastrophic famines.
- Our abuse of the natural environment and the increasing danger of collapse of important segments of the biosphere.
- The potential exhaustion of key resources without adequate available substitutes.
- The exponential growth of an increasingly unstable economic system, coupled with an increasing have/have-not gap.
- The absence of effective control or adjudication systems for the globe, especially with respect to war and nuclear weapons, and to the five problems listed above.

This chapter is not intended to duplicate the recent outpouring of excellent books, articles, and curriculum units in these areas (environmental education, international education, peace studies, population studies, etc.). Instead, it presents an approach for dealing with all of these topics from a systems perspective, with special attention to the *interrelationships* among the different problems.

We need to emphasize the interrelationships because dealing with the problems one at a time is difficult and misleading, and because understanding the importance of each problem without reference to the others is impossible. Each problem is so intertwined with the rest that the use of the word "problem" itself is misleading — we are really dealing with a world "macro-problem," of which each of these problems is only a facet.

Why is population growth a problem? Because it means increasing demand for limited food and other goods, increased pressure on our environment and our supplies of resources, all of which in turn mean an increased danger of war. Why is the environment a problem? Because destroying it means destroying ourselves, but preserving it means limiting the growth of population, restricting the use of pesticides and other chemicals in agriculture, cutting back on the waste of many resources, and restraining economic growth, all of which would severely strain our fragile international control systems. And so on.

Dealing with all of these interactions is difficult, especially from a curriculum point of view. We are used to dealing with one topic at a time in the classroom, and in any case the "experts" we depend on are *specialists*, representing their own narrow viewpoints. Thus we get curriculum units or materials on population which present the facts and the processes of population growth very clearly, but which explain the importance — the *meaning* — of the topic only vaguely, often just with a few photographs intended to depict poverty, hunger, or crowding.

Worse yet, the people who are charged with *solving* these problems also tend to view them from a narrow, specialized perspective. So we get "solutions" to the problems of food production which increase poverty, economic programs which support population growth, resource policies which degrade the environment and environmental policies which waste resources, and peace-keeping proposals which exacerbate the causes of war.

Part of the difficulty in coping with a macro-problem is structural: the person in charge of one department is paid to solve the problems in his department, not to worry about the side-effects of his "solutions" on some other department's problems. Part of the difficulty is semantic: the very notion of "side-effects" as things that are somehow peripheral is very misleading. (One wry definition of a side-effect is, "Any consequence of our actions which we don't want to think about or be responsible for.")

But the largest part of the difficulty is that we lack the conceptual tools to think or communicate easily about such interactions. Six topics have 30 potential interrelations. When we write about the topics or discuss them in class in a normal sequence, one after the other, we can easily emphasize only five, or at the most ten, of those interactions. Our words and sentences are linear, and not well adapted to describing networks of ideas or non-linear systems. A more holistic, systematic approach is required.

The framework which we use as a way of avoiding these difficulties is adapted from a futures research tool called the "Cross-Impact Matrix." The "cross-impact" part of the name refers to its intention, which is to examine the impact of each portion of the problem on each other portion. The "matrix" part refers to the square grid which is used to insure that the examination is done systematically and covers each possible "cross-impact."

The cross-impact exercise is rather long (it takes up the remainder of this chapter), but it provides a valuable format for units on global survival ranging from a three-day workshop or three-week curriculum unit all the way to an entire one-semester course. The description of the exercise provides a very brief introduction to each of the problem areas and to a few of the alternative possibilities in each area, but this should be supplemented — if at all possible — by some of the excellent sources listed in Appendix C.

EXERCISE 23: *Cross-Impact Matrix on Global Survival*

I. *Background:*

The hypothesis that we are examining is that the world faces a series of major problems which — quite apart from their individual seriousness — are so interconnected that they cannot realistically be thought of as separate problems, but must be dealt with as components of a world macro-problem. These components are:

- Population Growth
- Food
- Environment
- Natural Resources
- Economics
- Global Management

However, this list is not yet in a useful form for our purposes. For instance, the impact of one of these areas on another (e.g., the impact of food production on the environment) is a complex relationship which changes as the status of each area changes. To help make the question of interactions more concrete, four alternative plausible courses of events are listed within each problem area (detailed explanations begin on the next page).

POPULATION GROWTH
- Continues
- Reduced by birth control
- Reduced by gender selection
- Reduced by increased death rate

FOOD
- Continued successful green revolution
- Food sources expanded by technology
- Better distribution
- Hunger

ENVIRONMENT
- Switch to non-fossil fuels
- Abandon "poison molecule" technology
- Limit new industrialization
- Continue to deteriorate (defensive adaptation)

NATURAL RESOURCES
- Continue to deplete (expand search, recovery, access)
- Modernize (recycle everything, minimize obsolescence, go nuclear, solar, etc.)
- Restrict consumption
- De-modernize

ECONOMICS
- Continued growth
- Steady-state (no-growth) economy
- Limit on goods only, all growth in service economy
- Limit on goods in "developed" nations only

GLOBAL MANAGEMENT
- Continued nation-state system
- Gradualist: economic and service web grows around U.N.
- Unionist: snowball approach
- Federalist: U.N. transformed into a world federation.

The alternatives listed under each area are by no means complete, or even necessarily the most likely possibilities; nor are they always mutually exclusive. They should, however, represent a diverse sampling for classroom purposes of the actual range of possible events. As the class goes over the introductions to the problems and the descriptions of the alternatives (below) they may wish to add possibilities for consideration. This is easily done — there is nothing special about the number four — as long as you write down an agreed-upon description of just what is meant.

II. *Descriptions of the Problem Areas:*

POPULATION

World population is currently growing at roughly the rate of 2% per year, which means that it is doubling every 35 years. For the poorest fourth of the world's peoples, population is increasing as fast as or faster than food production or real wealth. In other words, population growth has cancelled the gains that might have been made through industrialization or modern agriculture.

a. Continued Growth:

If population continues to grow at its present rate, we will need to double the world's basic life support services in 35 years just to maintain the present poor standard of living. Just to stay even in this "Red Queen's Race" requires that in one generation we double the number of houses, the number of schools, the number of hospitals, the capacity of our agriculture, our production of energy and portable fuels, our access to scarce resources, our supplies of fresh water, *everything*.

b. Birth Control:

To effectively reduce the growth rate by means of birth control would require substantial interventions in many cultures, a stronger and more enforceable decision-making level, and improvements in the technology of birth control.

c. Gender Selection:

An alternative to direct birth control that would involve less cultural intervention has been described by Garrett Hardin, as follows. In population growth, the number of males is essentially irrelevant; it is the increase of female babies over their mothers' generation that counts. Instead of attempting to reduce the number of female babies by reducing the total number of babies born, a more culturally acceptable method in a number of peasant societies would be to reduce the *percentage* of female babies. This is perfectly feasible with current technology, and a shift in the birth ratio from approximately 49:51 to approximately 37:63 (female: male) would be sufficient to stabilize a population of India's type in about 65 years.

d. Increased Death Rate:

However, if we are unable to reduce the growth rate either through birth control or gender selection, and we are also unable to maintain the treadmill pace of a 35 year doubling time, then the growth rate will be reduced through an increase in the death rate. Whether this occurs through ever more devastating famines or through the overwhelming of public health systems by the combination of poverty and density, or both, the effect would be to shorten the average life span until the death rate is once again in equilibrium with the birth rate.

FOOD

Approximately 1/4 of the world's population is starving or chronically malnourished. Solutions to this problem generally are proposed under three headings: increasing the productivity of agricultural crop-land; expanding our food-production base beyond its present limits of "crop-land"; and eliminating current inequalities in food distribution.

a. Green Revolution:

Our civilization has been built on a tremendous increase in the agricultural productivity of land and labor. The techniques that make up our modern agriculture and which we are attempting to export as the "Green Revolution" are: mechanization, mono-cropping, hybrids and genetic tailoring, inorganic nitrogen fertilizers, and pesticides. But while we tout the "Green Revolution" as a solution to the world's hunger problem, these techniques are proving increasingly troublesome here at home and in other areas where they have been applied. Mechanization requires huge areas devoted to single crops of high-yield plants. Unfortunately, the combination of vast acres and lush production is an invitation to pest infestation and plant diseases. This requires, in turn, the extensive use of lethal pesticides and plant sprays. But insects reproduce much more rapidly than their natural predators, and therefore often become immune to the pesticide by genetic selection while the predators do not. Thus, by eliminating the predators, the pesticide often precipitates an even larger pest explosion, requiring the continual development of new and more lethal pesticides. Similarly, the tremendous yields produced by modern techniques enable us to remove huge quantities of vegetable matter from the land, along with the large quantities of nutrients and minerals contained therein. To replace these, and to increase yields still further, the farmer must turn to artificial fertilizers. Unfortunately, the inorganic nitrogen in fertilizer depresses and eventually paralyzes the nitrogen-fixing bacteria in the soil, thus requiring ever increasing amounts of fertilizer while making it impossible to get out of the fertilizer trap.

b. New Food Sources:

An alternative to continuing the "Green Revolution" with its attendant instabilities and dangers is to greatly expand our sources of food. This generally involves massive investments of technology, as in dam-building, desalting ocean water, and/or building extensive irrigation systems to bring large desert or arid areas into production. Other proposals are for extended use of hydroponics, sea-farming, and aqua-culture. All of these suggestions have in common the problem that greatly expanded application would require that the world invest successively larger and larger portions of its material wealth and labor into food production, thus reversing a long-term historical trend. Other suggestions in this area include substantial revisions of culturally ingrained eating preferences (e.g., algae-burgers, fish-meal protein supplements, and the almost total elimination of natural meat).

c. Equalize Distribution:
A third strategy for solving the hunger problem stems from the observation that the world's present food production is distributed very unevenly and could, if carefully rationed, provide a minimum healthful diet for many more people than it currently supports. Like stringent birth control, such equalization of distribution would require a greatly increased level of global decision-making and enforcement, strong enough in this case to dictate terms to even the most powerful nations.

d. Hunger:
The fourth possibility is that the preceding three efforts will fail and that hunger — through its effect on the death rate — will limit population and therefore limit the demand on agriculture. The grim picture of the transitional period makes us appalled by such a "solution," but our best efforts may not prevent its occurrence if population is not stabilized by some other means.

ENVIRONMENT

Man's disruptive impact on his environment has increased drastically with his increasing numbers and his increasingly extensive and "non-biological" technology. Such disruptive impacts range from our ancient (but now greatly enhanced) capacity for deforestation and desert-making to such modern pastimes as the injecting of a wide assortment of persistent chemical and radioactive poisons into the air, soil, and water.

a. Switch to Non-Fossil Fuels:
Since one of our most pervasive polluters of the air and the waters is our use of coal and oil, one starting place in coping with environmental pollution would be a concerted effort to switch to non-fossil fuels. Of the nuclear alternatives, uranium fission also presents considerable problems of waste disposal, while hydrogen fusion (which would be virtually non-polluting) may be beyond our technical or economic grasp — at least in this century. The remaining alternatives are the "natural" energy resources: sunlight, wind, falling water, the tides, and the earth's internal heat. All of these have the drawback that they are dependably

available only in a few favored locations, and the two of these that are the most widely available — wind and sun — are both intermittent and costly (in terms of other resources) for the amount of power generated.

b. Abandon "Poison-Molecule" Technology:

The other portion of our technology which is especially disruptive is our introduction into the environment of huge quantities of artifically produced chemicals, ranging from pesticides and detergents to aluminum cans and most plastics. Any long-term solution to this part of the environment problem must include severe limitations on this type of product. Where mingling with natural systems is unavoidable, degradable substitutes will have to be found. Where no substitute exists for the non-degradable substance, it must be contained within a tightly closed recycling loop.

c. Limit Industrialization:

A third approach would be to limit, not the type of industrialization, but rather the amount and extent of industrialization. (Of course, the two might be done simultaneously.) A global set of restrictions on new industrialization and on gross physical interventions in the environment would, however, involve a considerable loss of sovereignty by all nations and would probably be greeted with considerable hostility by the non-industrialized nations.

d. Defensive Adaptation:

Finally, failing effective positive remedies, it is assumed that we would continue to practice defensive adaptation to a deteriorating environment. It is, of course, much more sensible to prevent poisons from entering the rivers or the air than it is to build purification plants to make poisoned rivers drinkable or to wear gas-masks in a smoggy city. But the inner logic of our social system often seems to compel the least reasonable course, if only because the price for the benefit (clean water, breathable air) is most likely to be paid by those who have no choice — those at the immediate point of consumption.

NATURAL RESOURCES

One effect of the Industrial Revolution was an explosive increase in the utilization of a wide variety of natural resources.

Until recently men have been able to assume that the total human demand was such a small part of the world's supply that we need have no fears of running out. The power of an exponential growth curve, however, is such that we are fast coming up against the limits of the total recoverable supply of a number of vital resources. Of these resources, the most critical ones seem to be the energy resources. With most of the other resources, especially minerals, poorer ores can be mined or other less suitable substances can be substituted (though such practices usually degrade the environment and exact a considerable cost in additional energy, thus aggravating the energy shortage problem).

a. Continued Depletion:

Present strategies for industrial countries focus on increasing the available supply of threatened resources. That is, technical, economic, and diplomatic efforts are concentrated on greatly expanding the search for, access to, and recovery of new deposits in ever more remote or inhospitable locations. There are two basic arguments for, and two against, this approach. The arguments in favor are that the approach has worked in the past, and that estimates of unknown resources are only estimates, which a major discovery could prove completely wrong. The arguments against this approach are that it ignores continually rising discovery and extraction costs and that, since the earth *is* finite, this approach simply postpones the inevitable reckoning.

b. Modernization:

An alternative solution would be to totally modernize our industrial economy: extensive closed recycling systems, minimization of obsolescence, and the eventual switch to a completely solar/nuclear economy. The problem is that this is easily said, but not so easily done. How does one go about making a fusion reactor that produces more power than it uses? How do we foster "uneconomically" long-lived products without seriously disrupting our economy? How do we go about collecting, sorting, dismantling and re-using the bewildering variety of products discarded daily around the globe? Even if we can figure out how to do these things, how do we pay for them?

c. Restrict Consumption:

Of course, instead of expanding supply or increasing the

efficiency of use, we can concentrate on reducing demand or at least reducing its current rate of growth. This will eventually be necessary in any case, since exponential growth can never be sustained indefinitely. Even so, it is only a temporary solution to the problem of impending shortages: e.g., at *projected* rates of consumption, we will run out of oil by 1990; at *current* rates of consumption, we will run out by 1995, a postponement of only five years.

d. De-Modernization:

Finally, if the first three strategies are insufficient, we will gradually have to revert to older forms and practices where this is possible. In the energy area, for instance, there is no shortage of fossil fuels *if* we include vast supplies of high-sulfur coal and/or coal which is available only through strip-mining on a presently incomprehensible scale.

ECONOMICS

The problem here is two-fold: stability and fairness. Existing industrial economies depend on continued exponential growth, yet there is good evidence that the technological/ environmental base which supports that growth is intrinsically unstable and becomes more so the longer current growth rates continue. Furthermore, any talk of restricting growth runs up against the problem of distribution: in a world with profound inequalities of distribution the promise of "progress" has been vital to the hopes of the "underdeveloped" nations and to the consciences of the developed nations.

a. Continued Growth:

The first and most likely possibility is that the built-in self-propelling growth mechanisms will continue to be stronger than any attempt to regulate them intentionally, until eventually some basic limit or irreplaceable scarcity is reached and the system flops over into a contraction mode, producing another severe depression.

b. Steady-State Economy:

The direct solution to this dilemma would be to somehow clamp a flat lid on economic growth and channel as much as possible of the wealth that would normally be invested in new productive capacity into increasing the "livability" of the planet, with special attention to the underdeveloped portions of the globe.

c. Limiting Goods:

A slightly more sophisticated approach would be to similarly limit only the portion of the economy devoted to the production of material goods and to rechannel all of the "profits" from this area into the service economy. However, no matter how the distributive system is arranged, it is unlikely that either this or the previous alternatives would be received at all well by the poorer nations, since it would lock them into the poor/rich dichotomy while making them dependent on the benevolence of the rich nations.

d. Limiting the Rich:

Provided that there still remains a good deal of room for economic growth before crucial limits are reached, it might also be possible to limit industrial increase in the "developed" countries only, for a fixed period of time, giving the "underdeveloped" nations time to catch up before stabilizing the global economy. The question remains as to whether, and under what circumstances, the "developed" nations would either sponsor or submit to such a program.

GLOBAL MANAGEMENT

The problem here, as in the preceding sections, stems from our vastly increased capacity for wreaking havoc on ourselves and on our life-support systems. The current nation-state system has no enforceable controls over the use of nuclear weapons, the squandering of vital resources, or the disruption of the biosphere.

a. Status Quo Extended:

Each year that this system continues there is a small, but real, risk of major catastrophe or irreparable harm. Although this risk cannot be computed, it can be estimated, and from this estimate we can, in turn, estimate the cumulative risk we run. Let us say, conservatively, that each year there is only an insignificant one chance out of one hundred that some accident (or maniac) will set off a major eco-catastrophe or push the nuclear button. This means that over a period of 70 years the chance of disaster is better than 50%. If there is one chance in 20 of disaster each year, it is an even money bet that we will destroy ourselves in only 14 years.[1] Clearly,

---

[1] Half-life — the period over which something with a constant risk level has a 50% chance of occurring — is computed the same way we computed doubling time from percentage growth rates in chapter four: the half-life equals 70 divided by the percentage chance of occurrence in any one year.

in the long run, such risks are unacceptable. Yet the trend is to draw more and more antagonists from more and more remote regions of the globe into the network of potential global conflict, thus continually increasing the risk of crisis.

b. Gradualist:

The counter strategy which is most apparent and which has the most official, if tacit, support can be termed the "gradualist" (or "Functionalist") approach, and is based on a theory and an observable trend. The theory is that most of big government is bureaucratic, not basically political; the observable trend is the very rapid growth of international corporations and agencies in the last 15 to 20 years. If we assume the theory is correct and that the trend will continue, it seems likely that a world government, in practice, will grow up out of the constant interlinking of international agencies, corporations and interest groups. The traditional objections to this approach are that it would result in an administrative government grown up around an ineffectual policy-making organization (presumably the U.N.) and that without an effective "head" it would be unable to do any effective long-range planning or establish coherent objectives and programs. In defense of the gradualist approach, one can point out that modern large governments are notoriously incapable of performing these functions anyhow, and that perhaps they could be better performed by non-governmental agencies.

c. Unionist:

Another objection to the gradualist approach is that we may not be able to afford the luxury of the time it would take. Two alternatives are the "Unionist" and the "Federalist" approaches. The Unionists argue for a snowball effect, that is, the alliance of several nations in an initial super-national Union which would continue to grow with the addition of new members. Once started, such a movement could generate considerable momentum, especially if it became clear that the advantages of membership were high and that the rights of the member nations were carefully safeguarded. The trick, of course, is to get the snowball started.

d. Federalist:

The second alternative would take longer to initiate, but would be considerably more rapid in its implementation. The model here is the formation of a "federal" government similar in structure to the original 13 states of the United States. In principle, a workable and mutually satisfactory world government could be devised to deal with the problem of war and other threats to the survival of the globe. This government would go into effect, supplanting the U.N., when its constitution had been approved by some designated portion of the planet's peoples. Though potentially the most rapid and the most "sensible" solution to the defects of the nation-state system, the Federalist approach is dogged by one question: could *any* governmental scheme be devised which would be acceptable to, say, 3/4 of the world's nations, or nations representing 3/4 of the world's peoples?

III. *Using the Cross-Impact Matrix:*

We now have a set of 6 problem areas and 24+ possible outcomes, four or more in each area. The task for the class is to look systematically at the interrelationships between these items, estimate the strength and direction (positive or negative) of each cross-impact, and record these estimates in the matrix. This is done going from left to right across each row, in the order in which the squares are numbered in the matrix on page 191, dealing with all four cross-impacts within each square before going on to the next square. This pattern allows the class to combine comments on similar cross-impacts.

Each of the entries to be made in the matrix represents the *impact of one of the alternatives* listed in the left-hand margin *on one of the general problems* listed at the heads of the columns. For instance, if the class concludes that continued exponential growth of population would make it *much* more difficult to solve our agricultural problems, then matrix entry 1.a should be a double negative (--). If the alternative being considered would make the particular problem *somewhat* more difficult to cope with, it would get a single minus sign, for "moderate negative impact." *No* impact is marked as a zero, a moderate positive impact is a plus sign, and a strong positive impact — "directly contributes to a solution" — gets a double plus.

An essential part of the exercise is the recording of brief descriptions of the *reasons* for making each matrix entry. This provides a memory aid when, as often happens, you suddenly look back eight or ten squares and say, "Good grief! Why did we do *that*?" It also helps you to maintain a degree of consistency in your interpretation and use of the different alternatives and problem areas.

Pages 190 to 201 contain an example of a completed matrix with explanatory comments to illustrate the kind of result we are talking about. This is not a crib to the "right answers," but a demonstration of how it was done on a previous occasion.

IV. *Interpreting Results and Drawing Conclusions*

In evaluating the matrix it is useful to keep in mind that the entries are, in effect, tabulations of the *side-effects* of the possible strategies or courses of events. Planners and decision-makers have to be concerned not only with the effect of a solution on a problem but with its possible effects on other areas as well. The "plus" entries represent positive side-effects (or "serendipities"); if they are not anticipated, the severity of the problem in the area receiving the serendipitous help may be overrated, with the consequence that excess time, money, and other scarce resources may be spent there and not in more urgent areas. If negative side-effects are not anticipated, the results are often disastrous precisely because the side-effects cross problem and discipline boundaries and, being human-initiated, often have rapid onsets. However, if the negative side effects are foreseen, they often can be mitigated or prevented by modifying the original strategy to include corrective measures.

If past versions of the matrix are at all reliable as a guide, the degree of such interconnectedness is extremely high. In the sample matrix on page 191, every row and every column contains at least one negative entry. More than thirty percent of the entries are rated as strong (i.e., double pluses or double minuses), while the zeros — indicating essentially no impact — constitute only one sixth of the entries.

But the matrix, of course, deals only with primary effects and thus only hints at the potential difficulties of actual planning. For instance, if two approaches to the resource problem seem equally feasible, a planner might choose the one with the best effect on economics; but this might also have a mild negative effect on agriculture, forcing the choice of the more drastic solution from among contemplated alternatives in that area, which in turn might have a disastrous effect on the environment, with critical side-effects for political stability of the globe.

Meanwhile, the other approach to the resource problem has its own train of second, third, and fourth-order implications. The planner thus faces a much more complex task than "merely" select-ing the least unworkable of strategies: he must patch, modify, and tailor each of the strategies until he finally has a truly integrated strategy — one that actually has a chance of coping with these urgent and potentially catastrophic problems.

The largest cause for concern about this discussion, however, is that the "planner" referred to above is entirely hypothetical. The planning function is fractionated into areas, specialties, and sub-specialties, and dispersed among myriad nations, corporations, and agencies. If a workable "solution-set" is as difficult to achieve by conscious intent as this exercise would indicate, then it is extremely unlikely that it will be achieved "automatically" by a system of competing interests where *no one* is responsible to or for the system as a whole.

The final step for you and your students, however, is to pretend to be a "World Planning Agency" responsible for producing a realistic synthesis of all the disparate pieces, and to discuss ways your "solution-set" could be put into effect. Since you will not have unanimity on either solutions or strategies, the discussion from this point on will be as open-ended as you care to make it.

V. *Example of a Completed Matrix:*

Reading the Matrix: The matrix records the impacts of the alternatives listed in the left hand margin on the general problem areas listed at the heads of the columns. The "code" is:

Strong negative impact	(--)
Moderate negative impact	(-)
No significant impact	(0)
Moderate positive impact	(+)
Strong positive impact	(++)

Thus, entry 1.a is "strong negative impact," indicating that continued exponential growth of population would make it much more difficult to solve our food production problem.

The matrix entries and the explanatory comments (below) are the work of an undergraduate class at the University of Massachusetts. Roughly similar results have been produced by high school juniors and seniors. Please note that this section is *not* a crib to the "right" answers, but an example of the *kind* of result you should expect. In any case, the important standard for this exercise is the quality and intensity of the discussion, not the "correctness" of the matrix entries.

	Population	Food	Environment	Resources	Economics	Global Management
Population: a) Continued growth b) Birth control c) Gender selection d) Increased death rate		1. a) -- b) ++ c) + d) 0	2. a) -- b) + c) + d) ++	3. a) 0 b) - c) - d) +	4. a) - b) + c) ++ d) -	5. a) -- b) + c) 0 d) --
Food: a) Green revolution b) Expanded food sources c) More equal distribution d) Hunger	6. a) -- b) - c) - d) ++		7. a) -- b) - c) 0 d) +	8. a) - b) - c) 0 d) +	9. a) 0 b) + c) 0 d) -	10. a) - b) - c) - d) --
Environment a) Go to non-fossil fuels b) Abandon "poison" tech. c) Limit industrialization d) Defensive adaptation	11. a) 0 b) 0 c) 0 d) +	12. a) + b) + c) 0 d) --		13. a) ++ b) 0 c) + d) -	14. a) - b) - c) ++ d) --	15. a) 0 b) + c) - d) --
Natural Resources: a) Increased exploitation b) Modernize c) Restrict demand d) De-modernize	16. a) 0 b) 0 c) + d) +	17. a) ++ b) - c) - d) --	18. a) - b) ++ c) + d) --		19. a) + b) ++ c) - d) -	20. a) -- b) + c) - d) -
Economics: a) Continued growth b) No-growth economy c) Limit on goods only d) Limit goods only in West	21. a) - b) + c) ++ d) 0	22. a) ++ b) - c) + d) +	23. a) - b) + c) + d) +	24. a) -- b) + c) + d) +		25. a) ++ b) --- c) - d) +
Global Management: a) Continued nation-state b) Gradualist c) Unionist d) Federalist	26. a) -- b) - c) 0 d) +	27. a) 0 b) 0 c) + d) ++	28. a) -- b) - c) ++ d) -	29. a) - b) 0 c) + d) +	30. a) 0 b) + c) + d) ++	

FIGURE 9–1
Sample Cross—Impact Matrix on 6 Global Survival Issues

Comments on Matrix Entries:

1. *Impact of Population on Food*
    (a) Each additional mouth compounds the food problem.
    (b & c) Both reduce the demand on agriculture, but they do so only gradually.
    (d) Increased death rate also reduces agricultural demand but resultant shortened life span increases the educational costs of modern agriculture.

2. *Impact of Population on Environment*
    (a) Again, each additional person imposes an additional load on the environment.
    (b & c) Reduction in numbers of people helps but is partly offset by increased life span and standard of living.
    (d) Reduced numbers are here combined with reduced life span and standard of living, for the least load on the environment.

3. *Impact of Population on Natural. Resources*
    (a) Population growth is a relatively weak factor in resource use compared with wealth per capita.
    (b & c) Both birth control and gender selection are likely to lead to increased standard of living, meaning more resource consumption.
    (d) Reduced lifespan would reduce numbers and reduce wealth per capita somewhat.

4. *Impact of Population on Economics*
    (a) Rapid population growth nullifies economic gains from industrialization and efforts to equalize income.
    (b) Birth control permits increased wealth per person but may limit labor supply for crucial changeover effects.
    (c) Gender selection also decreases population growth but without reducing the available labor force.
    (d) Reduced life span means reduced efficiencies in many areas — especially education of a skilled labor force.

5. *Impact of Population on International Systems*
    (a) Pressures of population on land and resources have been a principal cause of war in the past.

(b) Birth control would limit such pressures, but relatively slowly.

(c) Gender selection would also reduce such pressures (though somewhat more slowly), but it would also result in large groups of young males for whom no women were available, thus increasing public volatility and the ease of raising armies.

(d) Increased death rate would result in increased willingness to risk death in war and increased incentive to solve shortage problems by force.

6. *Impact of Food on Population*
   (a, b, & c) Increased food supply, from whatever source, would remove one present limit on population.
   (d) Failure to increase food supplies would "solve" the population problem by increasing the death rate.

7. *Impact of Food on Environment*
   (a) Both pesticides and artificial fertilizers are anti-ecological.
   (b) Although with care they *need not* be harmful, most major efforts to expand the food base (e.g., the Aswan Dam, the Amazon Basin Project), have been.
   (c) Would not change current environmental impact.
   (d) Reduced demand on agriculture would mean reduced environmental impact.

8. *Impact of Food on Natural Resources*
   (a) Modern agriculture is increasingly mechanized.
   (b) Most suggested expanded food sources would involve extensive outlays of resources and energy.
   (c) No change from present.
   (d) Increased demand for food would draw capital away from industrial production toward agriculture.

9. *Impact of Food on Economics*
   (a, b, & c) Increased food supplies, in poor nations, would be an important first step in the equalization of wealth. However, both the "Green Revolution" and the equalization of distribution tend to deprive small peasant farmers of employment, driving them from the land. Expanded food

sources might well be labor-intensive enough to supply employment but might also require skilled labor imported from the "advanced" nations.
(d) Extended famine in poor nations would cripple efforts to industrialize them.

10. *Impact of Food on Global Management*
(a, b, & c) All three of these options would make many nations dependent on a few advanced nations while making the latter responsible for catastrophic failures which are a real risk due to the system's inherent instability. (For one example, see Ehrlich's scenario "Eco-Catastrophe.")
(d) A hungry man (or nation) is likely to steal.

11. *Impact of Environment on Population*
(a, b, & c) No predictable effect.
(d) Continued environmental deterioration is likely to increase the death rate somewhat, thus limiting population growth.

12. *Impact of Environment on Food*
(a) Hydrocarbon pollutants in the air reduce agricultural yield; abandoning fossil fuels would mean cleaner air, more food produced.
(b) Without pesticides, yields would drop, but this would be partly compensated for by the elimination of other chemical pollutants (such as smog) which presently reduce yields.
(c) Effects counter-balance (e.g., less farm land paved over for roads, but fewer tractors to till it).
(d) Extensive pollution could cripple our agricultural capacity.

13. *Impact of Environment on Natural Resources*
(a) Provided it is possible, it helps solve both problems.
(b) Difficult to tell until replacements are known.
(c) Helps keep consumption from growing.
(d) Many pollutants are unrecovered resources; pollution is equivalent to waste.

14. *Impact of Environment on Economics*
(a) A switch to non-fossil fuels would be very expensive,

possibly depressing the advanced economies while being
beyond the reach of poorer nations.

(b) Similarly, we use throw-away chemical technology because
it is cheap: any replacement is likely to have reduced
economic efficiency.

(c) A tautological solution.

(d) The total cost *to society* of pollution is almost always higher
than the cost of prevention.

15. *Impact of Environment on Global Management*

(a) It is hard to see any unambiguous effect.

(b) Halting biocidal technology probably would not endear the
West to the nations that want it so badly, but it would
reduce the much more serious destabilizing threat of a
major eco-catastrophe.

(c) The "developing" nations are not likely to appreciate an
end to "development," no matter how lurid an example the
major polluters make of themselves.

(d) When one country's pollution threatens or destroys
another's livelihood, we can expect bitter recriminations
and perhaps even the first "pollution war."

16. *Impact of Natural Resources on Population*

(a & b) Neither increased exploitation nor modernization
should have much effect either way on population control
policies.

(c & d) Both restricted consumption and demodernization
should "help" the population problem, but only in the
unpleasant sense of reducing life span.

17. *Impact of Natural Resources on Food*

(a) Increased exploitation of resources would be a boon to
mechanized agriculture.

(b) "Modernization" would involve strict restraints on the use
of pesticides and artificial fertilizers.

(c) All three alternatives for increasing the food supply depend
heavily on capital investment which would be restricted by
limits on resource use.

(d) And demodernization of our resource-use pattern would
rule out any hope of feeding the "starving nations."

18. *Impact of Natural Resources on Environment*
    (a) Increased exploitation often means extraction from remote, dangerous, and/or fragile environments, with considerable risk to the local ecology (e.g., off-shore drilling at Santa Barbara, the Alaskan Pipeline).
    (b) In minimizing waste, a "modern" technology would also minimize pollution and environmental impact.
    (c) Limiting the resource input would at least keep down the quantity of the deleterious output.
    (d) Demodernization would be ecologically sound at premodern economic levels, but the cost to the environment in strip mining and air-pollution of just reverting to coal as our primary fuel at present demand levels would be extreme.

19. *Impact of Natural Resources on Economics*
    (a) Increased exploitation of resources would at first have a beneficial effect on distributing wealth globally. This would eventually be undermined as the increased costs of recovery make all labor less productive and, thus, all goods more expensive in human terms.
    (b) "Modernization" would increase costs in the short run, but is likely to prove more efficient in a number of respects in the long run.
    (c) Restricting resource use would not hurt the economic welfare if we only knew how to run an international economy without growth as an incentive. But we don't.
    (d) A reversion to pre-modern technologies would completely undercut the "productivity" on which the present economy rests.

20. *Impact of Natural Resources on Global Management*
    (a) The acute dependence of powerful industrial nations on poorer nations for critical resources conjures up visions of either neo-colonialism by the powerful or international blackmail by the resource owners.
    (b) Modernizing Western technologies would decrease the dependence/threat level while leaving some "old-fashioned" resources available for developing countries to use in a transitional period.

(c & d) Restricting resource use or abandoning modern technology entirely is unlikely to be popular in countries where the demand for increased material goods is very high.

21. *Impact of Economies on Population*
    (a) It is argued that continued growth is necessary for the poorer nations to reach the standard of living where birth control becomes feasible, but this ignores the fact that the material standard of living is not growing significantly in those countries; economic growth simply finances increased population levels instead.
    (b) The steady-state economy would, at the very least, eliminate one prop to continued population growth.
    (c) Limiting only the material economy would remove one support to growth while channelling economic resources into services such as education and family planning which enhance chances for population control.
    (d) Limiting goods only in the developed nations would retain the "channelling" effect but it would continue to provide material support for population growth.

22. *Impact of Economics on Food*
    (a) Continued economic growth finances vigorous capital investment in agriculture, (although the indirect effects via pollution might not be so helpful).
    (b) The steady-state economy would limit increases in agriculture as well as goods and services.
    (c & d) Limiting goods, only, might restrict supplies of tractors and fertilizer, but it would channel considerably more energy into the "services" of agriculture: weather prediction, soil testing, genetic development, cooperative marketing, pest-proof storage, and other applications of expertise to farming.

23. *Impact of Economics on Environment*
    (a) Other things being equal, continued economic growth will destroy the life-support capacity of the environment.
    (b, c, & d) All three remedies would at least limit the sheer quantity of effluent from the production of goods in the industrial nations.

24. *Impact of Economics on Natural Resources*
    (a) The conclusion for the input side of the economic machine is the same as for the output side: other things being equal, continued growth will exhaust the resources available.
    (b, c, & d) Again, all three strategies restrict the key element, consumption in the West.

25. *Impact of Economics on Global Management*
    (a) As long as there is the illusion of "progress," not even the poorest need despair.
    (b) Without growth the world becomes a zero-sum game, with dog-eat-dog strategies to match.
    (c) This is a little better, but not much; you can't eat advice.
    (d) Although this would restrict the flow of goods imported from the developed nations, it would hold out to the poor nations the real hope of catching up, while enabling them to conserve foreign exchange to buy Western technical services and expertise.

26. *Impact of Global Management on Population*
    (a) It is difficult to see how global population can be stabilized at reasonable levels with the current fragmented nation-state system.
    (b) In a gradualist scenario, international agencies would eventually gain the capacity for such control but given the long lags in population dynamics, it is likely to be a case of too little at first, and then too late.
    (c) The combined clout of the, presumably Western, proto-unionist combine might have some effect on population policy, but it is difficult to see how it could be much without being open to charges of blatant imperialism.
    (d) A federalist world government would at least possess the authority to set population standards: whether any *representative* world body would do so is another question.

27. *Impact of Global Management on Food*
    (a) Although cold-war tensions may spur aid in grain, tractors, and experts to particular key or client states, effective global and long-range solutions to the problems of feeding

the planet seem unlikely under the fragmented nation-state system.

(b) In a gradualist sequence much more aid would be switched from unilateral to international-agency channels. Although such international agencies would be unlikely to develop the clout to "solve" these problems, they could begin thinking globally and, at the very least, try to remove hunger from the realm of international power brokering.

(c) In a unionist pattern, the capability and willingness to deal with problems globally might develop considerably faster, but it is clear that the first obligation of the Union would be to feed its own members. (In a hungry world, this might, in fact, be a considerable incentive for joining the Union.)

(d) A federalist government — or any other true world government — would at least have the capacity to deal with agriculture as a global problem and to generate the resources to finance and enforce whatever strategies are decided on.

28. *Impact of Global Management on Environment*
(a) This is a classic case of the "commons" — a resource owned in common (the earth's air and waters) but with unrestricted use by individuals (nations) — and, as Garrett Hardin has shown us, this leads progressively and inevitably to tragedy if it is allowed to continue.

(b) In a gradualist scenario, international agencies would grow up to police the commons; whether they would do so in time, with sufficient strength to avoid disaster, is an open question: we simply don't know the capacity for abuse of the environment.

(c) Since a unionist movement would most likely begin with the Western nations, it would contain within itself at a fairly early date both the principal culprits and the principal victims of environmental disruption and thus be able to effect adequate solutions to the major problems without waiting on the rest of the globe.

(d) While a federalist world government would possess the capacity to solve environmental problems, it would almost certainly be dominated by nations for whom food production and increased standard of living take precedence over environmental concerns.

29. *Impact of Global Management on Natural Resources*
    (a) Not only are the resources for research and action
        fragmented in a nation-state system, the exploiter also
        gains a considerable short- and medium-term competitive
        advantage over the nation which invests in research on
        solutions. (E.g., if one nation conducts a crash program
        to develop and install a complete fusion energy system, it
        would drastically cut world demand for fossil fuels,
        bringing down prices and extending useful lifetime. A
        competing nation would save three ways: the costs of the re-
        search, the costs of a crash conversion program, and the
        high costs for conventional fuels which they would other-
        wise have had to pay.) Still, the cold war and the military
        significance of the resource shortage might supply
        considerable incentive in solving these problems.
    (b) It is hard to see how international agencies, even if some-
        what stronger than today, could have much influence on
        the resource problem, although international cooperation
        on fusion research has shown potential for cooperative
        solutions.
    (c) This case could go either way. A nascent world union
        consisting of the developed nations could bring tremendous
        combined technical and financial resources to bear on
        solving the problems of shortage, but it would also con-
        stitute a fearsome capacity for neo-imperial exploitation.
        On balance, the Union would probably use its power to
        fill its short-term needs.
    (d) Once again, the capacity is present; it would only be a
        question of whether a representative global government
        would rate resources very high against seemingly more
        urgent short-term problems.

30. *Impact of Global Management on Economics*
    (a) The international monetary system manages to keep
        tottering along, but it is both wasteful and unlikely to
        effect any fundamental reform while nations compete
        economically against nations.
    (b) A strengthened world bank, complete substitution of inter-
        national drawing rights ("paper gold") for gold as a
        monetary standard, continued negotiated reductions of

tariffs and a rapid increase in the proliferation of multi-national corporations — all of these would effectively diminish the economic sovereignty of nations and their real capacity to wage economic warfare on each other, while greatly increasing the economic efficiency of the whole system.

(c) Political union implies some kind of rationalization of economic alignment. While this would benefit Union members it would also place non-Union members at more of a competitive disadvantage (of course, this would be one of the incentives for continued growth of the Union).

(d) All solutions to the problems of economic stabilization and equity of distribution probably depend on the actual development of effective world government; the Federalist path would be the fastest route to a world government in the near future (say the next one-half century) of the possibilities considered here.

NOTES

175. On the identification of problem areas, see: Chase, *The Most Probable World* [23]; Ehrlich and Ehrlich, *Population, Resources, Environment* [124]; Ehrlich and Harriman, *How to be a Survivor* [121]; Meadows, *et al.*, *The Limits to Growth* [195]; Boulding, *The Meaning of the Twentieth Century* [19]; and Scott, *Teaching for a Change* [73]. Naturally, these different authors do not break down the global threats to our survival in precisely the same way, but all refer to problems that can be discussed meaningfully under these six headings.

176. I am indebted to Willis Harman and his staff at the Educational Policy Research Center for the term "macro-problem." (See Harman, Markley, and Rhyne, "The Forecasting of Plausible Alternative Future Histories.") [7]

177. Exercise 23 is a watered-down, non-quantitative version of the cross-impact matrix technique, which involves repeated solutions of sets of quadratic equations in an iterative process, usually on a

computer. For details, see pages 41 to 43 of *The Potential of Educational Futures*, edited by Marien and Ziegler [65], or Selwyn Enzer's paper on "Delphi and Cross-Impact Techniques" in *Search for Alternatives*, edited by Franklin Tugwell. [15]

179-188. The descriptions of the problem areas are an attempt at an organized synthesis of a wide range of materials, nearly all of which are included in Sections II, VI, and VII of the bibliography. Most of the general background can be found in: Chase, *The Most Probable World* [23]; Ehrlich and Ehrlich, *Population, Resources, Environment* [124]; Meadows, *et al.*, *The Limits to Growth* [105]; and Hardin's essay, "Tragedy of the Commons," in *Environment: Readings for Teachers*, edited by George Ivany. [62]

179. The phrase "Red Queen's race" refers to a famous passage in *Through the Looking Glass*, by Lewis Carroll:

> [Alice and the Red Queen have been running furiously until finally Alice collapses, out of breath.]
> Alice looked round her in great surprise. "Why, I do believe we've been under this tree the whole time! Everything's just as it was!"
> "Of course it is," said the Queen. "What would you have it?"
> "Well, in *our* country," said Alice, still panting a little, "you'd generally get to somewhere else — if you ran very fast for a long time as we've been doing."
> "A slow sort of country!" said the Queen. "Now, *here*, you see, it takes all the running *you* can do, to keep in the same place. If you want to get somewhere else, you must run at least twice as fast as that." (Gardner, *The Annotated Alice*, p. 210.) [306]

180. Hardin discusses the gender selection possibility in *Exploring New Ethics for Survival.* [130]

180. Albert Rosenfeld, the science editor of Saturday Review/World indicates that current techniques for gender selection are between 80 and 85% accurate. (Rosenfeld, "If Oedipus' Parents Had Only Known," *Saturday Review/World*, September 7, 1974, pp. 49 and 52.) [148] See also "Boy or Girl?" by Alan L. Otten, on the

editorial page of the *Wall Street Journal* for June 20, 1974. [140]

180. The figures on the stabilization of India's population are from the results of a computer simulation I conducted in 1972. The simulation was run under several different sets of assumptions, and the figures given (a ratio of 37:63, female to male, producing stability in 65 years) are based on what I felt to be the "best" set of assumptions.

The most important of these assumptions is that there would be a synergistic effect between gender selection and birth control. If we assume (for some societies) that the principal reason for having children is to have sons to work the farm and support the parents in their old age, then it would seem reasonable that such parents would be more open to the idea of birth control after they have had three or four sons (two of whom are likely to survive); this does, in fact, correspond with the experiences in many agricultural peasant societies. With a 50:50 birth ratio, this means an average of 6 to 8 births before the couple is willing to consider birth control. With gender selection, a typical family can have 3 boys out of four children, and may be willing to stop there. Thus, gender selection is likely to make birth control more attractive and more effective in patrilocal peasant societies.

Gender selection, if implemented, would produce some fairly exotic effects on the social structure, one of which — the effect on the role of women — is perhaps worth special comment. The impact of any abrupt social change depends a great deal, of course, on a whole host of factors in the existing society, but we can guess that a shortage of women would tend to push the position of women fairly strongly in one of two directions.

If the present situation is such that a young woman has a great deal of say over who she will marry, or at least the right to refuse to marry, then she has control over what would be a scarce and extremely valuable resource — herself — and she can exploit that control to greatly increase her power and improve her position in the society. If, on the other hand, arranged marriages are common, then her *parents* control a scarce resource and will try to tighten their control over her, thus worsening her position in society.

However, societies in which a young woman can be compelled to marry as her parents direct are becoming increasingly rare, so the general effect of gender selection would be to enhance the status of women, not worsen it. (Furthermore, gender selection would not work for long in a society in which the parents can compel their daughter to marry at their direction, because female children would quickly become valuable *to the parents*, causing the birth ratio to swing back too fast.)

180. For more on the "green revolution," see especially *The Closing Circle,* by Barry Commoner. [118]

182-186. Section VI of the bibliography is devoted to "Economics and Environment: The Growth Debate."

190-201. The comments on the matrix entries have been edited and condensed, but are otherwise unchanged. Prior to working on the matrix, the class had read Ehrlich and Ehrlich, *Population, Resources, Environment* [124], and Chase, *The Most Probable World.* [23] An excellent follow-up to this exercise is *The Limits to Growth* [105], by Meadows, *et al.*, which deals with the interaction among these issues. Students may be especially interested in comparing their own conclusions with the policy recommendations at the end of *Limits.*

CHAPTER X
Society and Foresight

In the first part of chapter one, we discussed some of the reasons why the continued stability and survival of our society increasingly depends upon long-range, anticipatory kinds of policy and decision making. The world has become so complex and the costs of failure so high, that we can no longer afford a short-sighted or reactive approach to problems. The United States will have to play a leading role in dealing with the issues which threaten the survival of world civilization. Coping with these global issues will inevitably create internal problems in the U.S., which will also have to be managed. For example, any move toward world-wide pollution controls, or limitations on industrial development, or any form of world government would have major impacts on American society.

In addition to the internal impact of these global issues, we face a growing list of domestic problems, some of which are unique to the U.S. and some of which we share with other industrialized nations. Indeed, our social agenda is over-crowded. Some of the older issues which are still with us and seem likely to persist are: racial inequalities, inadequate housing, a chaotic transportation system, the increasing unmanageability of our cities, persistent high levels of crime, poverty, unemployment, and inflation, a cumbersome and inequitable tax system, and an increasingly over-burdened educational system. Some of the science-related problems which will be of increasing importance are: shortages of energy and natural resources, increasing pressure on the natural environment, the need for social control of new technologies, the ethical issues posed by the "biological revolution" (psycho-active drugs, genetic engineering, test-tube babies, etc.), and the threat to privacy from electronic surveillance and computerization. In addition, we have some relatively new social issues which are complicating matters still further: growing dissatisfaction with older social goals and definitions of the quality of life, a proliferation of changing life-styles, increased political polarization, and high levels of alienation among the young.

Though certainly not complete, this is still a pretty awesome list. Nevertheless, these are all issues that can be dealt with *if* we can generate the political will to establish the necessary long-range programs, instead of expecting instant results from easy answers. There will be no quick or easy answers because — as with the global survival problems — these issues are all interrelated; the immediate causes of each are largely to be found among the consequences of the others. Foresight, patience, and a shared sense of purpose will be the keys to managing successfully.

But will we manage successfully? It is by no means certain that we will, since it is precisely our lack of these key attributes in the past which has created this swollen social agenda. Lack of foresight, particularly, is the problem which underlies all the rest. Our ability to cope with the future will depend in large part on what we do to create a more forethoughtful citizenry.

Once again, this chapter consists primarily of a single, long exercise. In this case, it is a group research project focused on this crucial underlying problem of lack of foresight, its origins and the ways it is built into our system. The project requires nine or ten hours of class time and considerable outside work, spread over two to three months. By its completion, students should have gained an increased understanding of our society as a functioning (and sometimes malfunctioning) *system*. They should also have gained some valuable experience in research and have a chance to feel real pride in the outcome.

EXERCISE 24: *Society and Foresight*

Procedure: Begin by discussing with students the history of some of the persistent problems in American life for which we have

generally failed to come up with satisfactory long-term solutions
(e.g., land use, housing, and transportation; city-management,
crime, poverty, and unemployment; energy, ecology, and
economics). In each case, policy has consistently been oriented
towards short-term benefits and quick solutions until and unless
the long-term problem reached a crisis point. (See Appendix C for
appropriate source material.)

Explain to the students that the class is going to undertake a
research project into the reasons why this pattern of shortsightedness exists, and what might be done about it. Begin the first
part of the project by distributing copies of page 208 to the class
and going over it with them, using the discussion which follows as a
guide.

After a chance for some discussion of each of the areas, divide the
class into seven research teams. One team is to research and write
the introduction and, later, edit the whole report. Each of the
remaining six teams is to thoroughly research and document (or
refute) the reasons for shortsightedness listed under one of the six
major areas and any other reasons related to that area which they
can discover. Each group should then prepare a written report on
its subject. (You may wish to use an approximate guideline of five
pages per student.) A draft of the report is to be submitted to you
for a quick editorial check, and then typed directly onto ditto-
masters. If possible, have the students themselves run off and
collate enough copies for each member of the class.

Schedule a separate class for the discussion of each area. Begin
with a brief oral presentation by the students on that research team.
Then throw it open for questions and a general discussion. When
the students have a good grasp of the background in that area, ask
the research team and the other students for their ideas on what
might be done to alleviate the situation.

In this discussion of possible remedies, try to guide the students
to be alert for damaging side-effects of their suggestions. If you
have previously done the matrix on global survival (chapter nine),
you can use that as an example of what you mean. Warn them
particularly about "remedies" which throw out what is good along
with what is bad. (For example, frequent elections may contribute
to short-sighted politics, but they are important for other reasons;
this is one instance where "symptomatic relief" is probably better
than a "cure of the underlying cause.") The research team for each

24 REASONS WHY WE LACK FORESIGHT[1]

POLITICS:

- Two- to six-year terms of office.
- Lack of public demand (or even tolerance) for anticipatory action.
- Tendency to praise or blame incumbent for situations his predecessor created.
- Vicious circle from lack of foresight--"the perpetual double bind."

ECONOMICS:

- Inability of market to function with very long reaction-times.
- "Discounted future values"--interest rates dominate social foresight.
- Paper economics applied to perishable real resources.
- "External" costs minimize true long-term costs.

FORECASTING ABILITY:

- Increasingly rapid change, thus increased difficulty (and necessity) of forecasting.
- Primitive methods.
- Scarcity of funding and of trained forecasters.

HISTORY/IDEOLOGY:

- Long period with the wealth and physical space to absorb mistakes.
- Faith in the inevitability of "progress."
- Patriotic belief that "the American system" is so good that it is self-guiding (or divinely guided).
- Fatalism (from religion, apathy, or felt impotence) and "presentism"-- live each day one day at a time.
- Withdrawal from future shock.
- Collapse of a shared sense of national purpose.

THE MEDIA:

- Lack of conceptual sophistication about the future.
- Lack of means for (and interest in) judging scientific competence.
- "Orthodoxy of optimism," derisive attitude toward those who warn of problems.

EDUCATION:

- Historical orientation toward the past.
- Traditional and glacially unresponsive bureaucracy.
- Built-in 10- to 50-year lag-time.
- Lack of recognition by parents and educators of the need for anticipation in a rapidly changing society.

---

[1]See pages 211 – 221 for discussion of each item.

topic is then responsible for preparing a shorter report on the remedies they would recommend, based on the class discussion and the team's own research.

The team that prepared the introduction will not, of course, have a report on recommendations to prepare; instead, they become the editorial committee for the whole group project. (They should be chosen, to begin with, for their writing and editing ability.) Their task is to take the seven original research reports and the six sets of recommendations and turn the entire thing into a readable short book. Have them prepare a title page for the whole book and for each chapter, with the names of each of the contributors clearly displayed, and in general do whatever can be done to encourage pride of authorship. (One way would be to write the preface yourself, and have them include your name in the list of authors on the cover.) If at all possible, find some way to get it published, even if just in a mimeographed edition for the school community.

Discussion: WHY WE LACK FORESIGHT

We are a very improvident nation — not always, nor in every area, but often enough to make it a conspicuous national habit. The American voter is a notoriously present-oriented individual; there is still ample wry truth in two of the oldest gag lines in politics: "Yes, but what have you done for me lately?" and "What has posterity ever done for me?" Businessmen are not much better; anything beyond 12 months is defined as "long-term," and *very* long-range forecasting — i.e., five to ten years — is considered to be "blue-skying," and not completely respectable. And (except for enrollment forecasts) education pays virtually no attention to the future — long-term or short-term.

In some cases, we have even grown so used to such behavior that it seems natural and proper. An example is our health care system, devoted almost exclusively to treatment of disease, even though preventive medicine is known to cost far less in dollars and human suffering. When we get sick, we want the doctors to make us well, but it rarely occurs to us to blame them (or ourselves) for the onset of the disease. The normal case, however, is for us to simply ignore a problem unti it turns into a crisis, and then to wish that we had taken preventive action earlier.

Perhaps it is misleading to say that we lack foresight. In many instances, such as the recent energy crisis, we have had ample evidence about the nature of the problem and the need for preventive measures for a surprisingly long time before the crisis was reached. The *crisis* comes because we refuse to believe or act on such advance information.

Why do we so often fail to look ahead? Why, even when we do look ahead, do we so often continue to act in a short-sighted manner? These questions are real, not just rhetorical. We act the way we do, not out of stupidity or moral defect, but because our traditions and our institutions encourage and support a more short-term, reactive approach. Nor is this completely without reason or merit. In many areas of our economic, social, and political life, we are a highly flexible and fast-reacting people. Historically, we have been able (with some important exceptions, like the Depression) to use our reactive ability as a substitute for foresight and anticipation. Costly though it was, we could afford to wait for a Pearl Harbor before mobilizing because our capacity to *react* was so large.

Unfortunately, we are facing a growing number of problems as the rate of change increases, and as we build our technological castles higher and more intricately, we are increasingly unable and unwilling to endure the crisis culmination of each problem. We are also less able to command instant solutions even when we mobilize our very considerable resources. It is one thing to throw dollars into a disaster-stricken town and expect it to be on its feet in a year; it is quite another to throw dollars into fusion research and expect to have fusion reactors going in a year or even in a decade. As problems become more technically complex, we can no longer count on getting immediate results, no matter how much we are willing to spend.

If we are going to generate the kinds of foresightful policies that will anticipate and avoid (or at least minimize) potential crises, we need to understand the social and traditional forces that work *against* foresight and anticipation. What follows is a look at six main areas of society and the roles they play in institutionalizing a reactive and past-oriented approach. The six areas are:

- Politics
- Economics
- Forecasting ability
- History/ideology
- Media
- Education

Several contributing factors are examined in each area.

Politics

The American political system has shortsightedness built right into its bones. We intend that our politicians be accountable to the people, and we try to achieve this by having them stand for re-election every two, four, or six years. The price we pay is that the *average* amount of foresight we can expect from them is 1, 2, or 3 years, because a politician can seldom afford to look beyond the next election. This is made even worse if the voters are very short-sighted (and have even shorter memories).

Take the case of the 1972 presidential election. The preceding four years were characterized by generally high rates of inflation and a recession. Highly inflationary policies were introduced in 1971 and 1972 to stimulate an economic recovery and boom during the summer and fall of 1972. To counterbalance the excess inflationary pressures, the government instituted wage and price controls in the summer of 1971, despite the evidence that such controls tend only to postpone the inflation, distorting the economy and producing a much higher rate of inflation when they are lifted.

Inflation was running at a "politically unacceptable" rate of $4\frac{1}{2}\%$ when controls were instituted; when they were lifted, six months *after* the election, inflation promptly soared to more than 10%, accompanied by persistent economic stagnation. In spite of all this, the public in 1972 rated Richard Nixon's handling of the economy very favorably, and this is believed to have contributed significantly to his landslide re-election. A small bubble of economic euphoria, timed exactly right for the campaign months, counted for far more than all of the preceding and following years of economic distress.

Another implication of this narrow time perspective of voters is that politicians are often unfairly blamed or credited for the results of their predecessors' actions. (It might be unfair to blame Richard Nixon for that first recession in 1970; it is certainly unfair to give him credit for the Apollo moon landings, although he got considerable political mileage out of them.) The result is that a political leader in office has a strong incentive to take credit for whatever long-term programs were financed and set into motion five, ten, or twenty years ago by his predecessors; at the same time, he has an incentive to keep taxes down and to spend money where there will be short-term benefits, rather than instituting and funding the long-term programs which we will need later. *He* will not pay the price, of course; his successor will.

This kind of approach can rapidly initiate a downward spiral, a "perpetual double-bind." An ounce of prevention is really worth a pound of cure. If a politician finds that all of his political and economic resources are exhausted in patching up the crises which his predecessor failed to prevent, he will have none left over to prevent current problems from becoming crises for his successor. His successor will then have to spend resources "by the pound" for cure, with no "ounces" left for prevention, thus perpetuating the cycle.

When immediate wants are pursued to the exclusion of long-term necessities, the efficiency of the whole system declines until eventually even the immediate wants cannot be met. Yet, with politicians forced to scramble to please a short-sighted populace, it often seems that the political system itself makes this trap almost impossible to avoid.

Economics

Like our government, our economic system is short-sighted because it is built that way. Take the whole system of prices and markets, the foundation of our economy. The basic assumption is that the market responds quickly to disparities between supply and demand. If demand exceeds supply, the price goes up, reducing the demand and increasing profits. This draws new producers and new resources back into the market, which increases the supply and drives the price back down again. If the supply increases too far and exceeds the demand, this drives the price down further, which drives some capital and resources out of the market, which reduces the amount of supply, which drives the price back up again. If the product is a necessity, a small shortage may produce a big increase in prices and, therefore, "windfall profits," but these high prices are also a big incentive to increase production rapidly, which is to society's benefit if the product is truly a necessity.

Unfortunately, this theoretical model makes little sense in a situation (like energy) where it may take five to ten years, or more, to increase production by a significant amount. The little up and down wiggles of the market are supposed to take place over periods of weeks or months, not decades. As we saw in chapter eight, it is as if the thermostat in your house took temperature readings only every six months. If it turns the furnace on in February, you're going to be awfully hot in July, and if it turns it off in August, you're going to be frozen out by January. In other words, a system that works perfectly well with one reaction time may be worse than useless with another, and this is happening to our economic system.

Energy is a good example. Up through the 1960's, there was a relative surplus of energy available, which would have produced very low prices if the government had not systematically intervened to discourage imports and new refinery capacity. As had been forecasted in considerable detail, this government policy combined with soaring demand, depletion of the most accessible supplies, and a tacit industry conspiracy, to produce a major energy shortage. (We should keep in mind, incidentally, that the Arab oil boycott of 1973-74 occurred because we were *already* experiencing a shortage; had we not made ourselves vulnerable, the boycott would have been pointless.) The result of the shortage, and of the vulnerability to foreign blackmail which it produced, was a strong demand for a crash program to achieve energy self-sufficiency. Yet, even with all the capital resources of the energy industry, and huge government subsidies to boot, most experts believe that President Nixon's goal of 7 years (1974-1980) to relieve the shortage and achieve energy self-sufficiency was wildly optimistic. It just takes longer than that to do the necessary exploration and research and to build the necessary facilities. In the meantime, prices stay high, the country remains vulnerable, and the public suffers.

Even when the demand is there, the market may not invest the necessary funds to increase production. In the first place, the longer the delay, the greater the chance that something will go wrong and thus the greater the risk of the investment. In the second place, the value of an investment depends not just on the expected profits, but on the amount of time that you must wait for those profits to be realized and on the interest rates during the intervening period.

Suppose I offer you a piece of paper promising to pay you $1,000 ten years from now. How much would you be willing to pay me for that paper today? At the moment, you can get a safe 7% return on your money in a long-term investment, and it happens that $500 invested at 7% will be worth about $1,000 in ten years (see chapter four). So, provided you don't think there is any risk in accepting it, my IOU for $1,000 ten years from now would be worth $500 to you right now. Businessmen go through a process like this to determine the *present* — or discounted — value of any *future* benefit. As a result, other things being equal, people have a strong incentive to invest in short-term projects instead of long-term projects.

Furthermore, what happens when we apply this kind of thinking to perishable resources like land, instead of replaceable items like factories? Let's say that you own some land with valuable timber on it, and you are faced with two choices: You can cut down all of the timber (called "clear-cutting") and sell it for two million dollars, after which the topsoil will erode away and the land will be worthless for timber-growing. Or you can cut down half the timber and sell it for one million dollars, and then in 20 years you can cut down half the timber again and sell it for 2 million this time (because of inflation), and in 20 more years you can cut down half of the timber and sell it for four million, and so on. Ignoring the sale value of the cleared land in the first case, and the first million dollars that you get in either case, which is worth more to you in the long run?

If you clear-cut the land, you can take your second million dollars and invest it at 10% interest, and your money will double every 7 years. (That's risky, but so is the other choice; your timber might be destroyed by forest fire or blight.) You would have two million dollars in seven years, four million dollars in fourteen years, and nearly eight million dollars in 20 years, compared with the 2 million dollars for the timber you might have sold under a conservation policy or the three million dollars you might have realized by clear-cutting the whole stand at the end of 20 years.[1] The disparity between the two choices grows wider and wider, the longer you extend the comparison.

| Year | CONSERVATION POLICY | | | CLEARCUTTING |
	Income	Interest	Total	Total
1 :	–	–	–*	$ 1 million*
21 :	$2 million	–	$ 2 million	$ 8 million
41 :	$4 million	$ 14 million	$ 20 million	$ 64 million
61 :	$8 million	$140 million	$168 million	$512 million

*Omitting $1 million in each case. The assumptions behind the table are that inflation is 3½% per year, and that 10% per year is a "normal" return on capital. Both rates are typical for the period since World War II, although they are not representative for the years 1973-1975. Note that even under a conservation policy most of the earnings come from interest.

---

[1] You get three million, not four, because half your trees are only half-grown.

"Obviously," the only sane thing for you to do is to clear-cut the land. Just as obviously, this kind of economics produces a nation without forests. The same dilemma faces the rancher trying to decide whether or not to overgraze his land, and the farmer trying to decide whether to practice expensive soil-conservation methods (or, for that matter, whether to say to heck with it and turn the farm into a sub-division).

There is an important and ironic corollary to this, which is that the more prosperous a society becomes (i.e., the higher the rate of real economic growth), the more short-sighted it becomes. Of course, the more shortsighted it is, the more it tends to destroy irreplaceable resources like land. The more basic resources it destroys, the more difficult it becomes to maintain the high growth rate, and eventually the economy shifts from rich-and-foolish back to poor-and-"wise," with a high value on perishable resources.

The shortsightedness of our economic system is further aggravated by what are known as "external costs." This is a polite euphemism that economists use when the public is forced to pay part of the cost of producing something while an individual or company retains all of the profits. For example, the pollution spewing out of a steel mill may triple the costs for clothing and laundry in the surrounding town. The pollution will also have an effect on the health of the townspeople and increase the bills for medical care not just in the present, but sometimes for many decades into the future. These costs of making steel are, of course, paid by the townspeople, not by the steel company. The same is true whenever the public pays for what, by rights, only the company and its customers should pay.

Since most of the costs which companies are successful in pushing off onto the public — especially the damage to health and to the environment — are long-term costs, this tends to further unbalance the relationship between short-term profit and long-term cost, making us even more short-sighted. In the previous discussion of timber land, for instance, the immediate profits of clear-cutting are compared with the long-term costs *to the owner* of foregoing future value from that forest. The comparison might be a little closer if the owner had to consider not only the value of the trees that will not be grown on it, but the value *to the public* of the streams that are polluted, the beauty that is destroyed, the species that are wiped out, and the supply of resources which is destroyed and denied to our children. It may be hard to state the values of these things in dollars, and it may be even harder to discount these values to find out what they are worth to us now, but without some way to internalize these costs, our economic system will continue to be automatically shortsighted.

Forecasting Ability

Another important reason why we lack foresight as a society is that foresight is becoming harder and harder to achieve. The higher the rate of change, the more new problems we have to cope with and the more we need to try to anticipate the future; at the same time, the higher the rate of change, the more inundated we are by unanticipated events and consequences, and the more difficult it becomes to anticipate anything (except the continued dislocations of change). The new discipline of "futuristics" has developed a number of new techniques for long-range social and technological forecasting, but these new methods have only barely offset the increasing volatility and "crisis-density" of our society. Like Alice and the Red Queen in *Through the Looking Glass*, we have to run harder and harder just to keep from falling behind. But for the layman — which includes the man in the street and most politicians, administrators, and businessmen — things have not stayed even, they have become continually less predictable; the result is an accelerating case of future shock.

Even the professional futurists have no claim to a crystal ball. The field is very new, the methods are still somewhat primitive and only partially validated, and a tremendous amount of work needs to be done, both to develop the methods and to apply them to the whole breadth of social issues. Unfortunately, for the reasons discussed above under "Politics" and "Economics," both government and business in the United States are relatively uninterested in the long-term future. Therefore, only a trickle of funding is invested in the development of forecasting abilities. This shortage of funding for basic research in forecasting, coupled with the newness of the field, means that there is also a severe shortage of people trained in forecasting. Most futurists are trained in some specialty and then branch out into applied forecasting, often on a part-time basis. As a result, the field as a whole loses both the research they would have done as students if they had trained in forecasting originally, and the basic research they would do if futuristics were their primary professional allegiance.

History/Ideology

Even where we have the ability to understand the future and anticipate future problems successfully, we tend as a nation not to be interested in making the effort to do so. The origins of this attitude are tangled up in our national history. For a long, long time we had sufficient surpluses to make up for misuse and the absence of planning. The total lack of a land-use policy, for instance, doesn't matter very much when there are billions of acres of unclaimed and unsettled land.

This long history of wealth and growth has greatly enhanced an ideological commitment to shortsightedness that is partly a fervent belief in the inevitability of "progress," especially economic and technological progress, and partly an equally fervent faith in the unguided wisdom of "the American system." The former — the notion that more technology means a better life — is finally being called into question. The latter is a sort of societal version of Adam Smith's "invisible hand," a belief that thousands upon thousands of short-term decisions made from personal self-interest will automatically add up to the best long-range policy for the group. As we saw in the discussion of "Politics" and "Economics" above, there are excellent reasons for thinking that exactly the opposite is true.

We have also inherited a strong strain of philosophical and religious fatalism and "presentism." Christianity has always had a basic, though sometimes played down, belief that the mortal world is unimportant except as preparation for the afterlife; the implication is that the only future that has any bearing on present actions is a future that lies after death, not the more immediate future here on earth.

Nor is this kind of passivity confined to Christianity. The poor and the powerless everywhere have tended to console themselves with a belief in a predetermined and unknowable, and therefore irrelevant, future: "Que sera, sera; what will be, will be." "Why should I worry about what I can't change? I just take it as it comes." "You just take care of today, and let tomorrow take care of itself." "I trust in the Lord, and accept whatever the future brings." "I'm like Job, I don't question what's the will of God." Such beliefs are an important psychological defense against unnecessary anxiety, frustration, and rage — but when fatalism becomes an article of faith, preached to all as moral and "true," it can reduce people's ability to change what *can* be changed.

Although we may have inherited a belief that if we take care of today, tomorrow will take care of itself, we have two additional reasons for lack of interest in the future which are quite modern. The first is that many people faced with overwhelming future shock cope with it by withdrawal: "Ah, who cares? I don't want to hear about it." The second is the pervasive feeling that we have lost any collective sense of national goals or national purpose. It is quite true that if you don't know where you're going, any road will take you there. Without a positive sense of our objectives, we are forced to fall back on the purely negative strategy of trying to avoid crises and disasters. The lack of coordination of our decisions which results is wasteful and (literally) pointless.

Media/Press

The fourth major reason for our lack of foresight as a society is the peculiar attitude towards the future, and the general incompetence in dealing with it, that have been displayed by the information media. Among other things, some parts of the media, particularly television, are not very good at coping with complex issues, and consideration of the future is seldom simple.

This is exacerbated by the fact that most newsmen have not grasped the fundamental distinction between a forecast and a prediction. In chapter three, we shared the tribulations of a hypothetical Professor Farsight, whose highly conditional forecast was turned into a flat prediction in a newspaper headline. The practice, however, is not hypothetical at all, but very widespread. One recent book (*The Limits to Growth*, by Donella Meadows, *et al.*) has been the victim of hundreds of cases of this kind of distortion. In the book the authors carefully and systematically lay out a number of alternative forecasts, some of which are based on policies which lead to disaster, and some of which are based on policies which lead to a relatively happy "equilibrium" world. The book was widely discussed in the press, and, in spite of the authors' repeated and emphatic statements to the contrary, nearly every columnist and TV commentator described the book as predicting inevitable disaster.

To complicate matters still further, most reporters, like most

Americans, have no basis for judging competence in the worlds of science and academia, so that when, for example, the National Academy of Sciences says that we are running out of oil, and the head geologist of Texaco says that there is plenty of oil, the newsman tends to report, "Scientists disagree about how much oil is available." In any case, newsworthiness is always treated as more important than competence, with sometimes bizarre distortions of the quality of information reaching the public.

Another related way in which the media contribute to the problem is the orthodoxy of optimism, which leads them to deride all who warn of potential difficulties as "doomsayers" or, even more idiotically, "doom-mongers!" It would hardly be original to point out that attacking those who warn of danger does not prevent disasters; instead, it prevents one from hearing about potential disasters in time to avoid them or prepare to cope with them. The point seems, however, to have escaped the notice of many Americans and most newsmen.

Education

The sixth, and in some ways the most important, source of our national myopia is our educational system. Historically, schools have been assigned a highly conservative role in society. Education is the guardian of continuity. Traditionally, its job has been to insure that the new generation resembles the old sufficiently for the existing institutions, social arrangements, and methods for handling people to continue to work.

Not surprisingly, the administration and management of education attracted people in psychological sympathy with the fundamentally conservative role of education. The result, over several centuries, has been a traditional and glacially unresponsive bureaucracy. But, in times of rapid change, "continuity" requires a fundamentally different approach. It can only be achieved by schools that not only keep up with change, but manage to anticipate it by at least some part of the lifetime of their students.

The depth of this bias toward the past is demonstrated very nicely in a recent (and otherwise admirable) article in *Educational Leadership* entitled, "What is Relevant for Today's Students?" The author, Galen Saylor, is a professor of Education at the University of Nebraska and a widely respected expert on curriculum development. In the article, he argues very cogently for changes in the content of the curriculum and in the manner of teaching it, reforms which he believes will make education more relevant to "today." Outside of the classroom, however, he is opposed to any significant change in the *structure* of education:

> One final point about what is relevant in today's schools. The school as an institution has three primary functions: (a) to contribute in significant ways to the transmission of the culture of our society; (b) to serve as a major agency in the socialization of the young; and (c) to contribute fully to the maximum development of each student. Most of us feel that our schools have not adequately fulfilled these essential functions in the past. But such inadequacies do not call for or justify demands that the school as an institution be radically uprooted, become merely one of many voluntary agencies for the schooling of the young, or serve simply as a vehicle for the radical reform of society.

Ignoring the exaggerated language in the last sentence, this is essentially a statement of conventional, past-oriented objectives, a concession that schools have failed to achieve them, and a denial that this failure warrants any "radical" change in education as an institution. One is forced to wonder why. Are the failures of education entirely the fault of teachers and not at all due to the structure of the institution? It seems an unlikely notion. Even if it were true, and a single set of reforms could correct the situation now, new situations would soon require new reforms. At some point it becomes more efficient to reform ("radically uproot"?) the institution itself to make it better able to anticipate and cope with change.

Saylor's straw men illustrate, however, an important dilemma facing any would-be educational reformer. If a school attempts to prepare students to cope with change, it is seen as *advocating* change and can expect to be roundly denounced for its "radicalism." Even the educational reformer tends to aim at bringing the schools "up-to-date," making them relevant to the present, without realizing that the structure of education makes this inadequate. We educate a child and expect him to use that education during the adult life which follows. This means an average delay of 30 years, from the middle of the education period to the middle of the adult life span. This time lag makes a mockery of our "current events" courses and other attempts to be very modern in our curriculum: whether we teach about the past or the present, it will all be history to the student when he must make use of it as an adult.

If schools today are educating tomorrow's adults, it really seems self-evident that they should concern themselves seriously with tomorrow's world. Yet, until very recently, such consideration of the future was almost forbidden among professional educators. It is still looked on as somewhat radical and faintly improper. Saylor, for example, manages to get through an entire article on "what is relevant for today's students" without making more than a single, oblique reference to the future. Ironically, that same issue of *Educational Leadership* started off with an editorial by Vernon Smith on educational taboos, which concluded as follows:

> The future is both the most critical educational taboo and the ultimate social reality. In earlier societies the future was the realm of religion. The task of the schools was the transmission of the past to the children of the present. But in one generation the future moved from the metaphysical to the physical. Man found the power to determine his future absolutely — he can destroy himself and life on the earth as we know it. And he has a growing number of alternative ways to do so, thanks to science, industry, and technology.

> A society with alternative modes of self-destruction cannot leave its future to chance. A democratic society cannot put its future in the hands of the elected or the powerful, for the future is the responsibility of every man. The future of mankind must become the central concern of the curriculum. Education must help children to learn to control their futures: to plan, design, and select from among various alternative futures.

This is, indeed, what education must do. But it will not be able to do it until educators and the public become more willing to tolerate educational change, and until the institutional structure of education is overhauled to make educational change more possible.

The Other Side of the Coin

We have had a quick glance at some of the ways that short-sightedness is built into the American system. It would be wrong to overstate the case, however. There are also (thank heavens!) some pressures in the opposite direction. If we have inherited strong strains of fatalism, apathy, and blind optimism, we have also been influenced by a tradition of long-sighted Yankee shrewdness. "Que sera, sera," is counterbalanced by "a stitch in time saves nine" — not to mention the Boy Scout motto. In the past few years, moreover, we have lost quite a bit of our belief in the inevitability of progress and in the inevitable unguided wisdom of the system.

In politics, in particular, we have occasionally been blessed with men and women who care deeply about the future of the country and are able and willing to look beyond the next election. In fact, some cities and even whole states in the nation are remarkable for their "governability" and their long histories of good government. The two are reciprocal, of course; good government anticipates and prevents the kinds of crises, frustrations, and inequities that breed hostility and destroy the basic sense of legitimacy and social cohesion that makes good government possible. As long as each successive mayor or governor makes most of the needed "stitches" in time, it is possible for such a tradition to endure for a considerable period. (It is not always the politicians who break faith, either. In some cases the public goes on a spree of irresponsibility, living off the efforts of the past and refusing to finance the necessities of the future.)

In education, the saving grace is that people learn and remember best what seems most important to them. Thus, if only one twentieth of schooling seems relevant to a student, he will probably remember that small part better than all the rest put together. Furthermore, the troubled state of both education and society has led a growing number of teachers and administrators to the conviction that education must abandon its preoccupation with the past and begin preparing students for the future. Their efforts, supported by intense student interest, are beginning to affect the educational structure and will begin to affect the general public as their students grow older.

And learning, of course, doesn't end with school. Education of the public can seem terribly slow and difficult for those attempting to bring it about, but it is heartening to consider the large number of adult Americans who have educated themselves about the environment just in the last decade.

Furthermore, there are signs that the public is becoming fed up with a reactive style of management and the continuing string of crises that it entails. The energy crisis, continued galloping inflation, the steady decay of our big cities, the sometimes disastrous effects of unchecked technology, and a growing awareness of the threats to our survival — all of these have contributed to a greater willingness on the part of the public to consider some basic long-range changes. If this is so, and some group or political leader can offer the public a convincing and fore-thoughtful vision of what ought to be done, then it seems possible that we may yet regain a sense of perspective and long-range national purpose.

It is a goal worth achieving. As C.P. Snow has put it:

> The world's greatest need is an appetite for the future.
> . . . All healthy societies are ready to sacrifice the existential moment for their children's future and for children after these. A sense of the future is behind all good policy. Unless we have it, we can give nothing either wise or decent to the world.

NOTES

205. In an interview conducted by G.R. Urban, Eric Jantsch had these comments on survival and the need for anticipation:

> The uniqueness of our situation is quite easy to explain: the time-scale on which we work has undergone a sea-change. In earlier times we had time to react to slow changes in our environment. It took thousands of years for man the hunter to become an agricultural worker and for the latter to become an engineer in electronics. Today we have such a dangerously short time-factor at play that we have to act in anticipation. To spread the word around about this is going to make some of us highly unpopular. I have already said that the full satisfaction of short-range demands will almost automatically involve us in

long-range disaster. So, to protect ourselves against long-range trouble, we ought to take restrictive steps right away, which people will not like. They will appeal to their protective shield ("hope" if you like) and shove the really important problems under the carpet. Alas, these problems will not go away. (Toffler, *The Futurists,* p. 226.) [14]

206. Franklin Tugwell's comment on the origins of our current difficulties is pertinent:

[This is] a time when we recognize that many of our most pressing problems are the long-term results of short-sighted policies or at least policies in which assumptions about the future were unexamined. (*The Search for Alternatives,* p. ix.) [15]

210. For comments on advance forecasts about the energy crisis, see the footnote to page 10, located on page 23.

211. For a further discussion of the pattern of inflation before, during, and after the wage/price controls of 1971-1973, see Milton Friedman, "Perspective on Inflation," *Newsweek.* [101]

212. An excellent summary of the reasons for the long delays in developing energy production capacity is an article by Les Gapay called "Elusive Goal" in *The Wall Street Journal.* [127]

214. In "The Carrying Capacity of the Globe," Jørgen Randers and Donella Meadows gave this summary of the problem of economic shortsightedness:

This acceptance of "the invisible hand" has, however, introduced a strong emphasis on short term benefits. When an action will bring both benefits and costs over time, individuals use the concept of net present value and discount the future implications so that they can determine whether or not an action is profitable — and hence should be taken. The result of this procedure is essentially that a value of zero is assigned to anything happening over 20 years in the future. In other words, actions are taken even though their cost to society 20 years hence will be enormous — simply because the benefits are larger than the costs in the short run. [108]

215. In the discussion of whether or not to clear-cut the timber land, two factors are left out which would unbalance the economic argument in favor of clear-cutting still further. In the first place, if you *do* clear-cut, that land may be worthless for growing more trees, but it still has some residual value, so you gain that in addition to the money you get for the trees themselves. On the other hand, if you keep the land in productive timber you must pay taxes on it every year, as well as other maintenance expenses, thus reducing still further the already small returns of a conservation policy.

216. On Alice and the Red Queen, see the footnote to page 179, located on page 202.

218. There is an excellent example of the denunciation by the press of those who warn of potential difficulties in the footnote to page 66, beginning on page 74.

219. Several comments on educational change, and resistance thereto, may be relevant at this point:

> Our educational enterprise is not only extensive, but it is also rich in tradition and even myth. The rich tradition has accumulated inertia making education cumbersome and slow to respond to a changing environment. Many educators and political leaders say that our educational system must be radically altered to meet the challenge of a rapidly changing world. Some believe that the present system can be modified to meet this need, and others think nothing less than a complete overhaul will suffice. (Hirsch, *Inventing Education for the Future,* p. 3.) [56]

> Educational systems everywhere are under great stress, in part because of the sheer lack of resources and in part because of the lack of relevance, a failure to change and adapt. (Brown, *World Without Borders*, pp. 115-116.) [115]

Supposedly, the decade of the sixties was one of school reform: in the curriculum, in the organization of the school classroom, and in instruction. But recent studies reveal that the appearance of change far outruns the actuality of it.

Despite emphasis on the need for identifying goals, few schools have a clear sense of direction. Despite the obvious futility of "teaching" the world's knowledge, schools still emphasize the learning of facts rather than how to learn. (John Goodlad, *et al.*, in Hostrop, *Foundations of Futurology in Education*, pp. 221-222.) [60]

See also "Resistance to Innovation in American Education," by David Nasatir (chapter 16 of *Inventing Education for the Future,* edited by Werner Z. Hirsch.) [56]

220. The Saylor quotation is from page 44 of the October 1973 issue of *Educational Leadership.* [72]

221. The "present orientation" of many curriculum experts (which is really a preoccupation with the *school's* present, not the present of the adult coming out of the school) is nicely illustrated by this comment from Morton Alpren's preface to *The Subject Curriculum: Grades K-12]:*

Because it seems more important to render a service to today's schools than to guess what schools of the 1980's might be doing, we sought to be as practical as possible. We sought to make direct application to the commitments made by the nation's schools today. (p. ix.) [42]

A little more attention to the students' future, instead of the schools' present, would benefit education greatly in the long run.

222. The passage by Vernon Smith is on page 9 of the October 1973 issue of *Educational Leadership.* [75]

223. The passage by C.P. Snow is quoted on page vi of *Search For Alternatives*, edited by Franklin Tugwell. [15]

Appendices

APPENDIX A
A Brief History of
Long-Range Forecasting

Man has been appropriately called the "time-binding" animal. Our ability to remember the past and anticipate the future is one of the essential elements of what it means to be human. Concern with the future is a universal trait; attempts to anticipate it and control it are found in every culture.

In our own society today we have many survivals of early attempts at prediction in our own and other cultures. Some, like the Tarot, the I Ching, the spirit medium, the seer, and the astrologer, are undergoing something of a renaissance. Others, like elaborate systems for interpreting omens, have vanished from our culture except in metaphor or superstition. Yet the predictive rituals in our Western tradition, both native and borrowed, are only a small sample of the amazingly varied and inventive procedures that have been devised by mankind.

Alongside these other predictive rituals has been the development of a system for empirical observation and the construction and testing of hypotheses, which we call "science." Science has developed considerable predictive ability in the more precise fields, such as astronomy, physics, and chemistry. Other fields, like meteorology and geology, are in the process of developing into good predictors. And, finally, the fields dealing with the interaction of life forms — such as ecology and the social sciences — are still in the process of devising good techniques for the collection of information.

There are several reasons that the latter are so far "behind" the others. First, it is not usually possible to perform truly replicable experiments in these fields. Second, the patterns of interaction are more complex, more statistical and more probabilistic (i.e., one electron behaves exactly like another; this is definitely not true for either muskrats or Parisians.) Finally, it is much harder for the observer in these fields to observe them without interacting significantly with them and distorting the results. (Note, however, that this classification of disciplines is rather arbitrary: particle physics resembles the social sciences in these last two respects more than it resembles "every-day" physics.)

This unequal development in the capacities of the sciences has placed modern man in the middle of a deadly dilemma. We possess relative mastery of the physical world around us without comparable understanding of ourselves or our biological environment. Science and technology have put us on a roller-coaster of social change and given us the capacity to completely destroy ourselves. The question facing us is whether we can develop sufficient skill at anticipation and planning in time to control this destructive capacity and guide our own social evolution. This is the setting which gives the modern attempt to develop a discipline of forecasting — "futuristics" — its urgency and importance for us all.

The Development of Futuristics

We have records of serious attempts to forecast the future development of human societies dating back to Plato and before. But, until the middle of the 20th century, all such attempts were characterized by being individual, sporadic, and essentially philosophical or recreational. This is simply because the best study of the future was — until recently — the study of the past. Of course, this strategy did not always work. To use the military as an example, history is littered with the defeats of traditionalist generals who failed to grasp the implications of new strategies or technologies. However, such innovations and the discontinuities they produced were the exceptions until recently, so that no one paid them much attention. But suddenly, in the first half of the 20th century, the generals got caught preparing for the last war (instead of the next one) twice in the same generation.

During World War II, it finally began to dawn on the American military that technological innovation and wholesale transformation of warfare had become the rule and not the exception. Following World War II this new insight was put into concrete form with the establishment by the Air Force of a civilian research and development corporation (RAND). RAND was chartered as a semi-private, non-profit "think-tank" and it became the first enduring organization devoted primarily to the systematic, on-going study of the future.

The development of RAND, and the other think-tanks which followed, has had a considerable influence on the study of the future as a discipline. RAND began by devoting its attentions almost entirely to the development and impact of new technologies. It soon became apparent, however, that the meaning for the military of a new gadget depended a great deal on the international political situation. Attempts to forecast the future development of international relations were found, in turn, to depend on an understanding of many broader social, economic, and political forces.

During the same period (from the mid-40's to the mid-60's) many non-military groups began to discover an urgent need for good, anticipatory thinking. The phenomenal success of corporations like Xerox, IBM, and Polaroid underscored the fact that financial success now depends as much on creativity in the laboratory and fast response to changing markets as on financial and administrative ability. Government officials in the early 1960's also discovered that their simplistic models of society were inadequate to anticipate the consequences of deliberate attempts at social change, thus producing strategies (especially in welfare and urban renewal) which were monumentally ineffective. Educators have also been battered by unanticipated forces ranging from Sputnik, Vietnam, and the drug culture to desegregation, the rise of the teacher unions, and the financial squeeze of the early 1970's. And for many individuals the need to anticipate the future has developed out of a runaway case of future shock — the feeling that everything is changing too fast and that we are moving out of control toward greater and greater risk of total disaster.

By 1965 enough individuals had become employed in response to this growing demand for them to realize that they were participating in the birth of a new discipline. The word "futurist" came into general use during this period and the World Future Society, which was founded in 1966, began publishing the journal *The Futurist* in 1967. (1967 was also the year of the first international conference on the future in Oslo, Norway.) The World Future Society has grown rapidly to some 15 thousand members in 1974, 15% from outside the U.S., and it is estimated that there are approximately two to three thousand professional futurists in the U.S.

The name of the profession that these futurists belong to is not so unanimously agreed upon. However, "futurism" sounds too much like an ideology, while "futurology" — besides being an awkward blend of Latin and Greek — sounds too close to astrology or scientology (associations most futurists would much rather avoid). So "futuristics" — literally, that which a futurist does — has become dominant by default, though not yet universal.

If futuristics is what a futurist does, what is it that futurists do? *Futuristics is the systematic study by basically rational or empirical means of the possible alternative futures of human societies and the special problems and opportunities relating to those futures.* It is this concern with rational methods and alternative futures which makes modern futuristics different from most earlier attempts at forecasting or prediction. To paraphrase a common definition of politics, futuristics is the art of *discovering* what is possible.

The basic approaches to long-range forecasting described in chapters three through nine (i.e., trend extrapolation, intuitive forecasting, group consensus, alternative futures, systems modelling, and cross-impact studies) are used in all of the many aspects of futuristics. But two branches of the field are, in addition, different enough in their approach and subject matter to be worth special comment.

Technological Forecasting

Technological forecasting is the art of forecasting the development, timing, and impact of new technologies.[1] It is the oldest

---

[1]Impact studies constitute a sub-category called "technology assessment."

branch of futuristics, the one with the most elaborate and detailed techniques, and the one still most associated with business and the military. Business and the military are, of course, primarily interested in the impact of new technology on economics and defense, and this has biased technological forecasting in these directions.

Recently, however, there has been a great deal of interest among social thinkers, political leaders, and the general public in assessing and perhaps controlling the social and environmental impacts of technology. Some of the great public debates of the 50's, 60's and early 70's have centered around issues of technology assessment: automation, the Pill, television, the automobile, electronic eaves-dropping and wiretapping, hallucinogenic drugs, and the super-sonic transport, to name a few.

The institutional result of this interest and these debates has been the establishment of the Environmental Protection Agency (EPA) and the Office of Technology Assessment (OTA). The EPA's charter takes a broad perspective on the word "environment," and the agency can require environmental impact statements which spell out in detail the effects of a proposed project on everything from marsh drainage to the integrity of a neighborhood. If the negative impact is too great, the agency can require counter-balancing additions or alterations, or it can block the project altogether.

The EPA is an administrative agency, established to implement the law and responsible to the President. The OTA, on the other hand, is a *legislative* research agency, reporting directly to Congress to provide Congress with information on the impacts of technology as a basis for better laws controlling technology. The OTA came about principally as a result of the supersonic transport (SST) controversy, when many Senators and Congressmen felt that they were getting a very one-sided, pro-SST, viewpoint from the administration and were being cut off from opposition viewpoints (including those of the President's own science advisor).

However, despite these beginnings, there is still considerable debate as to whether (and if so, how) we can design systems for controlling technology which will not interfere excessively with our individual freedoms. The tentative answer which seems to be emerging is that we can control "big" technologies like the SST (which was so big that no corporation could finance it without government help), but that we may never be able to satisfactorily control little "kitchen-table" technologies like LSD or electronic bugging.

Future Studies

The other somewhat different branch of futuristics is "future studies" — the subject of this book. The objective of future studies is the development of future-oriented educational techniques, curriculum materials, and classroom methods designed to increase the student's awareness of future possibilities and his ability to choose constructively among them. The justification for future studies is at least four-fold:

- The problems we are facing are increasingly long-range and global; the decisions we make today on the basis of short-term political considerations and inadequate information will affect the ability of our children and grandchildren to survive. We need leaders trained to understand long-range problems and willing to pursue long-range objectives.

- However, elitist futuristics, where only the leaders possess the crystal ball, would spell the end of democracy and freedom. Facing urgent long-range problems, as we are, we will have to choose between survival and democracy unless the public is both willing and able to understand and deal with long-range issues.

- We are currently living in a time of very rapid change. Already we can see many individuals around us caught up in the disorientation of "future shock," making decisions less appropriate to today than to yesterday. In the future, both personal competence and good psychological health will depend on developing from an early age the skills, habits, and attitudes of long-range thinking and anticipation.

- Educators have grasped much less well than students the fact of rapid change and the long "lead-time" involved in education. In response to demands for "relevance" the schools have shifted grudgingly from a sole interest in the past to a partial interest in preparing students for "the real world" — i.e., the world of today. But student demands for relevance are a plea for some kind of information, *any* information, about the world which they will actually live in and which they know will be very different from today — the future.

The first university-level course in futuristics was taught in 1966, the first pre-college course in 1967. Despite that near-equal beginning, university-level courses increased much faster in number than pre-college courses during the subsequent five-year period. Rojas and Eldredge have estimated that in 1973 there were approximately 400 colleges and universities in the United States offering futures courses.

> In 1971 about 200 colleges had such offerings; in 1970, the figure stood close to 75; about 30 schools were involved in 1969; perhaps 16 in 1968; and only 3 in the previous year.

Although efforts by pre-college teachers to incorporate a future orientation had become fairly numerous by the early 1970's, these were almost entirely individual and isolated efforts. One of the first attempts to provide a focus for these efforts was the Futuristics Program, started at the University of Massachusetts in 1969 to train futurist-educators, to develop future-oriented techniques and classroom methods, and to act as a clearinghouse of ideas and experiences for teachers and administrators in the field. Subsequently, in 1972, several of its members established the Future Studies Teacher Preparation Program, the first under-graduate program to train and certify new teachers in this area.

In 1973-74, in many ways a year of transition, the educational establishment suddenly became aware of and began to respond to the growing interest in future studies at the elementary and secondary levels. Some of the related events of the year are worth mentioning:

● November, '73: Research for Better Schools, Inc., hosts a conference on education and the future.

● February, '74: publication of Toffler's *Learning for Tomorrow.*

- March, '74: The Association for Supervision and Curriculum Development holds its annual conference with the theme "Developing Curricula for Human Futures."

- April, '74:' The Northeast Regional Social Studies Conference has future studies as its theme.

- June, '74: The American Association of Colleges for Teacher Education devotes the summer issue of the *Journal of Teacher Education* to the theme "Inventing the Future."

- July/August, '74: Webster College (Mo.) hosts a four-week summer school of futures studies.

- August '74: The Program for Applied Social Science and the Future, University of Minnesota, holds its first annual "Futures Curriculum Workshop."

- October, '74: Three different future studies conferences are offered for teachers — in Chicago (presented by the Dept. of Futuristics of the International Graduate School of Education, Denver); in Bethesda, Md., (presented by the World Future Society); and at the University of the Virgin Islands.

The contrast with preceding years is rather startling. It now seems likely that the number of elementary and secondary teachers involved in future studies has caught up with and will shortly surpass the number of college teachers in this field. (In a recent survey, Richard Stock identified 571 future studies teachers at the secondary level alone.)

Teachers at all levels have incorporated a wide range of content into future studies, some of it familiar and some not: long-range forecasting, utopian and dystopian literature, science fiction, environmental education, issues in global survival, war/peace studies, history, anthropology, values clarification, vocations and career counseling, and community development, to name some of the most important ones. Although the appropriate combination of subjects has been different for different classes and different age levels, the effect of the unifying framework of "the future" has generally been to relate the individual subjects to each other and make them more meaningful and interesting for the students.

Conclusion

Futurists can be found to debate the likelihood or probable timing of just about any future event. But this disputatiousness should not obscure some basic areas of common agreement. There seems to be, for instance, a strong consensus that we are entering a critically important transitional period, from even the broadest historical perspective. The dangers have never been greater, and neither have the opportunities. For the first time, the survival of the whole species is in question; also for the first time, we are beginning to sense the possibility of truly understanding ourselves and controlling our own fate.

Buckminster Fuller caught the sense of this nexus of problems and opportunities in the title of his book, *Utopia or Oblivion*. If we survive at all, the social and technical tools we will have to develop in order to survive will be powerful enough to build a magnificent world to live in, if we so choose. But it is becoming painfully obvious that we shall neither avoid the disasters nor be prepared to take advantage of the opportunities unless we develop much more far-sighted social perspectives and decision-making processes. Futuristics is the attempt to create new mechanisms for foresight, so that we can understand our choices better and choose more wisely among them.

NOTES

229. Donald Michael has commented as follows on the uniqueness of the human time perspective:

> Man lives in a more extended time dimension than do other animals; he reacts not merely to the immediate present, but to a present extended into the past and future by his ability to foresee and plan results in the light of experience. In Korzybski's phrase, man is a time-binder. No other animal has the intellectual potential to have the slightest interest in reading tea leaves. (*The Unprepared Society*, p. xi). [34]

231. On the development of RAND and the other think tanks, see *The Non-Profit Research Institute* [310], by Harold Orlans, or *Think Tanks* [304], by Paul Dickson. I have drastically oversimplified both the changing pattern of interests and the reasons for its occurrence; however, the overall pattern has been a shift from hardware to social issues, to the point where RAND now draws 35% of its funding from sources other than the Air Force and even, in the late 1960's, established a New York City-RAND to work on the social and administrative problems of that city. (Orlans, pp. 112 and 118).

232. Membership information is courtesy of the World Future Society, June 1974. *Mankind 2000*, edited by Robert Jungk and Johan Galtung, is the outgrowth and report on the Oslo conference. See particularly "The Professional Futurist" (pp. 244-250), by Edward S. Cornish, for a discussion of the early history of the field and the problems of semantic coinage and definition. [8]

232. In the preface to *Search for Alternatives*, Franklin Tugwell summarized the development and orientation of modern futuristics as follows:

> The growth of futures studies in the last decade has been closely tied to the increasing commitment among social scientists to producing more operational knowledge in order to improve the quality of public policies. Experts in policy analysis have long understood that rational, goal-directed choices are possible only on the basis of some conceptions of the future, even if they are fuzzy or unrecognized, or both. At the same time, rapid transformative change combined with increasing density, complexity, and interdependence have forced upon our institutions, private and public alike, the need to handle a constantly growing volume of difficult decisions, decisions which more and more involve, by necessity, long range consequences. Perceiving these conditions, a growing clan of analysts has set to work to improve our ability to: 1) understand the predictive behavior of policy makers and key institutions; 2) forecast what is foreseeable with care and elegance; 3) imagine what might be — that is, fashion images of plausible alternatives; and,

finally, 4) help determine the strategic availability of the more desirable outcomes. Perhaps the most surprising fact of all of this is the degree of attention and support futures analysts have attracted in so short a time and in the face of considerable skepticism on the part of professional colleagues.

Whether their work is motivated by a generalized sense of unease and jeopardy or by a desire to take a direct hand in improving our institutional ability to deal with the future, most modern futurists share a common perspective which distinguishes them from the religious prophets and literary speculators who were the futurists of the past. The key to this perspective is its unyielding non-determinism. Modern futurists view the future as a field of choice; they are concerned not so much with predicting what *will* be as with knowing what *might* be, and how this knowledge fits into the context of public policy and action. (pp. vii-viii.) [15]

232. For a good general introduction to technological forecasting, see *Technological Forecasting and Long Range Planning* by Robert U. Ayres. [1]

235. The Rojas quote is from pages 217-218 of *Learning for Tomorrow*, edited by Alvin Toffler. [78]

APPENDIX B
Sample Scenario
For a
Commission Simulation

This scenario was first prepared in early 1972 for use in in-service workshops for teachers on the future of education. (It was updated a year and a half later by inserting Gerald Ford's name in place of Spiro Agnew's.) Both the scenario and the simulation are considerably abbreviated because of the time constraints of the workshop format. A less hurried approach is preferable, with several interim meetings and ample time for outside research. Nevertheless, this has proved to be an effective and enjoyable exercise when time is limited.

THE PRESIDENT'S COMMISSION
ON EDUCATIONAL REFORM
January 22, *1981*

Background:

The American system of education is on the verge of collapse. Teachers are demanding higher pay, more security, and better working conditions. The courts have relentlessly imposed heavier and heavier financial and social burdens on the schools. Taxpayers, over-promised and over-taxed for years, are in revolt. And disgusted students, led by the radical "Ivies," have turned increasingly to sabotage. The ingredients for the crisis have been simmering for nearly three decades:

1) *Busing.* In 1954, the Supreme Court ruled that "separate but equal" school systems were in fact unequal, and therefore illegal because they discriminated against a class of citizens. The 1960's saw the forced desegregation of the nation's schools, culminating in the first half of the Seventies with a wave of massive busing decisions in most major northern cities and their suburbs.

2) *Teachers.* The unions were born in the fifties out of frustration at the miserable wages and menial status of teachers. Riding the baby boom, the resulting teaching shortage, and the new atmosphere of freedom and militancy, the unions helped improve the teacher's position considerably by the late Sixties. Faced with a teacher surplus and critically deteriorating classroom environments, the unions continued to expand in the Seventies, but turned their emphasis to job security and better working conditions.

3) *Students.* The militancy and unrest in our colleges in the Sixties was mirrored in the secondary schools in the Seventies. Now the "Ivies" (or "Ivanites," after their mentor, Ivan Illich) have produced a consistently growing demand for the abolition of mandatory public schooling. As their numbers have passed 25% of all high school students (with solid majorities in many major cities) without succeeding in their objective, there has been a definite switch from earlier militant non-violence to a new strategy of systematic sabotage and harrassment.

4) *The Public.* For twenty years educators and politicians have made education the solution and scapegoat for every social ill. Education has been the supposed cure for: Racism, Poverty, Unemployment, The Drug Problem, Alienation, and The Missile Gap. Meanwhile, the problems are still with us, the subjective perception is that the quality of education has deteriorated greatly, and property taxes have more than

quintupled. The taxpayer is fed up. Starting with a rash of school-bond and tax-increase failures in 1969, the taxpayer's revolt and the subsequent financial crisis in the schools have now become a national epidemic.

The Situation

The Supreme Court opened the final can of worms last June, when they ruled "Serrano" into law: the old property tax was found illegal as a means for financing education and all schools must now be funded on an equal basis within each state. Based on California's experience since 1974, this would mean a quadrupling of suburban taxes. The Court, however, did leave open a loophole, implying that with equal funding some retreat from busing might be feasible. Edward Kennedy, the Democratic candidate, whose stand favoring busing had weakened in the face of mounting black opposition to white "cultural imperialism," immediately added to his campaign a "deal" for the liberals and the affluent: total educational reform and an end to busing were promised, in exchange for a drastic "soak-the-rich" form of school financing.

Drawing substantial support from a surprisingly wide range of ethnic and income groups, Kennedy decisively trounced incumbent President Gerald Ford. In his inaugural address yesterday, President Kennedy claimed his near-landslide as a "vigorous mandate for social and educational change," and revealed that his first act of office would be to appoint a blue-ribbon Commission on Educational Reform.

The Task

You are the members of the President's Commission on Educational Reform, representing four groups: parents/taxpayers, teachers, students, and social planners. During the next two hours, each of these groups will meet separately to discuss the educational problems facing us and to arrive at the policies which you, *as representatives of your group*, will recommend to the Commission as a whole.

Each discussion will be taped. At the end of the three hours, you should sum up your results clearly into the recorder and designate one individual to present them to the Commission as a whole. YOU MUST COME TO AN AGREEMENT ON WHAT TO DO. How you do it is up to each group separately.

Obviously, this exercise is more suitable for teacher workshops than for most classroom situations. It is included to illustrate the basic elements of writing a scenario and preparing the instructions for a commission exercise. The most important thing to remember is to invent lots of believeable detail, using well-known people or creating plausible characters wherever possible.

Just in case someone is reading this without having read chapters three and five: the purpose of a scenario is *not* to predict the future *nor* to advocate a particular future. In fact, the better the scenario, the more unlikely it is to "come true" because of the richness of details. The scenario above, for example, describes a radical movement of high school students (called "Ivies") which gathers steam in the mid-seventies. Even if such a movement had arisen, it is highly unlikely that it would have chosen that particular nickname. The same applies to political events; e.g., it appears that Ford will not be eligible to run again in 1980 if he wins in 1976.

Incidentally, "Serrano" is the name of a court case in which the California Supreme Court held that the local property tax was an unconstitutional way to finance public schools, because an equal tax effort produced very unequal funding for different school districts.

APPENDIX C
Resources
For Teaching the Future

The bibliography at the end of this book is organized in a conventional manner. That is, books are listed alphabetically by author within a few general categories, and there is an attempt to be reasonably inclusive. Such a list is primarily a reference guide for people who are already acquainted with the general area covered; it is the place to go for further resources if you wish to explore some particular aspect in greater depth. A typical bibliography is not, however, very helpful for the person just starting to explore a new field, because it does not provide any guidance on where to start or how to get the best overview.

By contrast, the purpose of this appendix is to help you get started. To be helpful, it must be extremely selective. Unfortunately, this also means it must be personal and idiosyncratic. Nevertheless, even a biased starting point may be better than no starting point at all.

The first section, below, lists ten books which together make up an essential basic library for teaching the future. The second section consists of ten more books for further reading, all of which could have been included in the first section and were excluded only with great reluctance. Section three describes a starter library in science fiction, section four lists useful periodicals, and section five describes twenty useful films on the future.

I. TEN ESSENTIAL BOOKS

LEARNING FOR TOMORROW, edited by Alvin Toffler [78]

Makes a powerful and compelling case for future-oriented education. Discusses the role of the future in individual psychology, with chapters on the future image of women and of black children; explores the role of future studies in the curriculum, especially the sciences, social studies, the humanities, and early childhood education; also describes resources, such as science fiction, games, and values clarification, and has a valuable appendix on the status of future studies. A must.

THE FUTURISTS, edited by Alvin Toffler [14]

A "reader's digest" of the best and most influential writing on the future during the formative years from 1962 to 1972. By my count, there are 20 winners out of 23 chapters; a few of the most notable are: Paul Ehrlich's "Eco-Catastrophe!" scenario, the chapter on the future from Margaret Mead's *Culture and Commitment*, the definitive essay on intuitive forecasting from Arthur C. Clarke's *Profiles of the Future*, Ted Gordon's lucid summary of "The Current Methods of Futures Research," and Kenneth Boulding's essay on the economics of "Spaceship Earth," to name just a few. An outstanding, non-technical summary of futures thinking.

THE MEANING OF THE TWENTIETH CENTURY,
by Kenneth Boulding [19]

Other societies have perceived themselves as being unique in history; Boulding writes persuasively that, in our case, this is really true. The 20th century is a pivotal point in history, unlike anything that has gone before and unlike anything that will follow. It will either be a temporary "Golden Age," followed by a collapse of civilization, or a transitional period between two great eras of human existence. The choice will be determined by what we do. A clearly written and influential statement of the meaning of our times in the perspective of the past and the future.

THE MOST PROBABLE WORLD, by Stuart Chase [23]

Stuart Chase is a popularizer in the highest sense of the word; his talent is for translating complex issues into clear, direct language for the enjoyment of the layman. Here, he presents a concise and readable overview of the major problems and possibilities which our society is most likely to face. Some of the topics covered include: technology, population, cities, energy, economics, automation/computers, leisure, the arms race, international relations, and the search for solutions. Highly recommended.

WORLD FACTS AND TRENDS, by John McHale [32]

A persistent problem in education is that we deal too much in generalities and our students seldom have a chance to grapple with the underlying facts. Yet when we do go looking for data to share with our classes, we usually find that it is packaged in incomprehensible ways. McHale's book is a compendium of about 150 superlatively clear and attractive large-format diagrams, charts, tables, and graphs. The illustrations and the accompanying text provide an excellent introduction to the process and the pace of change, particularly as it has affected human technology, social systems, and the environment. An indispensable aid to classroom teaching.

THE SYSTEMS VIEW OF THE WORLD, by Ervin Laszlo [92]

Laszlo begins by explaining what is meant by a "systems approach," how it has developed and transformed the sciences, and why it is superior to linear and atomistic ways of understanding the world. He then demonstrates what it means to apply a systems perspective to the natural world and to the human world. A very readable, non-technical introduction to one of the most important and fundamental insights of our time.

THE SILENT LANGUAGE, by Edward T. Hall [55]

If ecology can be called the "systems approach to biology," cultural anthropology has a good claim to being called the systems approach to the study of man. Hall presents a clear and delightfully anecdotal look at the concept of culture and at the problems of communication between different cultures. Especially valuable for its discussion of time and the different ways it is perceived in different societies.

ENVIRONMENT: Readings for Teachers,
edited by J.W. George Ivany [62]
      An extraordinary number of books on the environment have been published in the last decade. Of the one's I've encountered, this provides the best combination of overall perspective, specific information, and suggestions for teachers. It includes 27 essays, ranging from "The Historical Roots of our Ecological Crisis," to "Ten Classroom Sessions in Ecology." Garret Hardin's famous article on "The Tragedy of the Commons" is especially recommended.

VALUES AND TEACHING, by Louis E. Raths, Merrill Harmin, and Sidney B. Simon [69]
      Future studies helps make us more able to achieve our objectives, but it does not tell us what our objectives should be. Better decision-making tools are pointless if we don't know what we want, or if our objectives are confused or contradictory. This is the case with many young people. They have absorbed a great number of conflicting precepts, often only half understood, from a great many different sources; the result is that they do not know what they value, or what they believe is good or worth working for. Raths, Harmin and Simon have worked out an effective strategy for helping students clarify their own values. The objective is not to inculcate a specific set of values, but to help the student arrive at his own system of values, a system which will hopefully be more consistent, more freely chosen, and more part of the student's conscious awareness. An essential component of education for the future. (See also: Simon, Howe, Kirschenbaum, *Values Clarification*.)

THE GUIDE TO SIMULATIONS/
GAMES FOR EDUCATION AND TRAINING
by David W. Zuckerman and Robert E. Horn [90]
      In chapters five and eight, three simulations (the President's Select Commission, the Thermostat, and Channels) were used to

illustrate parts of the process of forecasting. In teaching future studies, however, simulations and simulation games are even more important as ways to present content. The biggest difficulty in thinking about the future of society, or any of its aspects, is that it is outside our own range of experience; and the greatest strength of simulation as a teaching strategy is that it provides opportunities for experiential kinds of learning about situations which cannot be experienced directly. Simulations are particularly important for studying the future, but they are also a valuable addition to the available teaching strategies in any field. Zuckerman and Horn's book is, hands down, the best resource guide in the field. The second edition describes over 600 games and simulations in some detail, with several useful articles at the end. If your school won't buy it for you, it's worth every penny of the $15 for a copy of your own. No teacher should be without it. (Also write to STEM, P.O. Box 393, Provo, Utah 84601 for a free catalog of their extensive list of inexpensive simulations.)

II. TEN BOOKS FOR FURTHER READING

If I seemed to be overworking the superlatives in section 1, it is because all ten of the books in that section are excellent. So are the ten books that follow, but some choices had to be made. The books in this section provide either a broader general background or more detailed information on a specific subject. In other words, each expands or amplifies in some way on the topics covered in the first ten.

FUTURE SHOCK, by Alvin Toffler [40]

A thorough and impressive documentation of accelerating change and its impact on individuals and society. Chapter 18, "Education in the Future Tense," was the forerunner of *Learning for Tomorrow*, and provided the original stimulus for many teachers now involved in future studies.

TEACHING AS A SUBVERSIVE ACTIVITY, by Neil Postman and Charles Weingartner [68]

A lively manual for teachers who want to make the approach and the style of their teaching as future-oriented as the content.

TEACHING FOR A CHANGE, by John Anthony Scott [73]

A follow-up to Postman and Weingartner for secondary social studies teachers. Scott argues that the social studies curriculum should be devoted to the major, critical problems facing American society; included are extensive descriptions of both content and methods.

DECIDING THE FUTURE: A Forecast of Responsibilities of Secondary Teachers of English, 1970 - 2000 A.D., by Edmund J. Farrell [54]

Do not be misled by the subtitle; although the last two chapters are of special interest to English teachers, the whole book is relevant to teachers in all fields. Farrell uses the Delphi method to study alternative possibilities for the future of education. It is one of the best Delphi studies in print, and one of the outstanding books on the future of teaching and schooling.

SEARCH FOR ALTERNATIVES: Public Policy and the Study of the Future, by Franklin Tugwell [15]

This book covers much the same territory as Toffler's *The Futurists* and is every bit as good. I chose between them solely on the basis that *Search for Alternatives* takes a slightly more advanced approach. Chapters of special interest are: Tugwell's introduction; John Platt, "What We Must Do"; O.D. Duncan, "Social Forecasting: the State of the Art"; Elise Boulding, "Futurology and the Imaging Capacity of the West" (heavy going, but worth it); Jay Forrester, "Counterintuitive Behavior of Social Systems"; and Bertram Gross, "Friendly Fascism."

THE STEP TO MAN, by John R. Platt [96]

The title page includes this accurate description: "This book is concerned with the evolving nature of man, social and intellectual, what he is and what he may become." The whole book is relevant to social studies and futures courses, but science teachers will find Chapter 2, "Strong Inference," of special interest, and teachers of U.S. History and Government will find Chapter 7, "The Federalists and the Design of Stabilization," of particular use. A very effective, readable, systems approach to human society.

THE LIMITS TO GROWTH, by Donella Meadows, *et al.*, [105]
This is the non-technical report on the results of an elaborate computer model of the life-support systems of the planet. *Limits* is a devastating critique of the assumption that growth is always good and can be continued indefinitely; it is also undoubtedly both the most famous and the most controversial book that has ever been published in long-range forecasting. An important and valuable book.

POPULATION, RESOURCES, ENVIRONMENT: Issues in Human Ecology, by Paul R. Ehrlich and Anne H. Ehrlich [124]
A thorough, clear, and informative text on these three important topics and their interrelationships. There is no better place to start if you need to acquire a good background in ecology; especially valuable for social studies teachers because it relates ecological issues to the practical and ethical problems of human societies.

SERIOUS GAMES, by Clark C. Abt [84]
A concise introduction to educational games and the reasons for using them, with numerous examples and suggestions for using them and for designing your own. A valuable supplement to *The Guide to Simulations/Games*.

ALTERNATIVE FUTURES FOR LEARNING: An Annotated Bibliography of Trends, Forecasts, and Proposals, by Michael Marien [317]
If you can still get it, this is your best guide to where to turn next in your explorations of the wider fields of future studies and futuristics. (Second best, and a useful and slightly more up-to-date supplement, is *The Hot List Delphi* [319], also by Michael Marien.)

III. GETTING STARTED IN SCIENCE FICTION
The assumption in this section is that you have not read much science fiction, if any, but you want to become familiar with it so that you can use it in your classes. Suggestions for student reading are listed in the bibliography; the ones here are intended for you. The reason for the two-pronged approach is that introducing an

adult to science fiction is a difficult proposition. Most people have formed fairly strong personal reading habits by the time they finish college, and it is well-known in science fiction circles that most adults who read it acquired a liking for it in their teens.

There are two reasons for this inertia, in addition to simple force of habit. The first has to do with the use of a single label for a very broad and diverse field. The statement, "I like science fiction," is at least partly a lie. I like some authors and some types of science fiction, but there are also some authors and types of science fiction I tend to avoid, just as I like or dislike certain authors and approaches in "mainstream" fiction. The problem arises when a newcomer to the field reads one story or novel, and judges the whole field on that basis, since the odds are substantially against his stumbling on a particular kind of writing he likes. One might just as well judge all conventional fiction by reading *Valley of the Dolls* or *Gravity's Rainbow*.

The second difficulty is the in-group language used in some science fiction. Every year, hundreds of books, both popular and scholarly, are published which attempt to describe and explain our own society to us. Yet the science fiction writer has to create in the reader's mind, within the span of a single story, a convincing and believeable image of a completely different society and set of circumstances. To do this in a single story, without intruding on either plot or characterization, the author must frequently make use of some of the literary conventions which have been adopted for describing various alternative possibilities in a fairly economical manner.

This is necessary, especially when writing short stories, but it makes it hard for the uninitiated reader to understand what is going on. For example, an author may make a passing reference to "an FTL drive," with no further explanation. The experienced reader will know that this stands for a propulsion device capable of moving a spaceship at a speed "faster than light," a common plot device which makes it possible for explorers to visit other solar systems and for societies to interact with each other across interstellar space. The science fiction author need not explain what it is nor how it works, any more than a conventional author needs to give a lecture on the function of subways each time one of his characters rides on one. He assumes the reader understands.

Young people are used to this; if they read anything but

textbooks, they frequently stumble across unfamiliar terms which the author blithely assumes they understand. Storing these up and puzzling them out is part of the process by which they learn, and it makes little difference to them whether it is a subway or a spacedrive if they have never seen either. Adults, however, are more likely to insist that an author explain any unusual terms, and they become irritated by "jargon" unless they understand the reasons why it is necessary.

The point is that you should be willing to persevere in your explorations. It takes a while to learn the literary conventions of any genre; science fiction is no exception. It also takes a while to learn enough about the field to know which authors and kinds of stories appeal to you, and which do not. The books described below have been selected to make this as painless and enjoyable a process as possible.

The richest fields for initial browsing are three massive anthologies of the best science fiction short stories, novellas, and novelettes:

THE HUGO WINNERS: Vols. I and II, edited by Isaac Asimov
The "Hugo" is science fiction's equivalent of the Oscar. (It is named after Hugo Gernsback, founding editor of the first science fiction magazine.) Each year it is awarded to the stories voted the best in each of several length categories. These two volumes contain the winners in the short story and novelette categories, spanning the 1950's and 1960's.

A TREASURY OF GREAT SCIENCE FICTION, edited by Anthony Boucher
Another massive 2-volume anthology, this one ranges more widely in terms of time and includes more stories that are durable and re-readable, rather than spectacular.

THE SCIENCE FICTION HALL OF FAME, Vol. I, edited by Robert Silverberg
A few years ago members of the Science Fiction Writers of America were asked to vote on their favorite science fiction stories of all time. (Volume I of the *Hall of Fame* contains the winners in the short-story category; Volume IIA and Volume IIB contain the first ranked novellas and novelettes.) These are "writers' choice,"

and include a number of stories which, through ideas or craftsmanship, had a major influence on other writers.

The different methods of selection used in these three anthologies — the best of the year, a single editor's preferences, and a poll of science fiction writers — produce uniformly good results, with surprisingly few duplications. Between them, they include nearly all of the really good short science fiction stories written prior to 1964. Accordingly, the titles that follow are principally those of individual novels, with the exception of four groups of stories which "hang together." The selection was based on enjoyability (I like them, at any rate) and diversity. They range from well-crafted pot-boilers (*The Rolling Stones*), first rate adventure (*The Demon Breed*), and dry humor (*Tales from the White Hart*), to thoughtful philosophy (*A Case of Conscience* and *A Canticle for Leibowitz*). Somewhere among them, you should be able to find what appeals to you.

TALES OF THE FLYING MOUNTAINS, by Poul Anderson [187]
Economic and social consequences of colonizing the asteroid belt. Some good yarns and an unusual excursion into educational philosophy.

THE FOUNDATION TRILOGY: FOUNDATION, FOUNDA-TION AND EMPIRE, and *SECOND FOUNDATION*, by Isaac Asimov [190-192]
The collapse and rebirth of a galaxy-spanning human civilization, presided over by Hari Seldon, the patron saint of futuristics.

A CASE OF CONSCIENCE, by James Blish [200]
An alien species without "original sin" presents a theological dilemma.

STAND ON ZANZIBAR, by John Brunner [204]
Population, artificial intelligence, and problems of rapid social change, dealt with in a disconcerting but very effective collage style.

TALES FROM THE WHITE HART, by Arthur C. Clarke [210]
The art of the tall tale applied to science, with a distinct British flavor.

CHILDHOOD'S END, by Arthur C. Clarke [207]
An almost mystical vision of the end result (and purpose) of human evolution.

BEYOND THIS HORIZON, by Robert Heinlein [217]
A frontier-style, extreme libertarian society against the background of an economic and technological system which works almost too well; at least three different plots going at once, all fun and all skillfully handled.

THE ROLLING STONES, by Robert Heinlein [232]
Pure entertainment, and one of the best of Heinlein's so-called "juveniles." Science fiction's wackiest family takes you on a hectic tour of a carefully extrapolated colonized solar system, about two centuries from now.

THE MOON IS A HARSH MISTRESS, by Robert Heinlein [228]
Heinlein's most complex and successful future society is a lunar colony in revolt against the heavy-handed management of the controlling nations on earth. The background involves a rich inter-weaving of the American Revolution, early Australian history, economics, comparative anthropology, and artificial intelligence. (One of the more memorable characters in the book is "Mike," the large central computer on the moon, who gradually acquires self-awareness and eventually becomes one of the main conspirators in the revolution.) This is my favorite among all Heinlein's novels, but it is only fair to warn you that at least one literary critic, Alexei Panshin, considers it to be among Heinlein's worst.

DUNE, by Frank Herbert [239]
Against the background of a swashbuckling inter-stellar empire, Herbert evokes an extraordinarily detailed and compelling image of a desert planet called "Dune," with special emphasis on the intricate ecosystem and the problems involved in transforming it on a planetary basis.

ISLAND, by Aldous Huxley [242]
On the assumption that you have read Huxley's dystopian novel, *Brave New World*, this is his less well-known but much more affirmative novel of a successful but vulnerable utopia — part

Skinnerian psychology, part humanistic idealism, and part
religious drug culture.

THE SHIP WHO SANG, by Anne McCaffrey [247]
       An enjoyable frivolity, written in a style somewhat reminiscent
of Georgette Heyer; nevertheless, this is one of the most thoughtful
looks at the positive side of the Cyborg question — when man (or in
this case, woman) and machine are melded into a new kind of
organism, what happens to the individual's humanity?

A CANTICLE FOR LEIBOWITZ, by Walter M. Miller, Jr. [248]
       Miller chronicles the long ascension of a new civilization from
the Dark Ages following the collapse of our own in a nuclear
holocaust. Profound, moving, and beautifully written.

THE SHAPE OF SPACE, by Larry Niven [251]
NEUTRON STAR, by Larry Niven [250]
ALL THE MYRIAD WAYS, by Larry Niven [249]
       Three collections of stories, many of them related. Among the
new generation of writers, Niven is the undisputed master of the
"old" science fiction — solid science, meticulously examined and
extrapolated; if you have ever been fascinated by black holes and
neutron stars, or the social implications of organ transplants, Niven
is for you. The science never interferes with the tale, however, and
Niven is also the creator of some of the most memorable characters,
vivid locales, and delightful aliens that anyone ever dreamed up.

THE DEMON BREED, by James Schmitz [258]
       A crackling good adventure story, with — as a bonus — a
highly competent heroine. (By heroine, incidentally, I mean a
"female hero," not the vapid decoration on the arm of some brawny
knight or pirate.)

THE YEAR OF THE QUIET SUN, by Wilson Tucker [268]
       A quiet, poetic, and very moving story "about" the future of
race relations in the United States. As with all good stories,
however, it is really about its main characters. In this case, the story
focuses on a beautifully created protagonist, a shy, brilliant, young
black, whose profession happens to be social forecasting.

LORD OF LIGHT, by Roger Zelazny [272]

A sweeping blockbuster of a novel, with the ancient Hindu pantheon recreated in heroic but human form on a distant colony planet. What seems to be fantasy at first, Zelazny transforms into a possible (if unlikely) reality. Zelazny is one of the best literary craftsmen in the field, and he is at his best in this attempt to create a grand mythic dimension in science fiction.

THIS IMMORTAL, by Roger Zelazny [273]

A much shorter tale, written in a light, wryly comic vein, but with all of Zelazny's craft brought to bear on both plot and characterization. The myth this time is Greek (though not the Olympian sort), and the setting is a painful resurgence of humanity following the demoralization caused by contact with a similar but substantially superior species.

DANGEROUS VISIONS, edited by Harlan Ellison [215]

Up through the mid-1960's, science fiction had a reputation for being almost antiseptically prim and proper. Ellison almost single-handedly broke down many of the existing, extremely narrow constraints by inviting more than thirty of the top writers in science fiction to cut loose and turn out good stories on topics that the magazine editors would have rejected as being too "dangerous." They did, and the result was both controversial and successful beyond Ellison's wildest hopes. Not all of the stories are dangerous, and not all are in the very top rank, but a good many are both; it was this combination of quality and daring which opened the doors for a more mature consideration of issues in science fiction. (Be warned, however, that some of the stories in DV are not for the squeamish.)

A final note on science fiction: Unless you have access to a good library, you should seriously consider joining the Science Fiction Book Club (Garden City, New York 11530). Their standard offer for new members is to send you four books (chosen from a fairly sizeable list) for the lordly sum of 10c and a promise to buy four additional books within a year (at approximately $2.00 each). If, for example, you started off with Asimov's *Foundation Trilogy* and the three large anthologies at the head of this list, the first four books alone would be worth many times the cost of a minimum eight book membership. (Even if you don't join, by the way, your school library definitely should.)

IV. PERIODICALS

There seem to be an extraordinary number of newsletters and miscellaneous publications in futuristics, but only three are relevant to the concerns of teachers with any consistency, and only one of these is at all essential. The essential publication is *The Futurist*, the journal of the World Future Society. It is a somewhat slick, large format magazine, published every other month. The articles are usually non-technical and informative, with good layout and nice graphics; many of the articles are suitable for use in high school classrooms. The address for information or subscriptions is: The World Future Society, P.O. Box 30369, Bethesda Station, Washington, D.C., 20014.

If you want to keep up with who is doing what on a little more than a bi-monthly basis, your best choice is the World Future Society *Bulletin*, which is published during the alternate months when *The Futurist* is not. It is a six-to-eight page newsletter, and a typical issue has general headings for: News, Publications, Courses, Conferences, People, Meetings, Reports, and Books. The address is the same as for *The Futurist*, and you must subscribe to both in order to get the newsletter. (Subscribing to both makes you a "comprehensive member" in the World Future Society, which brings you some additional fringe benefits.)

A worthy supplement to *The Futurist* and the *Bulletin* is a monthly newsletter called *Footnotes to the Future*. The format is generally similar to the *Bulletin*, and in some ways the coverage is more professional, though it is not as good a source of information on what people in the field are doing. The address is: P.O. Box 48, Annapolis, MD., 21404.

Plans are currently under discussion for the eventual creation of a future studies journal and an information exchange specifically for elementary and secondary school teachers. There is some chance that these will be in the organizational stage by the time this book is published; if so, details and subscription information will be given in *The Futurist*.

V. FILMS ON THE FUTURE

Not knowing anything about the films that were available to

supplement futures teaching, I decided that the best way to learn would be to see a great number of them. The result was a course called "The Future on Film," taught in the fall of 1973, during which we screened and critiqued 68 films relating to the future in general or to the future of some important aspect of society. In the process, we identified some good films and learned something about ordering and using films. The suggestions below are drawn from that experience.

Your first step in obtaining films should be to locate and get in touch with the nearest regional office of Modern Talking Pictures, a company which acts as a distributor of free films to schools on behalf of corporate and governmental clients. If your librarian or AV director does not have the address, try the Yellow Pages of the nearest major city or write to the central office at 2323 New Hyde Park Road, New Hyde Park, N.Y., 11040.

Among the best films they distribute are those in the "21st Century" series from CBS, narrated by Walter Cronkite. If you want to show a number of films on a limited budget, these will be your most important resource. However, they are in great demand, so order as far in advance as you can — 18 months in advance is not too soon. With less than a year's notice, give them as many alternate dates as you possibly can. In any case, you should order all of your free films first, since you can usually obtain rental films on much shorter notice.

After calling or writing Modern, your next step should be to write for three additional resources. *Films on the Future: A Selective Listing*, by Marie Martin, is available for $3 from the World Future Society (see page 258). "Futures on Films," by David C. Miller, is free from the University of California Extension Media Center, 2223 Fulton Street, Berkeley, CA 94720; ask for "Lifelong Learning: EMC TWO-72." Finally, VNV Communications (628 El Camino Real, Arcadia, CA, 91006) will send you a free list of their "Futurist Film Series: Towards the Year 2000." These generally excellent (and expensive) films are available from other distributors, but VNV also sells matching student texts and teacher guides to go with most of the films in the series.

As a supplement to these general suggestions, here are the 20 best films from "The Future on Film":

Title: *Future Shock*
Distributor: Contemporary/McGraw Hill
Length: 42 minutes.   Color.   Cost: $33.00.
Range of usefulness without preparation: grades 9 - 12.
Range of usefulness *with* appropriate preparation: 6 - 12.

   Based on Toffler's book and narrated by Orson Wells; excellent introduction to any futures course.

Title: *World of the Future: Crisis in the 800th Lifetime.*
Distributor: EMC/Berkeley.
Length: 22 minutes.   Color.   Cost: $25.00.
Range of usefulness without preparation: 8 - 12.
Range of usefulness *with* appropriate preparation: 6 - 12.

   A shorter and earlier film based on Toffler's book; more straightforward and factual than the first film, but with less powerful visual impact.

Title: *America: On the Edge of Abundance.*
Distributor: University of Indiana
Length: 60 minutes.   Black and white.   Cost: $17.00.
Range of usefulness without preparation: 10 - 12.
Range of usefulness *with* appropriate preparation: 7 - 12.

   Begins with an impressionistic view of the materialistic success story of the United States and concludes with an interesting discussion of the consequences of abundance.

Title: *Civil Disorder.*
Distributor: *
Length: 80 minutes.   Black and white.   Cost: $
Range of usefulness without preparation: 10 - 12.
Range of usefulness *with* appropriate preparation: 7 - 12.

   A three-part documentary prepared by Public Broadcasting on the Kerner Commission (the President's Commission on Violence in the United States); presents a powerful and thoughtful look at the causes of urban disorder and the future of race relations in the U.S.

---

*At presstime, this is no longer available from our distributor; check your nearest university or commercial film library.

Title: *The Remarkable School House.*
Distributor: Modern Talking Pictures.
Length: 30 minutes.   Color.   Cost: Free.
Range of usefulness without preparation: 6 - 12.
Range of usefulness *with* appropriate preparation: 4 - 12.
   Concerned with innovative classroom techniques such as: computer assisted instruction, simulation-games, open classrooms, and individualized instruction.

Title: *Population Ecology.*
Distributor: Boston University.
Length: 19 minutes.   Color.   Cost: $10.00.
Range of usefulness without preparation: 7 - 12.
Range of usefulness *with* appropriate preparation: 5 - 12.
   Sticks to the narrow subject of population and covers it quite thoroughly. No shock tactics, just simple, straightforward information.

Title: *Tomorrow's Children.*
Distributor: Planned Parenthood.
Length: 20 minutes.   Color.   Cost: $12.50.
Range of usefulness without preparation: 7 - 12.
Range of usefulness *with* appropriate preparation: 5 - 12.
   A film concerning the effects of over population on food supplies, natural resources, and open living space; a good introduction to some of the problems facing tomorrow's children.

Title: *Tragedy of the Commons.*
Distributor: EMC/Berkeley.
Length: 34 minutes.   Color.   Cost: $25.00.
Range of usefulness without preparation: Not applicable.
Range of usefulness *with* appropriate preparation: 9 - 12.
   A graphic illustration of the article of the same title by Garret Hardin. The article is very specific and technical; the film is more emotional and psychological.

Title: *Population and the American Future.*
Distributor: Modern Talking Pictures.
Length: 50 minutes.   Color.   Cost: Free.
Range of usefulness without preparation: 8 - 12.

Range of usefulness *with* appropriate preparation: 6 - 12.

The report of the President's Commission on Population and the American Future; outlines the problems and the commission's suggestions for solutions.

Title: *Sorry No Vacancy.*
Distributor: *
Length: 27 minutes.   Color.   Cost: $
Range of usefulness without preparation: 7 - 12.
Range of usefulness *with* appropriate preparation: 5 - 12.

Paul Ehrlich, William Paddock and others discuss the reality and urgency of the population explosion.

Title: *Up To Our Necks: The Garbage Problem.*
Distributor: Boston University.
Length: 26 minutes.   Color.   Cost: $12.50.
Range of usefulness without preparation: 7 - 12.
Range of usefulness *with* appropriate preparation: 4 - 12.

Good general explanation of types of waste and how to deal with each. More emphasis could have been placed on initial causes and possible prevention — recycling, etc.

Title: *Waste: Recycling the World.*
Distributor: EMC/Berkeley.
Length: 22 minutes.   Color.   Cost: $25.00.
Range of usefulness without preparation: 7 - 12.
Range of usefulness *with* preparation: 4 - 12.

Contains elements of both optimism and pessimism about the problem without overstressing either; numerous and diverse solutions are proposed.

Title: *Water: The Effluent Society.*
Distributor: EMC/Berkeley.
Length: 22 minutes.   Color.   Cost: $25.00.
Range of usefulness without preparation: 9 - 12.
Range of usefulness *with* appropriate preparation: 7 - 12.

---

*At presstime, this is no longer available from our distributor; check your nearest university or commercial film library. The producer is Malibu Films.

Concerned with water use, waste, and pollution, basically in the U.S. Shows how water is polluted and wasted, and indicates ways to make better use of it; the key word is "recycling."

Title: *Alone in the Midst of the Land.*
Distributor: NBC.
Length: 27 minutes.   Color.   Cost: $15.00.
Range of usefulness without preparation: 9 - 12.
Range of usefulness *with* appropriate preparation: 5 - 12.
  A somewhat scary, but very effective ecology film; discussion of possible solutions should follow the film or the emotional effect may be overpowering.

Title: *Pollution is a Matter of Choice.*
Distributor: NBC.
Length: 53 minutes.   Color.   Cost: $25.00.
Range of usefulness without preparation: 10 - 12.
Range of usefulness *with* appropriate preparation: 7 - 12.
  An excellent film that can be used not only to illustrate the pollution crisis, but also to demonstrate the complexity of coping with real issues in an actual society.

Title: *Introduction to Feedback.*
Distributor: IBM/Modern Talking Pictures.
Length: 10 minutes.   Color.   Cost: Free.
Range of usefulness without preparation: 7 - 12.
Range of usefulness *with* preparation: 4 - 12.
  Introduces the idea of feedback and negative feedback. The examples used are simple and clear.

Title: *Incredible Machine.*
Distributor: Bell Telephone/Modern Talking Pictures.
Length: 14 minutes.   Color.   Cost: Free.
Range of usefulness for science classes: 7 - 12.
Range of usefulness for art or graphics classes: K - 12.
  Absorbing film on computer graphics and simulation of many phenomena, including voice. Nice visual effects — even young children should enjoy watching.

Title: *The Computer Revolution.*
Distributor: Modern Talking Pictures.
Length: 60 minutes.   Color.   Cost: Free.
Range of usefulness without preparation: 8 - 12.
Range of usefulness *with* appropriate preparation: 6 - 12.

   Walter Cronkite explores the presence of computers and the great effect that they have on our lives. (The two 30-minute reels may be shown separately.)

Title: *Ultimate Machine.*
Distributor: EMC/Berkeley.
Length: 30 minutes.   Color.   Cost: $22.00.
Range of usefulness without preparation: 9 - 12.
Range of usefulness *with* appropriate preparation: 7 - 12.

   Computers — their basic design and how they work, simply stated; a good view of their range of usefulness in business, teaching aids, medicine, technology, etc.

Title: *Tomorrow Today.*
Distributor: Contemporary/McGraw Hill.
Length: 30 minutes.   Color.   Cost: $18.00.
Range of usefulness without preparation: 5 - 12.
Range of usefulness *with* appropriate preparation: 4 - 12.

   Simulations — computer, mechanical and combinations: Walter Cronkite lands a simulated SST, turns somersaults in simulated moon gravity, and plays Space War. Walter's antics make this the most entertaining of the 21st Century series.

   In the description above, the grade ranges are only approximate; they represent an average of the responses given by teachers reviewing the films, and do not reflect experience in classrooms. Most films are available from more than one distributor (e.g., the Cronkite/21st Century films are available from McGraw-Hill — for a price), so check with the film libraries which are near you or which you know give good service. Prices also vary from one distributor to the next and from year to year.
   The films listed above do not, unfortunately, represent the whole spectrum of interests. In some areas, such as computers, population, and ecology, there seem to be many well-made films to choose from. In other areas, we struck out every time.

(Paradoxically, the worst group of films were consistently those about media, communication, and films themselves.)

Addresses for the distributors mentioned are given below; a more complete list is available in the World Future Society catalog by Marie Martin.

Boston University School of Education
Abraham Krasker Film Library
765 Commonwealth Avenue
Boston, MA 02215

Contemporary/McGraw-Hill Films
1221 Avenue of the Americas
New York, N.Y. 10020

Extension Media Center
University of California
Berkeley, CA 94720

Modern Talking Picture Service, Inc.
2323 New Hyde Park Road
New Hyde Park, N.Y. 11040

NBC Educational Enterprises
30 Rockefeller Plaza
New York, N.Y. 10020

Planned Parenthood — World Population
267 West 25th Street
New York, N.Y. 10001

University of Indiana
Audio-Visual Center
Bloomington, Indiana 47401

Although movies have an undeniable potential for great impact, filmstrip-based audio-visual packets can be nearly as effective, at less cost and with greater flexibility. Two filmstrip units related to future studies were included in *Learning* magazine's annual review of the best audio-visual materials available (A-V 75):

Ecology: The Man-Made Planet
Shelter: The Cave Re-examined
Energy: Transactions in Time
Food: An Energy Exchange System
Mobility: From There to Here
Communications: One World-Mind

All of a six-part set entitled Dimensions of Change. *Doubleday Multimedia*. Record or cassette. Set of six filmstrips: $125, record or cassette. (Junior high — high school).

The series gives a unique look at many of mankind's dilemmas and suggests possible solutions. A comprehensive teacher's guide includes writing and discussion questions and simulation games. The judges felt "this fast-paced, high-powered series, with its excellent graphics, is flexible enough to be used in science, social studies and English classes."

- *Ecology: The Man-Made Planet*. Examines man's depletion of irreplaceable resources and his interrelationship with other earth systems.
- *Shelter: The Cave Re-examined*. Looks at man's use and abuse of shelter.
- *Energy: Transactions in Time*. Examines some of the alternative solutions to the energy crisis.
- *Food: An Energy Exchange System*. Shows how technology can help us tap new food sources.
- *Mobility: From There to Here*. Explore's man's need to develop modes of transportation that won't lead to loss of green land.
- *Communications: One World-Mind*. Introduces some of the ways mankind might gain greater control over communications systems of the future.[1]

2000 A.D.

Newsweek, Inc. Record or cassette. Filmstrip, a map of Futura City and two booklets of Thermo-Fax masters: $47, record; $49.95, cassette. (Junior high — high school.)

---

[1] *Learning*, December 1974, page 72.

The filmstrip, two booklets of Thermo-Fax masters of supplementary readings and activities, and a large map of Futura City make up this current affairs study kit. The filmstrip uses facts and projections to look at the future. Raises questions about housing, population, communications, technology, the family. The judges felt "it would be best for advanced junior high students and above."[1]

---

[1] *Learning,* December 1974, page 70.

Bibliography

I. APPROACHES TO FORECASTING

1. Ayres, Robert U. *Technological Forecasting and Long-Range Planning*. New York: McGraw-Hill, 1969.
2. Bell, Wendell and James A. Mau (eds.). *The Sociology of the Future*. New York: Russell Sage Foundation, 1971.
3. Benveniste, Guy. *The Politics of Expertise*. Berkeley, CA: Glendessary Press, 1972.
4. Bundy, Robert. "Purposes and Characteristics of Forecasts" and "What Fundamental Beliefs About the Future Do You Hold?" Syracuse, N.Y.: Mimeograph by author, 1971.
5. Clarke, Arthur C. *Profiles of the Future*. New York: Bantam Books, 1958.
6. de Jouvenel, Bertrand. *The Art of Conjecture*. New York: Basic Books, Inc., 1967.
7. Harman, W.W., O.W. Markley, and Russell Rhyne. "The Forecasting of Plausible Alternative Future Histories: Methods, Results, and Educational Policy Implications." Menlo Park, CA: Mimeograph by Educational Policy Research Center, Stanford Research Institute, March, 1970.
8. Jungk, Robert and Johan Galtung (eds.). *Mankind 2000*. London: Allen and Unwin, 1969.
9. Lanford, H.W. *Technological Forecasting Methodologies: A Synthesis*. New York: American Management Association, 1972.
10. Martino, Joseph P. (ed.). *An Introduction to Technological Forecasting*. Washington, D.C.: Gordon and Breach/The Futurist Library, 1972.
11. Miller, David C. and Ronald L. Hunt. *Futures Curriculum Guide*. San Francisco: DCM Associates, 1973.
12. Miller, David C. and Ronald L. Hunt. *Futures Learning Resources Guide*. San Francisco: DCM Associates, 1973.
13. Prehoda, Robert W. *Designing the Future: The Role of Technological Forecasting*. Philadelphia: Chilton Book Co., 1967.
14. Toffler, Alvin (ed.). *The Futurists*. New York: Random House, 1972.
15. Tugwell, Franklin. *Search for Alternatives*. Cambridge, MA: Winthrop Publishers, Inc., 1973.

16. Watt, Kenneth E. F. *The Titanic Effect: Planning for the Unthinkable.* New York: E. P. Dutton, 1974.

II. THE FUTURE OF SOCIETY

17. Bell, Daniel. *The Coming of Post-Industrial Society: A Venture in Social Forecasting.* New York: Basic Books, 1973.
18. Bennis, Warren G. and Philip E. Slater. *The Temporary Society.* New York: Harper and Row, 1968.
19. Boulding, Kenneth E. *The Meaning of the Twentieth Century.* New York: Harper Colophon Books, 1964.
20. Brown, Harrison. *The Challenge of Man's Future.* New York: Viking Press, 1954.
21. Brzezinski, Zbignew. *Between Two Ages: America's Role in the Technetronic Age.* New York: Viking, 1970.
22. Buchan, Alastair (ed.). *Europe's Futures, Europe's Choices.* New York: Columbia University Press, 1969.
23. Chase, Stuart. *The Most Probable World.* New York: Penguin Books, 1969.
24. De Tocqueville, Alexis. *Democracy in America.* New York: Harper and Row, 1966. (Originally published 1835-1840.)
25. Drucker, Peter F. *The Age of Discontinuity: Guidelines to Our Changing Society.* New York: Harper and Row, 1969.
26. Dyckman, John W. "Transportation in Cities," *Cities: Their Origin, Growth and Human Impact.* Edited by Kingsley Davis. San Francisco: W.H. Freeman, 1973.
27. Heller, Alfred (ed.). *The California Tomorrow Plan.* Los Altos, CA: William Kaufmann, Inc., 1971.
28. Kahn, Herman and Anthony J. Wiener. *The Year 2000: A Framework for Speculation on the Next Thirty-Three Years.* New York: Macmillan Company, 1967.
29. Kahn, Herman and B. Bruce-Briggs. *Things to Come: Thinking about the Seventies and Eighties.* New York: Macmillan, 1972.
30. Lapp, Robert E. *The Logarithmic Century.* Englewood Cliffs: Prentice-Hall, 1973.
31. Lundberg, Ferdinand. *The Coming World Transformation.* Garden City, N.Y.: Doubleday and Co., Inc., 1963.

32. McHale, John. *World Facts and Trends.* New York: Collier Books, 1972.
33. McHale, John. *The Future of the Future.* New York: Braziller, 1969.
34. Michael, Donald. *The Unprepared Society: Planning for a Precarious Future.* New York: Basic Books, 1968.
35. Newman, Joseph (ed.) *1994: The World of Tomorrow.* Washington, D.C.: *U.S. News and World Report*, 1973.
36. Norman, Maxwell H. *Dimensions of the Future: Alternatives for Tomorrow.* New York: Holt, Rinehart and Winston, Inc., 1974.
37. Norman, Maxwell H. (ed.). *College Students Look at the 21st Century: Selected Readings on the Future with Student Critiques.* Cambridge, MA: Winthrop Publishers, Inc., 1972.
38. President's Research Committee on Social Trends. *Recent Trends in the United States.* New York: McGraw-Hill, 1933.
39. Shuman, James B. and David Rosenau. *The Kondratieff Wave: The Future of America until 1984 and Beyond.* New York: World Publishing. 1972.
40. Toffler, Alvin. *Future Shock.* New York: Random House, 1970.
41. _____. *Saturday Review/World*, Golden Anniversary Issue: Part 2 — The Next 50 Years. August 24, 1974.

III. EDUCATION

42. Alpren, Morton (ed.). *The Subject Curriculum: Grades K-12.* Columbus, Ohio: Charles E. Merrill Books, Inc., 1967.
43. Coombs, Philip H. *The World Educational Crisis: A Systems Analysis.* New York: Oxford University Press, 1968.
44. Davis, Douglas. "The Soft Sell," *Newsweek.* July 23, 1973, p. 11.
45. Dede, Chris and Draper L. Kauffman, Jr. "The Role of Futuristics in Education," in *Controversies in Education.* Edited by Dwight W. Allen and Jeffrey C. Hecht. Philadelphia: W.B. Saunders Company, 1974.

46. Dewey, John. *The Child and the Curriculum* and *The School and Society*. Chicago: University of Chicago Press, 1956. (Originally published 1902 and 1900 [rev. 1943] respectively).
47. Dewey, John. *Democracy and Education: An Introduction to the Philosophy of Education*. New York: The Macmillan Company, 1916.
48. Dewey, John. *Education Today*. New York: Greenwood Press, 1940.
49. Dewey, John and Evelyn Dewey. *Schools of Tomorrow*. New York: E.P. Dutton and Co., Inc., 1962. (Orig. pub. 1915.)
50. Drier, Harry N., Jr. and Associates. *K-12 Guide for Integrating Career Development into Local Curriculum*. Worthington, Ohio: Charles A. Jones Publishing Co., 1972.
51. Eldredge, H. Wentworth. "Teaching the Future at North American Universities," *The Futurist*. Vol. VI, No. 6, December 1972, pp. 250-252.
52. Fader, Daniel N. and Morton H. Shaevitz. *Hooked on Books*. New York: Berkley Publishing Corp., 1966.
53. Farber, Jerry. *The Student as Nigger: Essays and Stories*. New York: Pocket Books, Inc., 1970.
54. Farrell, Edmund J. *Deciding the Future: A forecast of responsibilities of secondary teachers of English, 1970-2000 A.D.* Urbana, Ill.: National Council of Teachers of English, NCTE Report #12, 1972.
55. Hall, Edward T. *The Silent Language*. Greenwich, CT: Fawcett Publishers, 1959.
56. Hirsch, Werner Z. and Colleagues. *Inventing Education for the Future*. San Francisco: Chandler Publishing Co., 1967.
57. Holt, John. *What Do I Do Monday?* New York: Dell Publishing Co., 1970.
58. Hopkins, Frank Snowdon. "Towards an Ameliorated World," *The Futurist*, December 1973.
59. Hostrop, Richard W. (ed.) *Education . . . beyond tomorrow*. Homewood, Ill.: ETC Publications, 1975.
60. Hostrop, Richard W. (ed.). *Foundations of Futurology in Education*. Homewood, Ill.: ETC Publications, 1973.
61. Hostrop, Richard W. (ed.). *Managing Education for Results*. Homewood, Ill.: ETC Publications, 1975.

62. Ivany, J. W. George (ed.). *Environment: Readings for Teachers*. Reading, MA: Addison-Wesley Publishing Co., 1972.

63. King, David C. *International Education for Spaceship Earth*. Foreign Policy Association, 1971 (2nd ed.).

64. Leonard, George B. *Education and Ecstasy*. New York: Dell Publishing Co., 1968.

65. Marien, Michael and Warren Ziegler. *The Potential of Educational Futures*. Worthington, Ohio: Charles A. Jones Publishing Co., 1972.

66. Mead, Margaret. *Culture and Commitment: A Study of the Generation Gap*. New York: Doubleday and Natural History Press, 1970.

67. Muller, Herbert J. *Uses of the Future*. Bloomington, Ind.: Indiana University Press, 1974.

68. Postman, Neil and Charles Weingartner. *Teaching as a Subversive Activity*. New York: Dell Publishing Co., 1969.

69. Raths, Louis E., Merrill Harmin, and Sidney B. Simon. *Values and Teaching: Working with Values in the Classroom*. Columbus, Ohio: Charles E. Merrill Publishing Co., 1966.

70. Reischauer, Edwin O. *Toward the 21st Century: Education for a Changing World*. New York: Alfred A. Knopf, 1973.

71. Rhodes, James A. *Vocational Education and Guidance: A System for the Seventies*. Columbus, Ohio: Charles E. Merrill Publishing Co., 1970.

72. Saylor, Galen. "What is Relevant for Today's Students?" *Educational Leadership*. Volume 31, No. 1 (October 1973), pp. 41-44.

73. Scott, John Anthony. *Teaching for a Change*. New York: Bantam Books, Inc., 1972.

74. Simon, Sidney B., Leland W. Howe, and Howard Kirschenbaum. *Values Clarification: A Handbook of Practical Strategies for Teachers and Students*. New York: Hart Publishing Co., 1972.

75. Smith, Vernon H. "Old Taboos: New Realities." *Educational Leadership*. Volume 31, No. 1 (October 1973), pp. 6-9.

76. Taba, Hilda. *Curriculum Development: Theory and Practice*. San Francisco: Harcourt, Brace and World, Inc., 1962.

77. Thompson, John F. *Foundations of Vocational Education: Social and Philosophical Concepts.* Englewood Cliffs, N.J.: Prentice Hall, Inc., 1973.

78. Toffler, Alvin (ed.). *Learning for Tomorrow: The Role of the Future in Education.* New York: Random House, 1974.

79. Vermilye, Dyckman W. (ed.). *The Future in the Making: Current Issues in Higher Education 1973.* San Francisco: Jossey-Bass Publishers, 1973.

80. _____. *Alternative Educational Futures in the United States and in Europe: Methods, Issues and Policy Relevance.* Paris: Centre for Educational Research and Innovation, OECD, 1972.

81. _____. *Alternative Futures in American Education.* Washington, D.C.: U.S. Congress, House Committee on Education and Labor, U.S. Government Printing Office, January 1972.

82. _____. *Journal of Teacher Education.* Thematic Section: Futurism in Education, Summer 1974.

83. _____. "Straight Talk," *Time.* July 22, 1974 p. 8.

IV. SIMULATIONS/GAMES

84. Abt, Clark C. *Serious Games.* New York: Viking Press, 1970.

85. Barton, Richard E. *A Primer on Simulation and Gaming.* Englewood Cliffs, N.J.: Prentice-Hall, 1970.

86. Inbar, Michael and Clarice S. Stoll. *Simulations and Gaming in Social Science.* New York: The Free Press, 1972.

87. Nesbit, William A. *Simulation Games for the Social Studies Classroom.* New York: The Foreign Policy Association, 2nd edition, 1970.

88. Raser, John. *Simulation and Society.* Boston: Allyn and Bacon, Inc., 1969.

89. Taylor, John L. *Simulation in the Classroom.* Middlesex, England: Penguin Books, 1972.

90. Zuckerman, David W. and Robert E. Horn. *The Guide to Simulations/Games for Education and Training.* Lexington, MA: Information Resources, Inc., 1973.

V. THE SYSTEMS PERSPECTIVE

91. Beishon, John and Geoff Peters (eds.). *Systems Behaviour.* London: The Open University Press/Harper and Row, 1972.

92. Laszlo, Ervin. *The Systems View of the World.* New York: George Braziller, 1972.

93. Parkman, Ralph. *The Cybernetic Society.* New York: Pergamon Press, 1972.

94. Parsegian, V.L. *This Cybernetic World: Of Men, Machines and Earth Systems.* New York: Doubleday, 1972.

95. Pattee, Howard H. (ed.). *Hierarchy Theory: The Challenge of Complex Systems.* New York: George Braziller, Inc., 1973.

96. Platt, John R. *The Step to Man.* New York: John Wiley and Sons, 1966.

97. Wiener, Norbert. *Cybernetics: Or Control and Communication in the Animal and the Machine.* Cambridge, MA: The M.I.T. Press, 2nd ed. 1961.

98. Wiener, Norbert. *The Human Use of Human Beings.* New York: Avon Books, 1950.

VI. ECONOMICS AND ENVIRONMENT: THE GROWTH DEBATE

99. Cole, H.S.D., C. Freeman, M. Jahoda, and K. L. R. Pavitt (eds.). *Models of Doom: A Critique of the Limits to Growth.* New York: Universe Books, 1973.

100. Daly, Herman E. (ed.). *Toward a Steady-State Economy.* San Francisco: W. H. Freeman and Co., 1973.

101. Friedman, Milton. "Perspective on Inflation," *Newsweek,* June 24, 1974, p. 73.

102. Forrester, Jay W. *World Dynamics.* Cambridge, MA: Wright-Allen Press, 1971.

103. Kohler, Heinz. *Scarcity Challenged: An Introduction to Economics.* New York: Holt, Rinehart, and Winston, 1968.

104. Meadows, Donella, *et al. The Dynamics of Growth in a Finite World.* Cambridge, MA: Wright-Allen Press, 1973.

105. Meadows, Donella, *et al. The Limits to Growth.* New York: Universe Books, 1972.

106. Meadows, Donella, *et al. Toward Global Equilibrium: Collected Papers.* Cambridge, MA: Wright-Allen Press, 1973.

107. Mishan, E.J. *Technology and Growth: The Price We Pay.* New York: Praeger, 1969.

108. Randers, Jørgen and Donella Meadows. "The Carrying Capacity of the Globe," *Sloan Management Review.* Volume 13, No. 2, Winter 1972, pp. 11-27.

109. _____. *The Steady State Economy, Daedelus,* Summer, 1972.

110. _____. "Thinking About Depression," editorial, *Wall Street Journal.* July 22, 1974.

111. _____. *Toward Balanced Growth: Quantity with Quality.* Washington, D.C.: Report of the White House's National Goals Research Staff, U.S. Government Printing Office, 1970.

VII. POPULATION, RESOURCES AND ENVIRONMENT

112. Bresler, Jack B. (ed.). *Environments of Man.* Reading, MA: Addison-Wesley Publishing Co., 1968.

113. Bresler, Jack B. (ed.). *Human Ecology: Collected Readings.* Reading, MA: Addison-Wesley, 1966.

114. Brown, Harrison and Edward Hutchings, Jr. *Are Our Descendents Doomed? Technological Change and Population Growth.* New York: Viking, 1972.

115. Brown, Lester R. *World Without Borders.* New York: Random House, 1972.

116. Callahan, Daniel (ed.). *The American Population Debate.* New York: Doubleday, Anchor Books, 1971.

117. Clarke, Gerald. "Time Essay: What Went Wrong," *Time.* December 10, 1973, pp. 49-50.

118. Commoner, Barry. *The Closing Circle: Nature, Man, and Technology.* New York: Alfred A. Knopf, 1971.

119. Detwyler, Thomas R. *Man's Impact on Environment.* New York: McGraw-Hill Book Co., 1971.

120. Disch, Robert (ed.). *The Ecological Conscience: Values for Survival.* Englewood Cliffs, N.J.: Prentice Hall, 1971.

121. Ehrlich, Paul R. and Richard L. Harriman. *How to Be a Survivor: A Plan to Save Spaceship Earth*. New York: Ballantine Books, 1971.

122. Ehrlich, Paul R., Anne H. Ehrlich and John P. Holdren. *Human Ecology: Problems and Solutions*. San Francisco: W.H. Freeman and Co., 1973.

123. Ehrlich, Paul. *The Population Bomb*. New York: Simon and Schuster, 1968.

124. Ehrlich, Paul R. and Anne H. Ehrlich. *Population, Resources, Environment: Issues in Human Ecology*. San Francisco: W.H. Freeman and Co., 1970.

125. Falk, Richard. *This Endangered Planet: Prospects and Proposals for Human Survival*. New York: Random House, 1972.

126. Foster, Phillips W. *Programmed Learning Aid for Introduction to Environmental Science*. Homewood, Ill: Richard D. Irwin, Inc., 1972.

127. Gapay, Les. "Elusive Goal," *Wall Street Journal*. July 24, 1974, p. 1.

128. Garvey, Gerald. *Energy, Ecology, Economy*. New York: W.W. Norton and Co., Inc., 1972.

129. Goldsmith, E. and the editors of *The Ecologist. Blueprint for Survival*. Richmond, Surrey, England: *The Ecologist*, 1972.

130. Hardin, Garrett. *Exploring New Ethics for Survival*. San Francisco: W.H. Freeman and Co., 1972.

131. Hardin, Garrett (ed.). *Population, Evolution, and Birth Control: A Collage of Controversial Ideas*. San Francisco: W.H. Freeman and Co., 1969.

132. Hardin, Garrett. *Science and Controversy: Population — A Case Study*. San Francisco: W.H. Freeman and Co., 1969.

133. Harrison, Gordon. *Earthkeeping: The War with Nature and a Proposal for Peace*. Boston: Houghton Mifflin Co., 1971.

134. Hunter, Robert E. *The Energy 'Crisis' and U.S. Foreign Policy*. New York: Foreign Policy Association, Inc. Headline Series No. 216, June 1973.

135. Landsberg, Hans H. *Natural Resources for U.S. Growth: A Look Ahead to the Year 2000*. Baltimore: Johns Hopkins Press, 1964.

136. McHale, John. *The Ecological Context*. New York: George Braziller, 1970.

137. Moorcraft, Colin. *Must the Seas Die?*. Boston: Gambit, 1973.

138. Nobile, Philip and John Deedy (eds.). *The Complete Ecology Fact Book*. New York: Doubleday, 1972.

139. Odum, Howard T. *Environment, Power and Society*. New York: John Wiley and Sons, Inc., 1971.

140. Otten, Alan L. "Boy or Girl?" *Wall Street Journal*. June 20, 1974.

141. Paddock, William and Paul Paddock. *Famine — 1975! America's Decision, Who Will Survive?* Boston: Little, Brown, and Co., 1967.

142. Park, Charles F., Jr. *Affluence in Jeopardy: Minerals and the Political Economy*. San Francisco: Freeman, Cooper and Co., 1968.

143. Pohlman, Edward (ed.). *Population: A Clash of Prophets*. New York: The New American Library, Inc., 1973.

144. Prinsky, Robert. "World Plan to Grow, Store Food," *Wall Street Journal*, June 3, 1974, p. 20.

145. Ridker, Ronald G. *Population, Resources, and the Environment*. Washington, D.C.: The Commission on Population Growth and the American Future Research Reports, 1972.

146. Rocks, Lawrence and Richard P. Runyon. *The Energy Crisis*. New York: Crown Publishers, Inc., 1972.

147. Rose, David J. "Energy Policy in the U.S.," *Scientific American*. Vol. 230, No. 1, January 1974, p. 21.

148. Rosenfeld, Albert. "If Oedipus' Parents Had Only Known," *Saturday Review/World*. September 7, 1974, pp. 49 and 52.

149. Sullivan, Edward A. *The Future: Human Ecology and Education*. Homewood, Ill.: ETC Publications, 1975.

150. Terry, Mark. *Teaching for Survival*. New York: Ballantine Books, Inc., 1971.

151. _____. "The Plowboy Interview: Paul Ehrlich," *The Mother Earth News*, Number 28, July 1974, pp. 7-13.

152. _____. *Population and the American Future*. New York: Commission on Population Growth and the American Future, New American Library, 1972.

153. —————————. *Resources and Man.* San Francisco: Committee on Resources and Man, National Academy of Sciences, W.H. Freeman and Co., 1969.

VIII. TECHNOLOGY AND SOCIETY

154. Bagdikian, Ben H. *The Information Machines: Their Impact on Man and the Media.* New York: Harper and Row, 1971.

155. Baier, Kurt and Nicholas Rescher (eds.). *Values and the Future: The Impact of Technological Change on American Values.* New York: The Free Press, 1970.

156. Best, Fred (ed.). *The Future of Work.* Englewood Cliffs, N.J.: Prentice-Hall, 1973.

157. Chinoy, Ely (ed.). *The Urban Future.* New York: Lieber-Atherton, 1973.

158. Greenberger, Martin (ed.). *Computers, Communications, and the Public Interest.* Baltimore, MD: Johns Hopkins Press, 1972.

159. Hamilton, Michael (ed.). *The New Genetics and the Future of Man.* Grand Rapids, MI: William Eerdman's Publishing Co., 1972.

160. Landa, Donald P. and Ryan, Robert D. *Advancing Technology: Its Impact on Society.* Dubuque, Iowa: William C. Brown Co., 1971.

161. Melville, Keith. *Communes in the Counter-Culture: Origins, Theories, Styles of Life.* New York: William Morrow and Co., 1972.

162. Miller, Arthur R. *The Assault on Privacy: Computers, Data Banks, and Dossiers.* Ann Arbor: University of Michigan Press, 1971.

163. Miller, Samuel and Pamela Roby. *The Future of Inequality.* New York: Basic Books, Inc., 1970.

164. Muller, Herbert J. *The Children of Frankenstein: A Primer on Modern Technology and Human Values.* Bloomington, Ind.: Indiana University Press, 1970.

165. Reilly, William K. (ed.). *The Use of Land: A Citizen's Policy Guide to Urban Growth: A Task Force Report.* New York: Thomas Y. Crowell Co., 1973.

166. Rosenfeld, Albert. *The Second Genesis: The Coming Control of Life*. Englewood Cliffs: Prentice-Hall, 1969.

167. Susskind, Charles. *Understanding Technology*. Baltimore: Johns Hopkins Press, 1973.

168. Taylor, John G. *The Shape of Minds to Come*. New York: Weybright and Talley, 1971.

169. Westin, Alan F. *Privacy and Freedom*. New York: Atheneum, 1967.

170. —————————. *Science, Conflict and Society: Readings from Scientific American*. San Francisco: W.H. Freeman and Co., 1969.

IX. PHILOSOPHY AND PRESCRIPTION

171. Cattell, Raymond B. *A New Morality From Science: Beyondism*. New York: Pergamon Press, 1972.

172. Dubos, Rene. *So Human an Animal*. New York: Scribners, 1968.

173. Muller, H.J. *Man's Future Birthright: Essays on Science and Humanity*. Albany, N.Y.: State University of New York Press, 1973.

174. Plato. *The Republic*. New York: Basic Books, 1968.

175. Platt, John. *Perception and Change: Projections for Survival*. Ann Arbor, Mich.: The University of Michigan Press, 1970.

176. Pollard, Sidney. *The Idea of Progress: History and Society*. New York: Penguin Books, 1972.

177. Russell, Bertrand. *Authority and the Individual*. Boston: Beacon Press, 1960. (Orig. pub. 1949).

178. Shapley, Harlow. *The View from a Distant Star: Man's Future in the Universe*. New York: Basic Books, Inc., 1963.

179. Taylor, Gordon Rattray. *Rethink: A Paraprimitive Solution*. New York: E.P. Dutton, 1973.

180. Theobald, Robert. *An Alternative Future for America II*. Chicago: Swallow Press, Inc., 1968.

181. Theobald, Robert (ed.). *Social Policies for America in the Seventies: Nine Divergent Views*. Garden City, N.Y.: Doubleday and Co., 1968.

182. Thompson, William Irwin. *At the Edge of History*. New York: Harper Colophon Books, 1972.

X. SCIENCE FICTION

183. *Anderson, Poul. *The Byworlder*. New York: Signet, New American Library, 1971.

184. Anderson, Poul, Gordon R. Dickson, and Robert Silverberg. *The Day the Sun Stood Still*. New York: Thomas Nelson, Inc., 1972.

185. Anderson, Poul. *The High Crusade*. New York: Macfadden Books, 1964.

186. Anderson, Poul. *The Star Fox*. New York: New American Library, 1964.

187. Anderson, Poul. *Tales of the Flying Mountains*. New York: Collier Books, 1970.

188. Asimov, Isaac. *Asimov's Mysteries*. New York: Dell Publishing Co., 1968.

189. Asimov, Isaac. *The Caves of Steel*. Greenwich, CT: Fawcett Publications, Inc., 1972 (orig. pub. 1953).

190. Asimov, Isaac. *Foundation*. New York: Avon Books, 1951.

191. Asimov, Isaac. *Foundation and Empire*. New York: Avon Books, 1952.

192. Asimov, Isaac. *Second Foundation*. New York: Avon Books, 1953.

193. Asimov, Isaac. *I, Robot*. New York: Pyramid Books, 1970.

194. Asimov, Isaac. *The Martian Way*. Greenwich, CT: Fawcett Publications, Inc., 1969.

195. Asimov, Isaac. *The Naked Sun*. London: Panther Books, 1960.

196. Asimov, Isaac. *Nightfall and Other Stories*. Greenwich, CT: Fawcett Publications, 1969.

197. Asimov, Isaac. *Nine Tomorrows*. Greenwich, CT. Fawcett Publications, 1959.

198. Asimov, Isaac. *The Rest of the Robots*. New York: Pyramid Books, 1966.

199. Biggle, Lloyd, Jr. *Monument*. Garden City, N.Y.: Doubleday and Co., Inc., 1974.

---

*Read before assigning, if you have severe censorship problems.

200. Blish, James, *A Case of Conscience*. New York: Ballantine Books, 1958.

201. Blish, James. *Cities in Flight*. New York: Avon Books, 1970.

202. *Brunner, John. *The Jagged Orbit*. New York: Ace Books, 1969.

203. Brunner, John. *The Long Result*. New York: Ballantine Books, 1965.

204. *Brunner, John. *Stand on Zanzibar*. New York: Ballantine Books, 1968.

205. Brunner, John. *The Whole Man*. New York: Ballantine Books, 1964.

206. Clarke, Arthur C. *The City and the Stars*. New York: Harcourt, Brace and World, 1953.

207. Clarke, Arthur C. *Childhood's End*. New York: Ballantine Books, 1953.

208. Clarke, Arthur C. *The Deep Range*. New York: Harcourt, Brace and World, Inc., 1957.

209. Clarke, Arthur C. *The Nine Billion Names of God*. New York: Ballantine Books, 1967.

210. Clarke, Arthur C. *Tales from the White Hart*. New York: Ballantine Books, 1957.

211. Clement, Hal. *Mission of Gravity*. New York: Pyramid Books, 1962.

212. de Camp, L. Sprague and Fletcher Pratt. *The Incomplete Enchanter*. New York: Pyramid Books, 1960.

213. Dickson, Gordon. *The Book of Gordon Dickson*. New York: DAW Books, 1973.

214. Dickson, Gordon. *Tactics of Mistake*. New York: DAW Books, 1971.

215. Ellison, Harlan (ed.). *Dangerous Visions*, Vols. I, II, and III. New York: Berkley Publishing Corp., 1969.

216. Heinlein, Robert A. *Between Planets*. New York: Ace Books, 1951.

217. Heinlein, Robert A. *Beyond This Horizon*. New York: New American Library, 1942.

218. Heinlein, Robert A. *Citizen of the Galaxy*. New York: Ace Books, 1957.

---

*Read before assigning, if you have severe censorship problems.

219. Heinlein, Robert. *The Day After Tomorrow*. New York: New American Library, 1957.

220. Heinlein, Robert. *The Door Into Summer*. New York: New American Library, 1957.

221. Heinlein, Robert. *Double Star*. New York: New American Library, 1957.

222. *Heinlein, Robert. *Glory Road*. New York: Avon Books, 1963.

223. Heinlein, Robert. *The Green Hills of Earth*. New York: New American Library, 1951.

224. Heinlein, Robert. *Have Space Suit — Will Travel*. New York: Ace Books, 1958.

225. Heinlein, Robert. *Magic, Inc*. Garden City, N.Y.: Doubleday and Co., Inc. 1951.

226. Heinlein, Robert. *The Menace From Earth*. New York: New American Library, 1959.

227. Heinlein, Robert. *Methuselah's Children*. New York: New American Library, 1958.

228. Heinlein, Robert. *The Moon is a Harsh Mistress*. New York: Berkley Publishing Corp., 1966.

229. Heinlein, Robert. *Orphans of the Sky*. New York: Berkley Publishing Corp., 1963.

230. Heinlein, Robert. *Red Planet*. New York: Ace Books, 1949.

231. Heinlein, Robert. *Revolt in 2100*. New York: New American Library, 1953.

232. Heinlein, Robert. *The Rolling Stones*. New York: Ace Books, 1952.

233. Heinlein, Robert. *Space Cadet*. New York: Ace Books, 1948.

234. Heinlein, Robert, *The Star Beast*. New York: Ace Books, 1954.

235. Heinlein, Robert. *Starman Jones*. New York: Dell Publishing Co., 1969.

236. Heinlein, Robert. *Time for the Stars*. New York: Ace Books, 1956.

237. Heinlein, Robert. *Tunnel in the Sky*. New York: Ace Books, 1955.

---

*Read before assigning, if you have severe censorship problems.

238. Heinlein, Robert. *Waldo*. Garden City, N.Y.: Doubleday and Co., 1951.

239. Herbert, Frank. *Dune*. New York: Ace Books, 1965.

240. Hoyle, Fred. *Ossian's Ride*. New York: Berkley Publishing Co., 1959.

241. *Huxley, Aldous. *Brave New World*. New York: Harper and Row, 1932.

242. *Huxley, Aldous. *Island*. New York: Bantam Books, 1962.

243. Lafferty, R.A. *Nine Hundred Grandmothers*. New York: Ace Books, 1970.

244. Le Guin, Ursula K. *The Left Hand of Darkness*. New York: Ace Books, 1969.

245. Laumer, Keith and Gordon Dickson. *Planet Run*. New York: Berkley Publishing Co., 1967.

246. Merrill, Judith. *Daughters of Earth*. New York: Dell Publishing Co., 1968.

247. McCaffrey, Anne. *The Ship Who Sang*. New York: Ballantine Books, 1969.

248. Miller, Walter M., Jr. *A Canticle for Leibowitz*. New York: Bantam Books, 1959.

249. *Niven, Larry. *All the Myriad Ways*. New York: Ballantine Books, 1971.

250. Niven, Larry. *Neutron Star*. New York: Ballantine Books, 1972.

251. *Niven, Larry. *The Shape of Space*. New York: Ballantine Books, 1973.

252. Nourse, Alan E. *Psi High and Others*. New York: Ace Publishing Corp., 1967.

253. Nourse, Alan E. *Tiger by the Tail*. New York: David McKay Company, Inc., 1961.

254. *Orwell, George. *1984*. New York: Harcourt Brace and World, 1949.

255. *Pangborn, Edgar. *Davy*. New York: Ballantine Books, 1964.

256. Pournelle, Jerry. *A Spaceship for the King*. New York: DAW Books, 1973.

257. Pratt, Fletcher and L. Sprague de Camp. *Land of Unreason*. New York: Ballantine Books, 1970.

*Read before assigning, if you have severe censorship problems.

258. Schmitz, James H. *The Demon Breed*. New York: Ace Books, 1968.
259. Schmitz, James H. *The Lion Game*. New York: DAW Books, 1973.
260. Schmitz, James H. *A Pride of Monsters*. New York: Collier Books, 1970.
261. Schmitz, James H. *A Tale of Two Clocks*. New York: Dodd, Mead and Co., 1962.
262. Schmitz, James H. *The Telzey Toy*. New York: DAW Books, 1973.
263. Schmitz, James H. *The Witches of Karres*. New York: Ace Books, 1966.
264. Simak, Clifford D. *The Goblin Reservation*. New York: Berkley Publishing Co., 1968.
265. *Stasheff, Christopher. *The Warlock in Spite of Himself*. New York: Ace Books, 1969.
266. Sturgeon, Theodore. *More Than Human*. New York: Ballantine Books, 1953.
267. Sturgeon, Theodore. *A Way Home*. New York: Pyramid Books, 1956.
268. Tucker, Wilson. *The Year of the Quiet Sun*. New York: Ace Books, 1970.
269. Vance, Jack. *The Languages of Pao*. New York: Ace Books, 1958.
270. Wyndham, John. *The Day of the Triffids*. New York: Fawcett Publications, Inc., 1951.
271. Zelazny, Roger. *The Doors of His Face, the Lamps of His Mouth*. New York: Avon Books, 1971.
272. *Zelazny, Roger. *Lord of Light*. New York: Avon Books, 1967.
273. *Zelazny, Roger. *This Immortal*. New York: Ace Books, 1966.

Books About Science Fiction

274. Armytage, W.H.G. *Yesterday's Tomorrows: A Historical Survey of Future Societies*. Toronto: Toronto University Press, 1968.
275. Atheling, William, Jr. (pseud.) See James Blish.

*Read before assigning, if you have severe censorship problems.

276. Amis, Kingsley. *New Maps of Hell: A Survey of Science Fiction*. New York: Harcourt, Brace, 1960.
277. Bailey, J.O. *Pilgrims Through Space and Time: Trends and Patterns in Scientific and Utopian Fiction*. Westport, CT: Greenwood Press, 1972.
278. Blish, James. *The Issue at Hand*. Chicago: Advent, 1964.
279. Blish, James. *More Issues at Hand*. Chicago: Advent, 1970.
280. Bretnor, Reginald (ed.). *Modern Science Fiction: Its Meaning and Its Future*. New York: Coward-McCann, 1953.
281. Davenport, Basil (ed.). *The Science Fiction Novel: Imagination and Modern Social Criticism*. Chicago: Advent, 1964.
282. Gunn, James. *Alternate Worlds*. Englewood Cliffs, N.J.: Prentice-Hall, 1973.
283. Hollister, Bernard and Thompson, Dean. *Grokking the the Future: Science Fiction in the Classroom*. Pflaun/Standard, 1973.
284. Knight, Damon. *In Search of Wonder: Essays on Modern Science Fiction*. Chicago: Advent:Publishers, Inc., 1967.
285. Lundwall, Sam J. *Science Fiction: What It's All About*. New York: Ace Books, 1971.
286. Panshin, Alexei. *Heinlein in Dimension: A Critical Analysis*. Chicago: Advent:Publishers, 1968.
287. Rose, Stephen and Lois Rose. *The Shattered Ring: Science Fiction and the Quest for Meaning*. Richmond, VA: John Knox Press, 1970.
288. Wollheim, Donald A. *The Universe Makers: Science Fiction Today*. New York: Harper and Row, 1971.

Science Fiction Readers and Textbooks

289. Allen, Dick (ed.). *Science Fiction: The Future*. New York: Harcourt Brace Jovanovich, Inc., 1971.
290. Disch, Thomas M. (ed.). *The Ruins of Earth: An Anthology of Stories of the Immediate Future*. New York: Putnam, 1971.
291. Dozois, Gardner (ed.). *A Day in the Life*. New York: Harper and Row, 1972.

292. Heintz, Bonnie L., Frank Herbert, Donald A. Joos, and Jane A. McGee. *Tomorrow, and Tomorrow, and Tomorrow* . . . New York: Holt, Rinehart and Winston, Inc., 1974.

293. McNelly, Willis and Leon Stover (eds.). *Above the Human Landscape: An Anthology of Social Science Fiction.* Pacific Palisades, CA: Goodyear Publishing, 1972.

294. Spinrad, Norman (ed.). *Modern Science Fiction*, Anchor Press, New York, 1974.

295. Stover, Leon E., and Harry Harrison (eds.). *Apeman, Spaceman: Anthropological Science Fiction.* New York: Doubleday, 1968.

Science Fiction Magazines

296. *Analog:* Science Fiction/Science Fact. Box 5205, Boulder, Colorado, 80302.

297. *Fantasy and Science Fiction.* Box 56, Cornwall, Connecticut, 06753.

298. *Galaxy Science Fiction.* 235 E. 45 Street, New York, N.Y., 10017.

299. *Worlds of If Science Fiction.* 235 E. 45 Street, New York, N.Y. 10017.

XI. MISCELLANEOUS

300. Ardrey, Robert. *The Territorial Imperative: A Personal Inquiry Into the Animal Origins of Property and Nations.* New York: Dell Publishing Co., Inc., 1966.

301. Ashton, T.S., Louis Hacker, F.A. Hayek, W.H. Hutt, and Bertrand de Jouvenal. *Capitalism and the Historians.* Chicago: University of Chicago Press, 1954.

302. Bramson, Leon and George W. Goethals (eds.). *War: Studies from Psychology, Sociology, Anthropology.* New York: Basic Books, Inc., Rev. ed., 1968.

303. Carroll, Lewis. See Martin Gardner.
304. Dickson, Paul. *Think Tanks*. New York: Atheneum, 1971.
305. Feinberg, Gerold. *The Prometheus Project: Mankind's Search for Long Range Goals*. New York: Doubleday Anchor Books, 1969.
306. Gardner, Martin. *The Annotated Alice* (consisting of: *Alice's Adventures in Wonderland* and *Through the Looking Glass*). New York: Bramhall House, 1960.
307. Greenspan, Alan. "The Politics of Inflation," *Wall Street Journal*, March 19, 1974.
308. Harris, Marvin. *Culture, Man, and Nature*. New York; Thomas Y. Crowell Co., 1971.
309. Norbeck, Edward. *Religion in Primitive Society*. New York: Harper and Row, 1961.
310. Orlans, Harold. *The Nonprofit Research Institute: Its Origin, Operation, Problems, and Prospects*. New York: McGraw-Hill, 1972.
311. Payne, Stanley L. *The Art of Asking Questions*. Princeton, N.J.: Princeton University Press, 1951.
312. _____ . "Democracies in Trouble," editorial, *Wall Street Journal*, March 19, 1974.
313. _____ . *Goals for Americans*. New York: President's Commission on National Goals, Prentice-Hall, Inc., 1960.
314. _____ . *The International Encyclopedia of the Social Sciences*. New York: The Macmillan Co. and the Free Press, 1968.
315. _____ . *U.N. Statistical Yearbook, 1972*. New York: U.N. Statistical Office, 1973.
316. _____ . "What America Thinks of Itself," *Newsweek*. December 10, 1973.

XII. BIBLIOGRAPHIES

317. Marien, Michael. *Alternative Futures for Learning: An Annotated Bibliography of Trends, Forecasts, and Proposals*. Syracuse, N.Y.: EPRC, Syracuse University Research Corp., 1971.

318. Marien, Micheal. *Essential Reading for the Future of Education: A Selected, Critically Annotated Bibliography.* Syracuse, N.Y.: EPRC, Syracuse University Research Corp., 1971.

319. Marien, Michael. *The Hot List Delphi.* Syracuse, N.Y.: EPRC, Syracuse University Research Corp., 1972.

320. Martin, Marie. *Films on the Future: A Selective Listing.* Annapolis, MD: World Future Society, 1973.

321. Miller, David C. "Futures on Films." Berkeley, CA: Extension Media Center, 1972.

322. Rojas, Billy. *Future Studies Bibliography.* Amherst, MA: University of Massachusetts, 1970, mimeographed.

Glossary

GLOSSARY

FUTURE STUDIES: 1. Education about the future and about methods for studying the future. 2. Loosely: futuristics.

FUTURISTICS: The systematic study, by basically rational or empirical means, of the possible alternative futures of human societies and the special problems and opportunities relating to those futures. [Also: FUTUROLOGY, FUTURE STUDIES, FUTURES STUDIES, FUTURISM, FUTUR-IBLES, PROGNOSTICS, LONG-RANGE SOCIAL FORECASTING.]

FUTURIST: One who practices futuristics. [Also: FUTUROLO-GIST, PROGNOSTICATOR, LONG-RANGE SOCIAL FORECASTER.]

THE FUTURE: 1. In modern futuristics: a spreading "web" or "tree" of alternative possibilities growing out of the present moment; a "zone of potentiality." 2. In common usage: the course of events which will actually occur.

A FUTURE: A possible course of events; one of the many strands in the "web" of alternative futures.

FUTURES: Plural of "a future" (above); alternative possibilities. [Also: ALTERNATIVE FUTURES, "FUTURIBLES."]

SCENARIO: An imaginative depiction of a possible course of events; often described in the past tense as history by a fictional character living at some future date. [Also: FUTURE HISTORY.]

TREND: A pattern of events in the past; the tendency or direction of movement of some past variable.

FORECAST: A conditional statement about a future possibility.

PRIMARY FORECAST: The extension of a past trend into the future. [Also: TREND EXTRAPOLATION, PROJECTION.]

SECONDARY FORECAST: A statement about any future possibility.

TERTIARY FORECAST: A statement about the most likely (or least unlikely) course of events, taking all factors into account, including deliberate human intervention and the effect of the forecast itself.

PREDICTION: A statement about a complete certainty. (Rarely used by futurists; exceptions usually occur in the negative: "Such-and-such will *not* happen.")

PROPHECY: 1. Any statement about the future made without a claimed basis in rational or empirical means. 2. Prediction. 3. Loosely: any statement about the future.

SYSTEM: Any mental or physical entity possessing interdependent components, organization, and a boundary.

SUB-SYSTEM: A system which can also be considered as a single component part of a larger system.

FEEDBACK: 1. The process by which the future behavior of a system is modified according to information about its present behavior. 2. The information so utilized.

EXPONENTIAL GROWTH: Increase of a quantity by a given percentage per unit of time. [Also: GEOMETRIC GROWTH, POSITIVE FEEDBACK.]

Index